Dear Ma

The Civil War Letters of Curtis Clay Pollock:
First Defender & First Lieutenant 48th Pennsylvania Infantry

John David Hoptak

SUNBURY
P R E S S

Mechanicsburg, PA USA

Published by Sunbury Press, Inc.
Mechanicsburg, Pennsylvania

www.sunburypress.com

For information about special discounts for bulk purchases, please contact Sunbury Press Orders Dept. at (855) 338-8359 or orders@sunburypress.com.

To request one of our authors for speaking engagements or book signings, please contact Sunbury Press Publicity Dept. at publicity@sunburypress.com.

ISBN: 978-1-62006-800-7 (Trade paperback)
ISBN: 978-1-62006-801-4 (Mobipocket)

Library of Congress Control Number: 2017955934

FIRST SUNBURY PRESS EDITION: October 2017

Product of the United States of America
0 1 1 2 3 5 8 13 21 34 55

Set in Bookman Old Style
Designed by Crystal Devine
Cover by Lawrence Knorr
Edited by Lawrence Knorr

Continue the Enlightenment!

Contents

---◆·◆·◆---

C URTIS CLAY POLLOCK was one among the more than two
million soldiers who donned the Union blue and fought in
defense of the United States during the American Civil War.
And, by war's end, he would be counted among the many hundreds of thousands of those soldiers who died to help ensure
that that nation might live.

He was among the very first to respond to his country's
call, volunteering his services immediately upon the outbreak
of hostilities in the spring of 1861. On April 17 of that fateful
year, just five days after the war's opening salvos at Fort Sumter
and in response to President Abraham Lincoln's first call-to-
arms, eighteen-year-old Curtis Pollock marched off to war as a
private in the Washington Artillery, a militia company recruited
from the young volunteer's hometown of Pottsville, Pennsylvania. The very next evening, the Washington Artillery, along with
four other companies of Pennsylvania volunteers, arrived in the
distressed nation's capital. As it turned out, these men, Pollock
included, would be the very first Northern volunteer soldiers to
arrive in Washington following the commencement of war and
would thus go down in history as the famed First Defenders.
Earlier that day, as the volunteer soldiers of these five companies made their way through the streets of Baltimore on their
journey south to Washington, they were assaulted by a vehement mob of pro-Confederate sympathizers who hurled not only
insults but also bricks, bottles, and stones. Pollock escaped
injury, but some of the Pennsylvanians were struck down and
injured during the melee, and thereby shed some of the very
first blood in what would prove to be America's bloodiest war.

Mustered into service as a three-month organization, the
Washington Artillery served a rather uneventful ninety-day
term of service garrisoning government buildings and fortifications in and around the nation's capital. In late July 1861, the
company was discharged, and its members returned home to
Pottsville to a hero's ovation. Yet the war was still very far from
over; indeed, it was just then still getting started and despite—or

A young Curtis Pollock, pictured in civilian clothes, in a photograph likely taken just prior to the Civil War, when he would have been about 18 years of age. [Courtesy of Mr. Jon Murray]

perhaps because of—the recent Union defeat upon the fields of Manassas, a palpable patriotic fervor still swept the land. All throughout the North, volunteers continued to answer their country's call, turning out by the tens of thousands to serve now not for just ninety days, but for "three years or the course of the war," whichever would come first. As was the case throughout the North, volunteer officers in the anthracite-laden coal fields and lush agricultural countryside of Schuylkill County, in east-central Pennsylvania, were busy recruiting men to serve in any number of these three-year regiments. Scores of companies were raised exclusively from Pottsville, the county's largest city and seat of government, while others were recruited from the county's many coal towns and farming villages. Thousands of Schuylkill County's sons decided to leave their picks, shovels, and plows behind to take up arms in defense of the United States. And among them, once again, was young Curtis Pollock.

On September 9, 1861, Pollock enlisted for a three-year term of service and several weeks later, on October 1, he was formally mustered back into service, this time as a corporal in the ranks of Company G, of the 48th Pennsylvania Volunteer Infantry, a regiment recruited almost entirely from Schuylkill County. At the time of his mustering into service with the 48th, Pollock was described as having a "fresh" complexion, grey eyes, and dark hair. And he was rather tall, too, standing 5'10½" in height, several inches above the 5'7" average of all Civil War soldiers. He listed his occupation as clerk, employed, no doubt, at his father's lumber yard in Pottsville. Like many other young soldiers and young men who were trying to find their own way in the world, Pollock yearned for a higher rank. He bristled at his corporal's commission, believing his previous ninety-day experience with the Washington Artillery had entitled him to at least the rank of sergeant. In the months ahead, Pollock pined and wrangled for higher rank, seeking an officer's commission. He would rely heavily upon the influence of his father, William, who had some connections, it seems, to local and state politicians. William's uncle, James Pollock, after all, had once served the people of Pennsylvania as the Commonwealth's Thirteenth Governor from 1855-1858. Curtis Pollock's efforts would eventually pay off, for in May 1862, he received a lieutenant's commission directly from Pennsylvania's wartime Governor Andrew Curtin. With this promotion, however, Pollock was advanced in rank over many other non-commissioned officers in the company and his promotion would trigger quite a controversy in the ranks of Company G and throughout the entire regiment. Pollock was even urged to resign to cool things down, but, stubbornly, the young, newly-minted lieutenant refused and, instead, worked hard to become the best officer he could be. Gradually, the controversy abated and the men came to respect Pollock both as a soldier and as an officer.

Pollock served with great personal bravery in the 48th Pennsylvania through all the regiment's many wearisome campaigns and sanguinary battles, seeing action in North Carolina, Virginia, Maryland, Kentucky, and Tennessee. Described by a fellow officer as being utterly "fearless of danger," the young lieutenant emerged unscathed through some of the war's bloodiest fights, including 2nd Bull Run, South Mountain, Antietam, Fredericksburg, and Knoxville. In the winter of 1863-1864, with the cessation of hostilities still nowhere in sight and with the impending termination of their initial three-year term of service, Pollock, along with most of the surviving veteran soldiers of the

48th Pennsylvania, decided to re-enlist for another three-year term, or, again, at least until the war's conclusion, whichever would come first. By the spring of 1864, and after having served in many various theaters of operation, the 48th Pennsylvania was back again in Virginia and once more in the thickest of the fray. By now, a seasoned, veteran officer, Pollock would survive the hell that was the Wilderness, Spotsylvania, and Cold Harbor, during which battles so many of the 48th fell, but on June 17, 1864, while assaulting Confederate lines east of the city of Petersburg, he was struck down by a rifle ball to his right shoulder. Although hopes were initially entertained for his recovery, the wound proved fatal. On June 23, 1864, Curtis Pollock drew his last breath, one month and five days shy of his twenty-second birthday.

From his initial enlistment in the spring 1861 until his death in late June 1864, Curtis Pollock spent more than 1,100 days of his short life in the uniform of his country. And as was true of so many other Civil War soldiers, all throughout his time in uniform—from the day after he first arrived in Washington with the First Defenders until a few days before receiving his fatal wound at Petersburg—Curtis Pollock wrote letters home, documenting his experiences and his thoughts on serving in the nation's bloody, fratricidal struggle. Many of these letters were written to his younger siblings; some were addressed to his father. Most, however, were written to his mother, Emily, whom he affectionately referred to as his "Dear Ma." Fortunately, many of these letters the young soldier wrote home survive. Indeed, copies of Pollock's letters home are held in the archives of both the Historical Society of Schuylkill County, in Pottsville, and at the United States Army Heritage and Education Center in Carlisle, Pennsylvania.

Growing up in Schuylkill County and as someone who has studied the Civil War for as long as I can remember, I was naturally drawn from a young age to the wartime history of my native region. My interest especially was with the First Defenders and principally with the famed 48th Pennsylvania Infantry. The letters of Curtis Pollock represent one of the largest known collections of letters written by any single member of either of these units and the idea of one day editing and annotating his letters for publication was a thought that never strayed too far from my mind. The letters are important for they provide us with a window through which to view the history of one of the war's most famous and most well-traveled regiments—the 48th

Pennsylvania—a regiment that served in many theaters of the war, under many different commanders, and in many of the war's bloodiest battles. For most of the conflict, the 48th Pennsylvania formed part of the Ninth Army Corps, which remains a relatively underrepresented corps in those vast, vast annals of Civil War historiography. The letters Pollock wrote from Washington as a First Defender in early 1861 are also important, for they allow us to glimpse the conflict from within the nation's capital during those heady early days of war. Much, much more than this, Pollock's letters home enable us to get a glimpse of the Civil War as seen from the inside, for they well chronicle and document the actions, experiences, and thoughts of a young man caught up in the nation's most severe trial and greatest tragedy; of a young man who, like so many others, volunteered to serve and ultimately gave his life fighting in defense of the nation.

In editing and annotating Pollock's letters, I kept as much of his original spelling as possible, though I sometimes added punctuation marks for clearer understanding and better readability. Sometimes, it was impossible to decipher a word and thus I inserted [illegible] into the text. My own commentary and annotations were sometimes added in brackets or in the footnotes, while I did my best to provide as much contextual history as possible, relying heavily upon the two regimental histories of the 48th Pennsylvania, Oliver Bosbyshell's *The 48th in the War* (1896) and Joseph Gould's *The Story of the Forty-Eighth* (1908). Additional sources consulted are in the bibliography.

I would like to thank Mr. Jon Murray, who owns the original letters written by Lt. Curtis Pollock, for his kindness in granting me permission to have the letters published. I would also like to thank the late Bill Stoudt for his work, a few years back, in first transcribing the letters, and the late Leo Ward, longtime president of the Historical Society of Schuylkill County, who connected Mr. Murray with Mr. Stoudt. Thanks go out also to a number of good friends and fellow historians of mine who have encouraged me along the way—too many to name individually but they know who they are—and to Ronn Palm, owner of the Museum of Civil War Images in Gettysburg, Pennsylvania, for allowing me to use several of his original photographs of 48th Pennsylvania soldiers in this work, to Dr. Michael Gray of East Stroudsburg University for his consistent support throughout this undertaking, and to Nick Picerno, for putting me in touch with a descendant of Curtis Pollock. Thanks are also due to the staffs at the U.S. Army Heritage and Education Center in

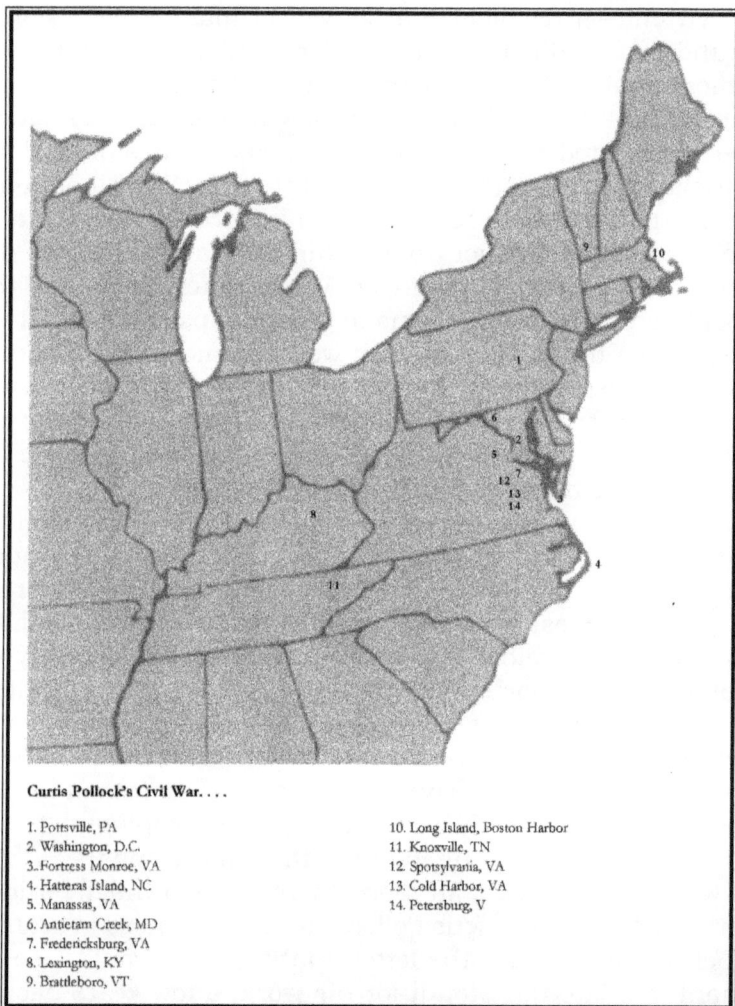

Curtis Pollock's Civil War. . . .

1. Pottsville, PA
2. Washington, D.C.
3. Fortress Monroe, VA
4. Hatteras Island, NC
5. Manassas, VA
6. Antietam Creek, MD
7. Fredericksburg, VA
8. Lexington, KY
9. Brattleboro, VT

10. Long Island, Boston Harbor
11. Knoxville, TN
12. Spotsylvania, VA
13. Cold Harbor, VA
14. Petersburg, V

As a First Defender and especially as a member of the 48th Pennsylvania Infantry, Curtis Pollock saw action in several different theaters of the war, campaigning in North Carolina, Virginia, Maryland, Kentucky, and Tennessee, as well as serving on recruiting duty in Vermont and Massachusetts. (Map by John D. Hoptak)

Carlisle and at the Historical Society of Schuylkill County in Pottsville. And thank you to Mr. Lawrence Knorr and everyone at Sunbury Press for saying 'yes' to publishing this manuscript.

Above all others, though, my unending thanks, appreciation, love, and gratitude goes out as always to my family—to my wife Laura and daughter Hannah, to my mom Colleen, my dad David and sister Angie—all of whom have always been and always will remain my sources of inspiration and pride. I am blessed and thankful beyond words to have all of you in my life.

CHAPTER ONE

With the First Defenders in Washington

April-July 1861

———•◦•◦•———

WEDNESDAY, APRIL 17, 1861, was a "very cold, raw, and disagreeable" day in Pottsville, Pennsylvania, yet the poor weather and cold temperatures did little to deter thousands of men, women, and children from lining the streets to cheer on the soldiers of the city's two militia companies as they marched off to war. With bands leading the way, the 244 members of the Washington Artillery and National Light Infantry marched down Centre Street to the depot of the Philadelphia & Reading Railroad where, amid much fanfare, they boarded train cars and readied for their journey to the state capital of Harrisburg. All along the parade route, these volunteer soldiers were greeted with thunderous cheers and a "perfect ocean of handkerchiefs waved by the ladies, who had taken possession of all the windows, and every available situation along the streets." When they arrived at the station the Pottsville Cornet Band struck up "Hail Columbia" and "Yankee Doodle." "The men were in good spirits," recorded the *Miners' Journal*, "but there were some, who though possessed of manly hearts, who could brave toil and danger without complaint or fear, who could endure suffering with stoical indifference, but who could not prevent the tear from starting to the eye when called upon to bid farewell to all their friends."[1]

Among those bidding farewell to his home and his family by marching off to war that afternoon was eighteen-year-old Curtis Clay Pollock, a private in the Washington Artillery. Born on July 28, 1842, Curtis was the first child born to William and Emily

---

1. *Miner's Journal*, reprinted in Francis B. Wallace, *Memorial to the Patriotism of Schuylkill County*, (Pottsville: Benjamin Bannan, 1865), 13-14; See Also, John D. Hoptak, *First in Defense of the Union: The Civil War History of the First Defenders*, (Bloomington, Indiana: AuthorHouse, 2004): 3-9.

Clay Pollock. A native of Milton, in Northumberland County, Pennsylvania, Curtis's father, William Pollock, was a lumber merchant by profession and a nephew of James Pollock, who, in the 1840s, served as a Whig in the United States House of Representatives and who, from 1855-1858, served the people of Pennsylvania as the Commonwealth's Thirteenth Governor. In October 1841, twenty-five-year-old William Pollock married Emily Clay, the twenty-four-year-old daughter of Reverend Jehu Curtis Clay, the prominent pastor of the Gloria Dei Episcopal Church of Philadelphia. Nine months after their marriage, William and Emily Pollock, now having settled in Pottsville, welcomed Curtis, their first child, into the world. Their second, a daughter Mary, was born in 1844, and over the next fifteen years, Emily would give birth to five more children: Margaret (1847); Julia (1848); James (1853); Francis (1854); and Anne (1860). It appears that William was doing quite well in the lumber business in Pottsville and comfortably supported his growing family. By 1860 the value of the family's home and property was placed at $2,500, while the census of that year also reveals that the Pollock's employed a twenty-two-year-old house servant named Mary Dalton. All of Curtis's younger siblings—excepting Anne, who was yet an infant—were attending school while eighteen-year-old Curtis declared his occupation as an engineer, though it is most likely he would have worked with his father in various capacities at the lumber mill.[2] Yet, whatever aspirations young Curtis may have had for his future were dashed the following year when those looming and long-threatening clouds of civil war at last erupted with a savage fury over the young American nation.

The first shots of America's deadliest war were fired at Fort Sumter, South Carolina, during the early morning hours of April 12, 1861. Following a thirty-four-hour-long bombardment, Major Robert Anderson, in command of the United States soldiers stationed inside the fort, raised the white flag of surrender. In response, President Abraham Lincoln—who had taken the Oath of Office just five weeks earlier and who now found himself confronted with the greatest crisis to ever befall the nation—called upon the militias of all the states remaining in the Union, seeking a total of 75,000 men to serve a ninety-day enlistment to quell the now hostile rebellion of Southern states.

2. 1860 U.S. census, Schuylkill County, Pennsylvania, population schedule, Pottsville, North East Ward, p. 40, dwelling 290, family 279, Pollock, William.

An 1833 "bird's-eye" view of Pottsville, Pennsylvania. The seat of government for Schuylkill County, Pennsylvania, Pottsville was home to two of the five First Defender companies as well as five of the ten companies of the 48th Pennsylvania Volunteer Infantry. (Courtesy of the Library of Congress)

Lincoln's call-to-arms was announced on April 15 and instantly a pronounced and profound patriotic fervor swept across the North as eager volunteers responded to their nation's call.

Among the very first to respond were the 244 volunteers of Pottsville's National Light Infantry and Washington Artillery, militia companies of long standing, which, upon offering their services to the distressed nation, were directed to proceed immediately to Harrisburg. Less than forty-eight hours later, on that wintry April 17, the soldiers of these two companies—Curtis Pollock included—paraded down Centre Street amid all that fanfare and celebration as the city turned out to bid farewell to their gallant volunteers. More than likely, Curtis's family was there, among the gathered thousands, and no matter whether young Curtis caught a glimpse of his mother and father and younger siblings as he marched his way through the city, their thoughts and prayers for a safe return surely traveled with him.

With snow flurries dancing to the ground, the volunteer soldiers of the two companies climbed aboard the train cars and, at 2:15 p.m., departed Pottsville. Later that evening they arrived in Harrisburg where they joined three other militia companies that had arrived earlier that same day: the Ringgold Light Artillery from Reading, the Logan Guards from Lewistown, and the Allen Infantry from Allentown. Taking up quarters in some of the city's hotels and saloons, the men enjoyed only a few hours' rest before waking early the next morning, anticipating an early departure for the nation's capital. Before setting out, Captain Seneca G. Simmons of the 7th U.S. Infantry formally mustered these men into Federal service, having them take the oath of allegiance by raising their right hands and swearing that they would obey the Constitution of the United States, the laws of the nation and of the state of Pennsylvania, as well as the orders of their superior officers. Once officially sworn into service as soldiers of the United States, the 475 soldiers of these five Pennsylvania volunteer companies—most of them unarmed and in various clothing and uniforms—climbed aboard the box cars of the North Central Railroad and at ten minutes past 8:00on the morning of April 18, set off from Harrisburg to Washington.[3]

Few—if any—of the men anticipated much trouble on the journey south and fewer still could have predicted that this was just the start of what would become America's bloodiest war. As the historian of the Allen Infantry later wrote, most of these volunteer soldiers "regarded the journey [to Washington] as a pleasant change from daily occupations, a picnic and [an] agreeable visit to the Capital."[4] But as they would soon find out, war was serious business and, indeed, trouble loomed directly ahead.

Because there was no direct rail line from Harrisburg to Washington, the eager, mostly naïve Pennsylvania soldiers would be forced to detrain at Baltimore and make their way two miles through the city to Camden Station where they would board a new train for the final leg of their journey. Baltimore was a hot-bed of secessionist sympathy and, when some Confederate-leaning citizens got word that northern volunteers were heading their way, they determined to prevent them from marching through their city. As the cars of the North Central Railroad drew to a halt, a mob of some 2,500 vehement secessionists rushed toward and swarmed around the train—approaching, said Captain James Wren of the Washington Artillery, "like a lot of angry wolves"— and soon began crowding around the nervous Pennsylvanians, screaming and yelling obscenities, threatening the volunteer soldiers while also raising shouts in support of Jefferson Davis and

---

3. Heber Thompson, *The First Defenders*, (N.P., 1910): 12; Hoptak, *First in Defense of the Union*, 18-19.
4. James Allen, Quoted in Thompson, 135.

Sixty-five-year-old Nicholas Biddle marched off to war as the personal servant of Captain James Wren of Pottsville's Washington
Artillery. In uniform, Biddle was struck down by a vehement mob
of pro-Confederate sympathizers in Baltimore as the company
made its way south to Washington. Wounded badly, many believe Biddle was the Civil War's first casualty. (From the John D.
Hoptak Collection)

the Southern Confederacy. The situation grew tense but, wishing
to avoid any kind of physical confrontation, the five companies
were ordered back on board the train where they awaited the
arrival of Mayor George Brown and the 120 members of the city's
police force who would escort them through the city. [5]

The crowd grew increasingly irate and more brazen in their
words and actions as the police finally arrived and led the
Pennsylvanians toward Camden Station. It must have been an
incredibly anxious march for young Curtis Pollock and his fellow volunteer soldiers. Excepting just 34 members of the Logan

5. Thompson, 137-138; Hoptak, *First in Defense of the Union*, 20-22.

Guards and a handful of officers with side arms, the Pennsylvanians were entirely unarmed and only a thin line of policemen protected them from the mob. Unable to control themselves any longer, the mob turned violent once the Pennsylvanians reached Camden Station. Bricks, stones, sticks, bottles, and a host of other projectiles were hurled at the volunteers as they attempted to get on board the awaiting trains. Several soldiers were struck, sustaining painful wounds. Among the injured was Nicholas Biddle, a sixty-five-year-old African-American who had escaped slavery and who now served as an aide to Captain James Wren of the Washington Artillery. Biddle was wearing the uniform of the Washington Artillery and the sight of a black man in uniform especially infuriated the already frenzied mob. Biddle was struck in the head with a brick leaving a wound deep enough to expose bone. Though no one sustained fatal injuries that day, the elderly Biddle along with several other soldiers in the ranks of the five Pennsylvania companies, shed some of the very first blood in what would prove to be America's bloodiest war. The events in Baltimore no doubt left the Pennsylvanians shaken and made them fully aware to the fact that the nation was now fully in the throes of civil war.[6]

Amidst the flying bricks and bottles and amidst the threats and obscenities, the Pennsylvania volunteers boarded the train cars at Camden Station and were soon on their way to Washington, where they would finally arrive sometime around 7:00 p.m. on the evening of April 18, following their long and eventful day's journey. Stepping off the cars, the soldiers were greeted by Major Irvin McDowell who then led them on a short march to their assigned quarters: the spacious chambers and committee rooms of the Capitol Building. There they would remain for the next several days, marveling at the interiors of the Capitol and fortifying the building against a Confederate attack most in the city believed to be imminent.

During those heady days following the attack on Fort Sumter, Washington was a city very much on edge. Most expected it would come under attack, especially after Virginia declared its secession from the Union and particularly after word arrived that Virginia forces had seized the U.S. Navy Yard at Norfolk and the Arsenal at Harpers Ferry. The Capitol, the White

---

6. Hoptak, *First in Defense of the Union*, 22-28; Thompson, 12-14; For more on Nicholas Biddle, see "A Forgotten Hero of the Civil War," by John Hoptak, *Pennsylvania Heritage*, (Spring, 2010).

When Pollock and the First Defenders arrived in Washington, they were initially quartered in the U.S. Capitol Building, which was just then under construction, as can be seen here in this photograph of President Abraham Lincoln's inauguration, taken in March 1861, one month before the start of the Civil War. (Courtesy of the Library of Congress)

House—Washington itself—was expected to be attacked next. The tension and anxiety was great but it began to subside once the Northern volunteers began arriving in the city, and the first to arrive were these 475 men from Pennsylvania, including young Curtis Clay Pollock. For their timely response and in recognition of the fact that they were the nation's first volunteer troops to reach Washington following the outbreak of war, these men would soon earn the title of "First Defenders." So relieved and so thankful were they for the prompt arrival of these Pennsylvania soldiers that for days afterward several high-ranking government officials traveled to the Capitol Building to meet and to personally thank these soldiers from Pottsville, Reading, Lewistown, and Allentown. Among them was Speaker of the House Galusha Grow, Secretary of War Simon Cameron,

Secretary of State William Seward, and, of course, President Abraham Lincoln, who shook hands with Pollock and all the other First Defenders.[7]

The excitement and the anxieties that defined the days immediately following Sumter continued to abate as thousands of more volunteers began to arrive in Washington in the wake of the First Defenders. The famed 6th Massachusetts arrived on April 19, followed by scores of other companies from throughout the North. And as the days and weeks passed, Private Curtis Pollock and his comrades settled into the routine of soldier life with the men spending almost every day of the next three months engaged in drill, parades, and in target practice. While they may have enlisted for the glory or for the adventure of soldiering, or for the chance to defend the nation on the field of battle, most of the soldiers of all five First Defender companies would, instead, spend the entirety of their ninety-day term of service stationed either inside Washington or in any number of the city's important military installations. Some of them were assigned to man the heavy guns inside the fortifications that ringed the city, while others were sent to either the Navy Yard or to the Washington Arsenal. For Curtis Pollock and most of his comrades in the Washington Artillery, orders arrived on April 28 to proceed to Fort Washington.

Located along the banks of the Potomac River just a few miles south of the city, Fort Washington, "an old-fashioned case-mate work, built of brick" in 1809, was destroyed in 1814 during the War of 1812, but was rebuilt ten years later under the direction of Pierre L'Enfant and Lieutenant Colonel Walker Armistead.[8] In 1861, Fort Washington was under the command of Major Joseph A. Haskin, an 1839 graduate of West Point and a thoroughly professional officer who had lost an arm while storming Chapultepec during the Mexican-American War.[9] Haskin and his small contingent of Regular Army soldiers stationed at Fort Washington immediately began drilling the volunteers from Pennsylvania, working "zealously and kindly" with them and "perfecting them in their duties as soldiers."[10] It was while stationed at Fort Washington that Curtis Pollock and the

7. Hoptak, *First in Defense of the Union*, 50-51.
8. William W. H. Davis, *History of the Doylestown Guards*, Doylestown, Pennsylvania: n.p., 1887, page: 119.
9. Ezra Warner, *Generals in Blue: Lives of the Union Commanders*, Baton Rouge: Louisiana State University Press, 1964, pages: 214-215.
10. Samuel P. Bates, *History of Pennsylvania Volunteers*, Vol. I, Harrisburg, Pennsylvania: B. Singerly, State Publisher, 1869, page: 8.

Pollock spent much of his ninety-day term of service with the Washington Artillery stationed at Fort Washington, situated along the banks of the Potomac several miles south of the capital. (From Picturesque America, *Vol. II, 1874)*

other members of the Washington Artillery, having already been in the service several weeks, finally received their uniforms.

Drill, guard mounting, and fatigue duty were the orders of the day as Major Haskin continued to transform his civilian volunteers into soldiers. Near the end of May, the various First Defender companies were officially incorporated and organized into a regiment. Because they were the first volunteers to respond and to arrive in Washington, most of the First Defenders naturally expected the honor of having their companies be organized into the ranks of the 1st Pennsylvania Volunteer Infantry. They were greatly disappointed, however, when, instead, they learned that they would become part of the 25th Pennsylvania Volunteers, which was the *last* of Pennsylvania's three-month regiments to be formally organized. In those hectic early days of the war, as state and federal military and civil authorities faced the monumental task of organizing tens of thousands of volunteer soldiers, the five First Defender companies were simply overlooked, and as Historian Samuel Bates, in his *History of the Pennsylvania Volunteers* pointed out, it was not until after 240 other companies of Pennsylvania volunteers were organized that the First Defenders "were remembered as a part of the Pennsylvania troops."[11] Curtis Pollock and the other members

---

11. Ibid.

of the Washington Artillery were reorganized and designated as Companies B & H of the 25th Pennsylvania. Having been officially organized, the time came for the members of the 25th to elect its leaders, a somewhat difficult task considering that the regiment's ten companies were located at various posts in and around Washington. In the end, it was Henry Lutz Cake, a lieutenant in the National Light Infantry, who was elected colonel. Born on October 6, 1827, in Northumberland, Pennsylvania, Cake later settled in Pottsville where he founded the *Mining Record* and where he became heavily involved in local politics and in the city's militia, joining the National Light Infantry. Cake's standing in the community, his experience in the militia, and his political connections all helped get him elected colonel of the 25th Pennsylvania Infantry, although there were some in the regiment, Pollock included, who had some doubts about Cake's qualifications and his leadership.[12]

Gradually, Pollock became accustomed to life in the military but grew increasingly frustrated with the inactivity. For Pollock, service in the uniform of the United States became monotonous, mundane, and tiresome. After spending the first week-and-a-half in the Capitol, he would spend the remainder of his ninety-day term of service stationed inside the brick walls of Fort Washington, marching, training, drilling, and going on and off guard duty. Rumors were rife that the men would soon be ordered into Virginia to confront the enemy but nothing ever came of it. If he had marched off to war seeking great adventure or seeking to achieve some romanticized images of military glory, he would find none of it while stationed with the First Defenders in Washington. He did, however, have a lot of time to write to his brothers and sisters, his father, and especially to his "Dear Ma," Emily, all of whom he had left behind in Pottsville.

Pollock's first letter home was dated April 19, 1861—the day after he and the First Defenders arrived in Washington—and he would write at least a dozen more while stationed in and around the capital during his first ninety-days in uniform. In his letters, Pollock wrote of the harrowing march through Baltimore, of meeting Lincoln, and of how he adjusted to soldier life. He recorded his impressions of his superiors—including Major Haskin at Fort Washington and Colonel Henry Cake—and he explained how he and his comrades spent their time. He spoke

---

12. Wallace, 508.

of the food, the seemingly non-stop drilling, the rumors of going on campaign, and of his desire to see action. Written during the first three months of the conflict, Pollock's letters home provide a window into the war's earliest days in the nation's capital and the early efforts in defending the city. More importantly, though, they chronicle Pollock's transition from civilian to soldier as he grew increasingly more accustomed to army life.

Washington Apr 19th

Dear Ma

We are quartered here in Washington for the present but news has just come that we [are to] go on board a war vessel in the harbor. Apr. 17th Started from Pottsville at 2 ¼ P.M. and had a pleasant ride to Reading where we waited two hours for the train for Harrisburg. We occupied our time by running around the streets and by 6 O'clock, [we] started for Harrisburg. Nothing of any importance occurred on the road and we arrived in Harrisburg at 8 ½ O'clock. We were then conducted to our quarters over [the] Lager beer Saloon. We stayed over night. We had our supper in the Saloon and had beans and pork with bread and butter and coffee without any sugar or milk. It was the dirtiest place I have been in for a long time. After a person was done [eating], they took the plate and threw what was left of it on the floor and then wiped the plate with a dirty towel. Well, enough of that. We had supper and breakfast there and the next morning started for Washington. After we got to Harrisburg and had our supper we commenced to drill and drilled until 1 ½ O.C. and then went to bed we had to sleep on the floor and on straw. A parcel of us went to a livery stable and brought [back] twenty-four bundles, which was scattered around the floor.

Apr 18th Got up at 3 ½ O.C[lock]. and commenced to drill again and drilled until 5 O'C. and then got breakfast and after breakfast started for the depot. We were then sworn in by Capt. [Seneca] Simmons and then waited for the cars.[13] Nothing occurred until we arrived in Baltimore when we were met by an immense crowd and the whole force of the city police

---

13. As Major of the 4th U.S. Infantry, Simmons was killed in action at the Battle of White Oak Swamp, on June 30, 1862.

(about 200)[14] we had two miles to get to the depot where the Washington train started from. We were hissed and hooted at and called all manner of hard names and the people were hurrahing for Jeff Davis and the Southern Confederacy. It would have taken very little to raise a row but we had no arms and we did not say any thing to them. Nick Biddle had his head cut open to the bone with a stone thrown by one of the Sescess.[15] We rode to Washington in a freight train got here at 7 o'clock. We were ordered to march to the Capitol where we now are.

We are now going to drill again.

So
C.C. Pollock

I [will] send you a few views of the city in another envelope.

———◆•◆•◆———

Afternoon 5 o'clock 1861
Capitol Washington Sunday Apr 28th

*D*ear Ma

I received your letter yesterday and was much pleased to get [it] as I had been anxiously expecting one for some time. I write a letter to you almost every day and would like to hear from you as often as possible. Lincoln was up here this afternoon and was all over the capitol shaking hands with all the soldiers. He is very tall but not at all bad looking.[16] Secretary Seward was along with him and he also shook hands all around. Mr. Seward is quite small not much taller than Uncle Joseph. I went to church this morning with Geo. Hill & Ed

---

14. The actual number was 120.

15. The wound to Biddle's head was a severe one, cutting him so deep that it exposed his skull. He survived the injury and passed away in 1876 at the age of 80. Upon his death, the surviving members of the Washington Artillery and National Light Infantry arranged for his funeral and raised funds for a headstone. Upon that stone it was inscribed that Biddle was the first man to shed blood in the Civil War.

16. Lincoln made his way around to each of the five companies and when he greeted the Washington Artillerists, he noticed Nick Biddle, with his head wrapped in blood-soaked bandages. He advised Biddle to seek further treatment in one of the city's hospitals but the elderly man refused, preferring instead, he said, to remain with his company. One member of the Pottsville company called on Lincoln to make a speech, but Lincoln declined. "Officers and soldiers of the Washington Artillery," Lincoln said, "I did not come here to make a speech. The time for speech-making has gone by, the time for action is at hand. I came here to give you a warm welcome to the city of Washington, and to shake hands with every officer and soldier in your company providing you grant me that privilege."

Shippen.[17] We went to Trinity Church and heard a good sermon from Dr. Butler of Cincinnati. We had quite a heavy rain this morning but it is now very pleasant but quite windy. Yesterday afternoon I was up at [the] Patent Office looking around and saw a great many different things of all kinds sorts & sizes and was only through one or two rooms. I saw [George] Washington's clothes which he wore during the Revolutionary War and his sword, tea set, water chairs, &c which he used to use. I also saw the Printing Press which [Benjamin] Franklin worked on. The Presents which the Japanese presented to [President James] Buchanan were also there and other interesting relics. I intend to go to the Smithsonian Institute tomorrow and I will give you an account of what I see in my next letter.

We are all getting along very well and are in very good spirits, though a few are complaining of not being well. There is now in the city between 15 & 20 thousand men and [we] are not afraid of the biggest [army] the Virginians can bring down on us, though no person in town now thinks there will be an attack made. We all got a blanket, two pair of shoes, and two pair of stockings last night from the government and are to get our uniforms on Tuesday. It seems very little like [a] Sunday here; it [is] all noise and bustle the men are working downstairs, rolling flour and there are several bricklayers at work putting up cooking apparatus for the men. The Capitol, large as it is, is completely filled up with soldiers and flour barrels and the other two stories have the soldiers while the cooking apartment is in the cellar. We also bake our own bread. I suppose you have heard that the government had seized 20,000 lbs. of flour and it is nearly all stowed up here. The other day I was down stairs helping to barricade the windows and doors so as to have the lower story safe in case of an attack.

Does Rob Hill come up every Saturday night to see Augusta? Tell Augusta I am very much obliged to her for her present and I shall prize it very highly for I have several times needed it very much. I have written a pretty long letter and I believe I have no more today so I will close.

With love to all friends and much to the family.

I remain your affectionate Son
C.C. Pollock

---

17. Shippen and Hill were privates in the Washington Artillery.

———•◦•◦•———

Fort Washington Sunday Afternoon
2 o'clock May 12th 1861

*D*ear Ma

I received Mary's letter yesterday afternoon and was much pleased to get it. I am now lying in my bunk writing this to you on Will Bartholomew's valise.[18] It is a very fine day but quite warm. Our guns are inspected every Sunday morning by Major Haskins and we have to keep them very clean. We are more satisfied with our position than we were at first and are getting along very comfortably. We got the butter and eggs on Thursday evening and had the first of them on Friday morning. They were brought down on the Philadelphia, the same vessel that brought us from Washington [to Fort Washington]. Mr. Campbell, Geo. Patterson, Col. Cake, J.W. Cake and his son Adam, Mr. Baber,[19] and some other Gentlemen were all on board and they got off and came up and were looking around the fort and they took <u>tea</u> with us (dry bread and coffee). After tea, we all went down to the boat and after it started we gave them three hearty cheers and a tiger. We all felt much better since they were here. They raised our spirits considerably. I got a dollar from Mr. Campbell when he was here and [$]2 before we left Washington. We are all pretty hard up for money here; nobody scarcely has any. There is not much use here for money but there are a great many little necessities that we can buy if we have the money.

We got our uniforms this morning; they came down in a steamer about 11 o'clock. It consists of a dark blue blouse and pants and light blue overcoat very much like the one we had. The one that I have fits me very well.

We can see Mount Vernon from here as it is just on the opposite side of the river and you can look at the picture in the dining room and see the river on which the fort stands. It is not against orders to go over there but none of the men could go if they wanted to as the few boats that are about here are always in use by the fishermen and the guard at [the] wharf

---

18. William Bartholomew was a twenty-two-year-old native of Pottsville, serving as a private in the Washington Artillery. He entered the U.S. Regular Army following his three-month term of service, rising ultimately to the rank of Captain.
19. These men were all residents of Pottsville, down to visit the troops.

have orders to fire on any soldier who attempts to go away in a boat. Today seems more like Sunday has, yet as it is very quiet all around and no work going on. We have had a great deal to do this last week we got a large supply of ammunition and twelve 36-pound guns and have been working this last week at getting them up into the fort. There are three guns mounted in our battery: two 36 pounders and one 24—and yesterday afternoon they were firing them off loaded with ball to see how far they range. We fired one ball across the river into Virginia; the first ball fired into that State. We have a chaplain here but he is in Washington at present so we had no services to day. We also have a Physician here and I believe he takes very good care of the sick from what the sick men say, but I hope I will not have a chance to find out what kind of man he is. A steamer went up the river this morning full of troops (I think from New York). I believe I have run out and have said everything that will be of any interest to you so I will close with much love to all.

I remain your affectionate Son
C.C. Pollock

The butter and eggs are very good.

----------◆•◆•◆----------

Fort Washington May 15th 1861

ear Ma

It is just sundown and I have been on duty all day mounting cannons. We commenced work at 8 o'clock and quit at 12, and commenced at 1, again until 5. We are kept busy almost all the time. We go on guard one day (24 hours) commencing at 8 o'clock in the morning until 8 the next morning then we have nothing to do that day but clean our guns. The next day we have to work in the fort at [what] they call police duty then the next day we are on fatigue duty (generally cutting down trees around the fort or bringing up things from the wharf). Last week we had to haul up the cannons from the wharf which is pretty hard work as some of them weigh about 7500 lbs. The day after we are on fatigue duty our turn generally comes to go on guard again for 24 hours, so you see our time is pretty well taken and as our facilities for writing are not very good you must not expect a letter every couple of days. I write though every chance I get. I received Augusta's needle case to day and am very much obliged to her for it as I think it is a very nice one and something I wanted very much. One of the company brought it down from Washington; he said either Major Campbell or Colonel Cake gave it to him. They are going to divide the company in a few days. I do not know which company I will be in but I would like to stay in the old [one]. We are getting along very nicely and are all very well satisfied as the men all say they do not want to leave until the three months are up. I commenced the latter part of this letter this morning as it got too dark last night to finish it. Frank Dewees and Lewis Snyder went to Washington on Monday last in a small schooner. I am very glad to hear that you have sent a box to me; a great many of the fellows are getting them. I would like it very well if you could send me a box of segars [cigars] as they are very dear here. You can get a box for $1.50. I would like you to send me some money also as I am completely out and I will have to have some to get my clothes washed with [it]. Col. Cake told one of our members who was in Washington the other day that he was going to have us removed to Arlington Heights about 4 miles from Washington on the other side of the river. It has been very warm here the last few days and we are all getting sunburnt pretty badly.

Tell Harry Dewees that I will write to him before long and that I would have answered his letter long ago but it is so much bother to get everything together. You first have to get a sheet of Paper and an envelope; next thing a lead pencil, which takes about a half an hour to find one; then you must find a small board somewhere about the fort to write on and the last thing is to get a soft seat somewhere and go to work. I am writing this letter on a rough board which I picked up. Frank Dewees[20] is trying to get an appointment as Paymaster in one of the Regiments. He does not want it circulated though until after he is appointed. It is nearly guard mounting time and as I am on fatigue duty to day I will have to close with much love to all.

I remain
Your Affectionate Son
C.C. Pollock

Tell Rob Hill to write to me.

---

20. Francis P. Dewees of Pottsville and was a 28-year-old private in the Washington Artillery.

--------•◆•--------

Fort Washington May 20th 1861

ear Ma

I received the box on Saturday and would have had written yesterday but I was on guard all day. Frank Dewees was in Washington and brought the box down with him. Will Patterson, Lewis Thompson, L. Garrigues & Dr. Woodnut all came down in the same boat and were here all day yesterday and left this morning for Washington. It is rumored about here that we are to [be] taken back to Washington to join our regiment which is now stationed at the Arsenal. The [steamer] *Baltimore* has just arrived from Washington with [Secretary of War Simon] Cameron's son on board; he has gone up to the fort with Major Haskins. You want to know in your last letter what we get to eat here but it is not much. We generally get a cup of coffee and a loaf of bread with a piece of fat pork or beef. The bread has to last us all day. At dinner we get a piece of meat and a tin cup of soup, either rice or bean, or else some of the potatoes which Mr. Haywood sent us instead of the soup and at supper we get a cup of coffee. So you see we live very plain and I do not suppose that many of us will get the gout. You must not believe all the idle reports that get to Pottsville about us; they are all falsehoods and the persons that send home some of these tales are hard up for something to write so they invent all sorts of Stories which have not a word of truth in them. We are all getting along very well and are all in good condition, there being but one person in the hospital. We had services yesterday but I could not get there as I was on guard.

The company was divided this morning. I remain in the old company under the command of Lieutenant [David A.] Smith and this afternoon was had an election of officers. Lieut. Smith was elected Capt.; [Francis] Wallace 1st Lt.; Philip Nagle 2nd Lt.; and Henry Russel 3rd Lt. Frank Dewees ran against him but was beaten. Capt. Wren was Capt. of the new company with Jos. Gilmour 1st Lieut.; Wm. McQuade 3rd [Lt.]; Cyrus Sheetz 2nd [Lt.]. We have had very unpleasant weather for the last day or so and the ground is very muddy. Mr. Haywood, Millholland, and Saml. Huntzinger were all down here last week. Cameron having given Haywood an order for a boat to bring them down, they were here about three hours and then they went back. Old Benny [was] very much pleased with his visit.

The things in the box are all very nice particularly the cakes and segars. Frank Dewees had a tin box inside from Miss E. Loeser which was full of some of the nicest things I have seen in a long time. It is now raining quite hard. I am setting in the officers' quarters writing this letter. You mentioned in the letter that you sent me a bottle of ink but there is none there but I could easily buy some in the Fort if I had some money. From what I have heard since I have been writing I do not know whether we will be likely to leave here very soon or not. I will write a letter whenever I get a chance and I think I will be able to write oftener as we have pretty much all the work done and are going to drilling. I will tell you in the next letter what kind of work we have to do.

From your affectionate Son
C.C.P.

Fort Washington May 28th 1861

Dear Ma
I received yours and Margie's letter the other day and was glad to hear from you. You always say something about my not writing often enough but we are kept busy almost all the time and the mail sometimes lays here two or three days before it starts for Washington as the steamers run very unregularly. I received a letter from Aunt Annie and Uncle Joseph sent me the [illegible] in it. I also received one from Grandpa in answer to the one I wrote him. I also wrote to Aunt Annie the day before I received her letter and I intend writing to Aunt Sarah in a day or two. The box is nearly empty except for the cigars which are particularly nice. I think I will act upon your suggestion and send it home to be filled again but I think it would not cost near as much to get another one made not so large and put a little more in it for me as Frank Dewees had more than half the box. The tongue was very good but did not last any time at all. B. Reilly told me to tell Mary that her cakes were extra good and the he would call and see her next New Years and get some more. This morning just before dinner we fired a salute of eleven guns on account of the death of Surgeon

General of the army.[21] The wind has been blowing very strong here for the last couple of days and is blowing quite strong yet Lieutenant Snyder who was at Sumpter has been here for the last couple of days superintending the work outside the fort but left yesterday for Alexandria as they are putting up fortifications there. There is nothing of any importance going on at present everything is very quiet. Last night the steamer *Baltimore* was down here and we received a lot of papers from some of the New York 7th Reg. who were aboard. Yesterday the flag stuck fast to the top of the flag staff and one of the regulars went up and got it loose. I have nothing more to say at present so I will close with much love to all.

Your affectionate son

C.C. Pollock

Fort Washington June 3rd 1861

ear Ma

Thomas Reilly is here and expects to start for home in the first boat that comes along so I will send you a few lines by him. We are getting along very well and everything goes on as smoothly as possible. Yesterday F.P.D.[22] gave a dinner in the officers' quarters and it was decidedly the dinner of the season. The bill of fare will be seen in this week's *Journal* as Lieut. Wallace will give a full account of it in his letter to the *Journal*. It has been uncommonly warm here for the last two or three days but we had a shower last night, but this morning it is very pleasant. There was a steamer came up yesterday morning from Aquia Creek where she had been engaged in the fight. She had three balls in her and had fired away all her ammunition She had aboard and has gone up to Washington for repairs. Last evening another steamer went down to take the place of the one that went up in the morning. I was at church yesterday morning and we had a very good sermon from the 20 Chapt Mathew 69-75 in. There are a great many [who] attend church and the room is generally very well filled. Henry Russel

---

21. Surgeon General Thomas Lawson, who had held the post since 1836, died on May 15, 1861, at age 72.
22. Most likely "F.P.D." refers to Francis P. Dewees.

& Oliver Bosbyshell[23] raise the tunes and they are going to raise a choir to sing in church. Mr. Russel was down on Friday & I spoke to him, he said you were all well. I wrote a letter to Aunt Annie and Grandpa yesterday and I also wrote one to Milton but have not got an answer yet. The men are now going out to drill and I will have to close.

We have just finished drill and I am very warm. The main guard is just getting ready to go up to the fort. I am not on guard to day but will be tomorrow and you can think of me being out in the hot sun parading up and down the ramparts. The last time I was on guard I was guard over the prisoners they have to work around the fort and you might have seen me parading after them with a musket over my shoulder. Frank Dewees was on guard with me and also [had] charge of some of the prisoners. There are about twelve prisoners in the guard house most of them being put in for desertion. I have no more to say at present.

Your Affectionate son
C.C. Pollock

———•◦•———

June 6th 1861
Fort Washington

Dear Ma

I received your letter on Monday and I now take this opportunity of answering it. There is nothing going on here just now except the regular routine of duty and it is very hard work to write a letter when you have nothing to say. Dory Patterson got a large box yesterday with a great many things in it among the rest was some molasses which is very nice to eat with the dry bread; if you send me another box I would like to have some with it. I received the currant wine which was very nice. I do not know what became of the inkstand as I never saw anything of it. I saw the box that Miss E. Loeser sent Frank; it was a large one and had plenty of good things in it. There was a large cup cake as large as a cheese box and a whole

---

23. Russel was a sergeant in the Washington Artillery, while Bosbyshell was a private; both were from Pottsville. Bosbyshell would later go on to serve alongside Pollock in Company G, 48th Pennsylvania, and, in the 1890s, he wrote a regimental history of the 48th.

Henry Lutz Cake was made colonel of the three-month 25th Pennsylvania Volunteer Infantry. Although Pollock had doubts about Cake's ability to lead, he proved a good and brave officer, later commanding the hard-fighting 96th Pennsylvania Infantry. (Courtesy of the Library of Congress)

piece of gingerbread about three feet long and about 1 ft & 13 [inches] in width, it was not broken at all and it was very good. He also had some Scotch cakes which I like uncommon well (He says that there is only one <u>person</u> in town that knows how to make them). I think there is very little possibility of us leaving here though the Regiment has been accepted by the war department and Col. [Henry] Cake can now do with us as he pleases. The men are very much dissatisfied with Col. Cake as he has done some very mean tricks and some say he has a brave heart but cowardly legs, and also that he is very deficient in military discipline, not knowing how to give out the simplest commands in a proper form even with the book before him.[24] I

24. Later and as colonel of the 96th Pennsylvania Infantry, Colonel Cake proved himself a brave

had no ink handy when I commenced this letter so I have written it with a lead pencil. I have tried to write as long a letter as I possibly can so I will bid you good bye for a while.

Your affectionate son

C.C. Pollock

I will write another letter of Sunday.

C.C.P.

I have just been looking over the latter part of your letter and find there are several questions that remain unanswered (so here goes): I am not personally acquainted with any of the officers of the fort. The one that we all liked best has just gone away. He was ordered to report at Headquarters in Wash. and left on yesterday morning his name is Capt. Perkins. The officers that F.P.D. talks so big about Messing with are our officers, he goes in there and eats with them but I do not believe they like it much. That story about mosquitoes is all nonsense. I have not made up my mind whether I will remain longer than three months but I will come home first and see about it then. I would like uncommon well to have a Lieut'cy in the Marine Corps. I rec'd the handkerchief and towel and are very nice I should like to get a shot at that, C.C.

I had an invitation to that hi'c ni'c.

Your affectionate Son

C.C.P.

Fort Washington June 14th 1861

ear Ma

I received your letter this evening and as what you said about us leaving here is rather bad for us I will answer immediately. The principal reason for us not wanting to go is that we were very much disappointed in regard to our officers Col. Cake in particular who the men say (who have been in Washington) does not know how to give a command correctly, not even the most simple ones and they say that if we should

---

and good commander, leading his soldiers at such places as Gaines's Mill, South Mountain, and Antietam before tendering his resignation to pursue political office.

go away from here that some other companies would have come to take our place so that it is just as an important a post as almost any other or rather it was at first when we did not know at what minute we might have been attacked and then again we have helped to put the fort in a very good state of defense after a great deal of hard work. I think it is most too much that anybody should accuse us of being afraid of leaving. As for my part I would much prefer leaving after such reports getting out about us but I was talking to the men about it this evening after supper and they [say] that Col. Cake shall never have a chance to command them if they can help it. And then another thing, he has told us a great many stories of what he would do for us but as soon as he got away from here he forgot all about them and some of the men who have been in Washington and who were talking to him about us leaving here says that he said that he did not care much about us leaving here if it were to happen to get into an engagement and any of us were killed he would be blamed for it. If Col. Cake was anything of a good officer we would have been with the regiment long ago and in Virginia some-place. Most of the men say that they will enlist after the three months are over but not under Cake and that they would follow Col. [James] Nagle or Capt. [David A.] Smith from one end of Virginia to the other. I made up my mind some time back that I would reenlist a second term but the company will be home and reorganized over again and get a full company which we have not got now on account of fifty of them going into Capt. Wren's company. I think I can persuade Harry & Bob Hill to come along as it would be much pleasanter for me. Major Haskins was in Washington the other day and says that Gen. [Joseph K.] Mansfield had an order written out for us to return to Washington and was just going to send it with and order for a boat to come & take us back when he was informed of it and he went and got the order withdrawn for he said that we were a very good set of men and had got all the work done about the fort and were just commencing to learn to drill & that he would like to have us a while longer.

Your affectionate son
C.C.P.

<u>Write soon.</u>

———◆•◆•◆———

Fort Washington June 15/61

*D*ear Ma

I received your letter last evening and a very short one it was. Mr. Campbell was down last night and went up again this morning and he franked a lot of letters for us. I am on guard today and am writing this letter in the guard room. It is now one o'clock and I go on guard at two for two hours and it is very warm though there is something of a breeze blowing just now. You need not send me any molasses as it is hardly worthwhile for it will not be long before we will be at home now. I would much rather have a *New York Ledger* as the stories in it will give me something to do now and then when nothing else is going on. Mrs. Campbell did not get down here as she would have had to stay overnight for there is only one boat runs down here but once a day and she comes down at 5 ½ P.M. o'clock and returns next morning at 8 ½. Reilly is the most intimate friend I have down here although I do not go with him as often as I used to do on account of his not bunking with me anymore. I received the box of cakes through one of the men who were in Washington & got it from Mr. Campbell. We have a dress parade here every evening and all the men in the fort have to be out. We drill four times a day and when the days are warm it is pretty hard on us, the drill hours are from 6 ½ to 7 ½ and from 9 to 10. and from 1 to 2 & 4 to 5 besides the dress parade at 6 ½. Last night some of the boys in the fort had a concert and we had some very good songs accompanied by several instruments. The men are complaining very much from the heat to day and there is no doubt but it is very warm. Some of the men are practicing at the draw bridge in the sally port. We [have] so little news here except what we get from friends who happen to get here now and then that what news we do hear of anything that occurs about here you know it before we do. Hoping you are all well I close with love to all.

Write Soon.

Your affectionate son
C.C. Pollock

While I was on guard I broke of this stem which I send you
C.C.P.

———◆•◆•◆———

Fort Washington June 18th 1861

*D*ear Ma

I wrote a letter to you yesterday but as I have something I want to say I will write you again tonight. We have just had roll call. 9 ½ o'clock and I have not time to write much. We have just heard that Major Haskins has been ordered with his company to go to Manassas Junction and if no other officer is sent here in his place Capt. Smith will be commandant but the men very often get up reports on their own account so I do not know whether to believe it or not. What I wanted to tell you most was that Will Bartholomew has an appointment in the 16th Infantry and is ordered to report to the Col. at Chicago. He got the appointment through Lin's[25] influence who is private secretary of Cameron and I think you might say something to him about mine. I would rather be in the Marine Corps but if that is impossible, why, I will take any one that I can get. You had better make application at once for I believe there are a great many applications. The men are calling to me to put out the light so I will close.

With much love to all
I remain your affectionate Son
C.C. Pollock

Direct your letters in care of Capt D.A. Smith Fort Washington Md.

———◆•◆•◆———

Fort Washington June 24/61

*D*ear Ma

I received your letter to day and I will now answer it as after tomorrow we will have to come down to stamps as they have decided that franking does not pay and I guess you will have to send me some stamps (as I am entirely out of money)

25. Lin Bartholomew was a young but very prominent attorney in Pottsville who, in 1860, was elected to a seat in the state House of Representatives. Apparently, he was well acquainted with Secretary of War Cameron and was able to help secure an officer's commission for Pollock's friend William Bartholomew in the Regular Army.

or else I will have to put an end to writing to you. There was a scouting party sent out Saturday and they went down the river about ten miles scouting around after battery's but could not come across anything. The Major sent down for three men to go out of our company but all wanted to go so they marched all of us up into the fort and three were picked out but I was not among the lucky ones. They went down in two row boats and had all their hands blistered when they got back. Lieut. Wallace tells me to night that we are to have a gun boat down here this week to go out with. One of the Lieuts. came down from Washington to day and says that Capt. Wren's company is to leave this week to join the regiment but I cannot say how true it is as so many reports come here except what we get from papers two or three days old. Tell Mary or Margie I would like them to write to me and tell me something about what is going on in town among the girls as all I hear is from Reilly who gets letters from Clem Evans and one of the girls; does Mary know who it is? I would like to know. I have never written to Clara Wolff yet but may do so before long; does she ever say anything about Dory Patterson writing to her as Dory keeps very quiet about her? Please answer as soon as possible and send the stamps as I want to write several letters and would do it tonight but it nearly tatoo but I shall write one to Aunt Sarah tonight yet. One of the men just brought in a glow worm. They are very beautiful but smell just like sulphur.

From your affectionate son
C.C. Pollock

———•◦•———

Fort Washington June 30, 1861

*D*ear Ma
I have been expecting a letter from you for the last couple of days but have not had it yet; it is now nearly a week since I heard from you last but I think I will get one to-morrow. Everything is going on smoothly and nothing new except a scouting party every now and then up or down the river. There was one sent out last night. One party went on land and the other on the river as there is some evidence that a correspondence is kept up between parties in Washington and the rebel forces and that it is carried across the river somewhere near

this point but they did not hear or see anything, though Capt. Smith thinks that they got wind of the affair through some of the men who were out in the country and got talking incautiously. Yesterday evening the *James Guy* went past here at full headway and directly afterwards we saw another boat coming after blowing her whistle and waving a red flag which signals were meant for the *Guy* but she did not hear or see them so we fired a blank cartridge to bring her to but she did not appear to mind it so they sent a ball after her (the first one that has been fired at anything since we have been here) and it struck the water about ten feet ahead of her, a very good shot considering She was about two miles off. She immediately turned around and the other boat soon caught up to her. The *Guy* soon after turned around and went on downstream while the other boat came back to the wharf and the Capt. told us that the *Guy* was taking dispatches to the *Freeburn* and that just after she had started another dispatch had come and he was sent after her. He said that the Capt. of the *Guy* said he did not want any more balls that near to him again. It is raining quite hard this afternoon but this morning it was very pleasant and we had an inspection and parade. The men mostly are at the same job that I am at i.e. setting in their bunks writing letters. There is nothing more to tell you so I will close with love to all.

I remain your Affectionate son
C.C. Pollock

Tell Harry to write.

Enclosed you will find a piece of the flag staff that Ellsworth took the flag from in Alexandria and the other is a piece of the step on which Ellsworth was standing when he was shot. I got them both from Frank Bannan who went to Alexandria soon after the murder had taken place.[26]

Yours truly
C.C.P.

---

26. Elmer Ellsworth studied law in Abraham Lincoln's office in Springfield, Illinois. He accompanied Lincoln to Washington in 1861 and, upon the outbreak of war, organized the 11th New York Fire Zouaves. On May 24, 1861, Ellsworth led his men into the streets of Alexandria, Virginia. There, Ellsworth removed the Confederate flag that had been defiantly flying atop the Marshall House Inn, and which had been seen daily in Washington. On his way down the stairs of the hotel, however, the proprietor shot and killed him. Ellsworth became a martyr; his death a symbol for the Union and anything associated with the event—including pieces of the flag and, apparently, pieces of wood from the step upon which he was standing when killed—became sought-after souvenirs. It is not known whatever became of the pieces Pollock sent home.

CHAPTER TWO

To War Once More:
With the 48th Pennsylvania from
Pottsville to Fortress Monroe

July–November 1861

EARLY ON THE afternoon of July 30, 1861, Curtis Pollock and his fellow soldiers of the Washington Artillery arrived back home in Pottsville, amid great celebration. The people of the city turned out in large numbers to cheer on their heroes, just as they had when the company first marched off to war three months earlier, in April. Pride filled their hearts to know that it was these men—their sons, their brothers, their husbands—who were among the first to answer the nation's call and were the very first volunteers to reach the distressed capital city of Washington, ahead of all other Northern volunteer soldiers. Although they did not see any battle action but rather spent the entirety of their three-month term of service in and around Washington, to be a First Defender was still a great distinction and these men would proudly carry that title with them for the rest of their lives. Already they had received the official Thanks of Congress. On July 22—one day following the Union defeat at 1st Bull Run—Representative James Campbell introduced a resolution that read, in part, "That the thanks of this House are due and hereby tendered to the . . . soldiers from Pennsylvania who passed through the mob of Baltimore and reached Washington on the 18th day of April, for the defense of the National Capital."[1] Now, on that July 30 afternoon, as they marched through their hometown of Pottsville and listened to a number of stirring, patriotic speeches welcoming them home, these First Defenders were receiving the thanks of their fami-

1. Thompson, 96.

lies, their friends, and their neighbors. It is probable the Pollock family was there, with William and Emily welcoming the return of their son Curtis, who had celebrated his nineteenth birthday just two days earlier.

Pollock's three-month term of service had officially expired on July 18 but he remained on duty at Fort Washington for nearly a week afterwards. It was not until July 24 that he and his comrades in the Washington Artillery started for home. They traveled first aboard the steamer *Philadelphia* to the Washington Arsenal where they bedded down for the night. Next day they hopped aboard train cars and set off for a return visit to Baltimore only this time there would be no attack from a frenzied mob. Harrisburg was finally reached on July 26 but further red tape delays would keep them there for an additional four days. On July 29, the men turned in their muskets, received their pay, and were honorably discharged from the service. The following afternoon they were back at home. But while the three-month terms of service for these men may have expired, the war was still a far way from being over.

At the outset of hostilities the prevailing thought among many was that the war would last just a few months and be decided after one strong show of force. The crushing Union defeat on the fields of Manassas, however, squashed these thoughts and helped the nation awake to the terrible realities of war as the people now girded themselves for a longer struggle. President Lincoln had already issued another call-to-arms. Instead of seeking 75,000 men to serve for ninety days, Lincoln now sought 600,000 men to serve for a period of three years, or until the end of the war, whichever would come first. Quotas for volunteers were imposed upon all the states and all throughout the North, from the major cities to the smallest of hamlets, men flocked to recruiting offices to offer their services.

To help meet Pennsylvania's quota, Governor Andrew Curtin authorized thirty-nine-year-old Colonel James Nagle of Pottsville to raise and organize a regiment of three-year volunteers. Nagle was not a professionally trained, West Point-educated soldier, but he did have much experience in martial affairs. In the summer of 1840, and at just eighteen years of age, he had organized the Pottsville Blues, a militia company that two years later would become the Washington Artillery. As its captain, Nagle led the Washington Artillery in the Mexican-American

Curtis Pollock in the uniform of a private. This photograph was likely taken during either the spring or summer of 1861 when Pollock served in the Washington Artillery. (Courtesy of Mr. Ronn Palm and the Museum of Civil War Images)

War, serving creditably in General Winfield Scott's celebrated 1847 campaign from Vera Cruz to Mexico City and seeing action at such places as Cerro Gordo and Puebla. Nagle and his company returned home in the summer of 1848, greeted by a

perfect ovation, which, if he had seen it, must have left a profound impression upon a then six-year-old Curtis Pollock. Upon
his return from Mexico, Nagle turned to more peaceful endeav-
ors, focusing on raising his family and on his house-painting
and wallpaper-hanging business. But in 1852 the people of
Schuylkill County elected him sheriff and throughout the next
eight years he held various high-ranking positions in the state
militia system. When civil war broke out in April 1861, Governor
Curtin summoned Nagle to Harrisburg where he initially helped
to organize and instruct the raw volunteers who were arriving
in the state capital. Believing Nagle's talents would be better
served in the field, however, Curtin commissioned him colonel
of the 6th Pennsylvania Infantry, a three-month regiment composed largely of Schuylkill County men. Nagle's 6th Pennsylvania served in the upper Shenandoah Valley, in a small army
commanded by General Robert Patterson and in the brigade led
by Colonel George Thomas—the future "Rock of Chickamauga."
And although they did not participate in any substantial battle
action, Nagle made a great and lasting impression on the soldiers
under his command. Indeed, in October 1861, long after the 6th
Pennsylvania had disbanded, a number of officers and soldiers
from that regiment collected funds to purchase a field glass as
a gift for their former commander, upon which was inscribed
"To James Nagle . . . From the Officers and Privates of his old
command, the late 6th Regiment P.V., as a Tribute of regard
for his Gallantry and Patriotism." In a letter accompanying the
field glass, Nagle's former subordinates in the 6th spoke of the
qualities that made him such a good officer: "For many years
past the military spirit and organization of Schuylkill County
have been chiefly sustained by your exertions. When the Nation's honor was to be maintained on the plains of Mexico, you
with a well-disciplined corps under your command, sprang to
arms and hastened to the field of conflict; in Cerro Gordo's terrific fight you stood calm and unmoved amid the leaden storm
of death which fell on every side, and by your presence of mind
and courage saved many gallant men from the fearful carnage."
The officers went on to say that "During the three months we
served together, though inflexibly firm and persistently indus-
trious in the performance and requirement of every camp and
field duty, yet such was the kindness of your demeanor, and
your tender regard for the health, safety and comfort of your

men, that we regarded you rather as a friend and father, than a mere military commander."[2]

The people of Schuylkill County had long held Nagle in high regard and many of those who were desirous of volunteering, sought to serve under his command—including Curtis Pollock who made mention of this in his June 14, 1861, letter from Fort Washington. Oliver Bosbyshell, a fellow First Defender who went on to serve alongside Curtis Pollock in Company G of the 48th Pennsylvania, described James Nagle simply as "Schuylkill County's foremost citizen-soldier." When Nagle received authorization from Governor Curtin on August 14, 1861, to form a regiment of three-year volunteers, he endeavored to do so almost entirely from the towns, townships, and coal patches of Schuylkill County. To this end, Nagle selected ten men, including two of his younger brothers, to open recruiting stations throughout the county, with each man expected to raise a company of approximately one hundred men. Daniel Kaufmann gathered recruits from such places as Port Clinton and Tamaqua, while farmers and coal miners from the areas around Silver Creek and New Philadelphia signed up under William Winlack. Joseph Hosking's company came principally from Minersville; John Porter's from Orwigsburg, Auburn, and the small settlements of Schuylkill Valley. The impressively named Henry Augustus Muhlenberg Filbert signed up volunteers from Schuylkill Haven and Cressona while the other five officers— James Wren, Henry Pleasants, Joseph Gilmour, and Daniel and Philip Nagle—established their recruiting stations in Pottsville. Recruiting was prosecuted vigorously and within a just a few weeks, the work of these ten officers was completed and a new regiment was born.[3]

Volunteers arrived in great number. Throughout August and into September, thousands of Schuylkill County's sons descended upon the recruiting offices to enlist. They came from all the county's municipalities, from many ethnic and socioeconomic backgrounds and from many different walks of life. They were young, for the most part, with many being farmers,

---

2. For a biographical sketch of Nagle, see Wallace, *Memorial to the Patriotism of Schuylkill County*, 501-504; the letter authored by the officers of the 6th PA Infantry accompanying their gift to Nagle is reprinted in Ibid., 85.

3. For more on the raising and recruitment of the 48th PA, see Oliver Christian Bobsyshell, *The Forty-Eighth in the War*, (Philadelphia: Avil Printing Company, 1895): 17-18; Joseph Gould, *The Story of the Forty-Eighth* (Philadelphia: Alfred M. Slocum Printers, 1908): 21-23.

*Described as Schuylkill County's "foremost citizen-soldier,"
Brigadier General James Nagle organized and led four different
regiments of Pennsylvania volunteers, including, most famously,
the 48th Pennsylvania, a regiment he organized in the summer of
1861. Nagle died of heart failure at age 44 in 1866. (Courtesy of
the Library of Congress)*

skilled and unskilled manual laborers, students, and clerks.
Of course, with Schuylkill County lying at the heart of anthracite coal country, many of these volunteers were professional
coal miners, willing to leave their picks and shovels behind to
take up the musket in support of the nation. A good percent-
age of these volunteers were of foreign-birth, from Ireland and
Germany mainly. Many were already veterans, having served in
various three-month organizations such units as the 5th or 6th

Governor Andrew Gregg Curtin, the wartime governor of Pennsylvania. (Courtesy of the Library of Congress)

Pennsylvania. And, of course, a good number of these volunteers were First Defenders, veterans of either the National Light Infantry or the Washington Artillery who, upon returning home, made the decision to reenlist, this time for a three-year term of service. Indeed, for the majority of the First Defenders—whether they were from Pottsville, Reading, Lewistown or Allentown—their Civil War service did not end upon the expiration of that initial three-month term of service. Most of them—including Curtis Pollock—reenlisted.

After signing up, the recruits were next sent—sometimes singly, oftentimes in groups—to Harrisburg. They gathered

there at the great training ground known as Camp Curtin where
they were introduced to the rudiments of soldier life and where
they waited to be formally mustered into service, provided, of
course, they successfully passed a physical examination. Those
who did not were sent back home. By mid-September, 1861, the
1,010 volunteers who had signed up under Kaufmann, Wren,
Pleasants, Gilmour, Hoskings, Winlack, Porter, Filbert, or under
either of the Nagle brothers—Daniel or Philip—had arrived in
Harrisburg. Among them was nineteen-year-old Curtis Pollock
who, on September 9, signed up to serve in Captain Philip Nagle's company, which was recruited principally from Pottsville.
Ten days later, on September 19 and still at Camp Curtin, the
volunteers were drawn up into line and sworn into service, and,
just like that, the 48th Pennsylvania Volunteer Infantry came
into existence, the regiment thusly designated because it was
the forty-eighth regiment of volunteers recruited and organized
in Pennsylvania since the commencement of war. The following
day Governor Andrew Curtin journeyed to the vast camp and
training ground that bore his name. He went there to present
the 48th Pennsylvania with their regimental flags. Two stands
of colors were presented that day, one by Governor Curtin on
behalf of the state, the other presented by a Mr. John T. Werner,
"one of Pottsville's patriotic citizens," who delivered it on behalf
of the people of Pottsville. Upon the upper left canton of this
latter flag was inscribed a fitting motto which the 48th would
proudly serve under for the next four years: "In the Cause of
the Union, We Know No Such Word as Fail." Governor Curtin
delivered an inspiring speech—his "glowing words," said Oliver
Bosbyshell, making "a deep impression upon the command."
With the ceremonies concluded, the soldiers of the 48th Pennsylvania awaited orders, ready to take to the field. In the meantime, Colonel James Nagle, commanding the regiment, took a
few moments to write a quick note to the editors of the *Miners'
Journal* in which he thanked the people of Pottsville for the flag.
"We feel very grateful," declared Nagle, "and return our most
sincere thanks for the beautiful National Flag [Werner] saw fit
to present to us—a flag we all swore to protect and defend, and
I have every reason to believe that the 48th will do its duty,
knowing our cause is just."[4]

---

4. Bosbyshell, 18-19; Wallace, 86-87.

Orders for the new regiment at last arrived on September 24: The 48th Pennsylvania was to proceed to Washington, D.C. The men were soon busy packing their gear and that afternoon, the regiment set out aboard the train cars of the Northern Central Railway. Once more, the trip to Washington would take them through the city of Baltimore. For Curtis Pollock and the other First Defenders aboard the train, memories of their unpleasant experiences of April 18 when they were verbally and physically assaulted while attempting to march through the city no doubt rushed back to their minds. This time, however, Baltimore was firmly under Union control and the soldiers expected little trouble. But trouble did indeed arise once more. When the train carrying the 48th made it to within seven miles of the station in Baltimore, someone, presumably a Confederate sympathizer, threw the switch to knock the train from the track. Two of the cars were thrown off track but fortunately for the regiment, no one sustained any serious injuries, only a "few bruises." It was, however, a very clear reminder of the hostility of some. This "fiendish" attack—as regimental historian Joseph Gould later termed it—caused a lengthy delay, while everything was sorted out and as the cars were literally put back on track.[5]

Baltimore was finally reached on the morning of September 25. Unloading from the train cars, the regiment marched two miles through the city. Most, including Curtis Pollock, thought they were marching to the train station; instead, they marched to the harbor. At some point during their journey from Harrisburg, Colonel Nagle received a new set of orders: instead of going to Washington, the 48th Pennsylvania was directed to proceed to Fortress Monroe, Virginia. It was not until the soldiers arrived at the wharf and began boarding steamers that they discovered this change of plans.

Located in Hampton Roads in southeastern Virginia and on the tip of the peninsula bounded by the York and James Rivers, Fortress Monroe was an important Union military installation throughout the Civil War. Following Virginia's secession on April 17, 1861, and recognizing its strategic importance, President Abraham Lincoln directed that the Federal garrison at Fortress Monroe be immediately strengthened, hoping to prevent it from falling into Confederate hands. Thousands of troops began arriving and it was not long before the hexagonal fortress was

---

5. Gould, 34.

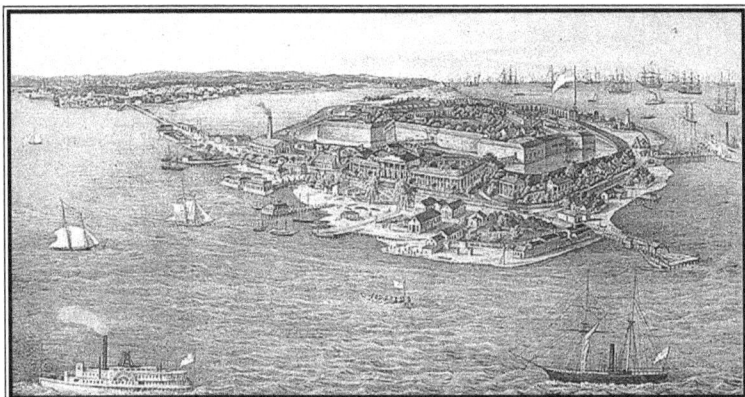

Fortress Monroe, Virginia, as depicted in this lithograph print by E. Sachse and Company. (Courtesy of the Library of Congress)

firmly secured. It would remain in U.S. hands throughout all four years of the conflict. In the middle of May, 1861, Major General Benjamin Butler arrived to take command of the fort. A pre-war lawyer and powerful Democratic congressman, Butler had no military background or experience but was nevertheless made a general since Lincoln needed all the support he could get from the other side of the political aisle. Soon after his arrival at Fortress Monroe, Butler made headlines by refusing to return escaped slaves who sought safe haven there. Since the Confederacy had been using slave labor to build fortifications, Butler deemed these escaped slaves as "contraband of war." His actions would be validated by Congress with the passage of the First Confiscation Act in early August 1861, which declared that any slave used for military purposes against the United States could rightfully be "confiscated." Seeking freedom, hundreds of escaped slaves soon began pouring into Fortress Monroe, which became known as "Freedom's Fortress." Butler's actions, approved by Congress and later applied across other occupied areas of the South, struck an early blow against the social and economic foundations of the Confederacy.[6]

The soldiers of the 48th Pennsylvania arrived at Fortress Monroe on September 26, 1861, after a rather harrowing ride down the Chesapeake Bay aboard the *Georgia*, a steamer Oliver Bosbyshell described as "a precarious old craft, likely to fall

6. Brian Matthew Jordan, "Fort Monroe During the Civil War." (2011, May 26). In *Encyclopedia Virginia*. Retrieved from http://www.EncyclopediaVirginia.org/Fort_Monroe_During_the_Civil_War.

CAMP HAMILTON – FORTRESS MONROE Vᴬ-.

The 48th Pennsylvania spent six weeks encamped at Camp Hamilton in the fall of 1861, nearby Fortress Monroe. Notice the "Camp of the 48th Pennsylvania" written upon this print. (Courtesy of the Library of Congress)

to pieces." The captain of the *Georgia*, said Bosbyshell, "wisely crept along close in shore, not knowing what moment the timbers of the old hulk would separate." For the soldiers of the 48th, many of whom had never traveled on water, it must have been an anxious voyage. Arriving safely, however, the regiment disembarked and marched around the high stone and brick walls of Fortress Monroe and across the "long, narrow road" that connected the fort to Hampton, where the 48th settled in at Camp Hamilton. By this time, Butler was gone, having been replaced by General John Wool, while General Joseph K.F. Mansfield held immediate command of the volunteer troops at Camp Hamilton. It was there, at Camp Hamilton, reflected regimental historian Joseph Gould, that the regiment "settled down into a soldier's life as naturally and contentedly as though we were old veterans."[7]

The 48th would remain at Camp Hamilton near Fortress Monroe for the next six weeks, the time the men spent in seemingly constant drills, parades, inspections, and picket duty. On October 3, Oliver Bosbyshell wrote to the *Miners' Journal* boasting that "Our regiment is fast becoming efficient in the many evolutions laid down in tactics under our able and much

7. Bosbyshell, 19; Gould, 34.

talented Colonel James Nagle. He is untiring in his efforts to make this a tip-top Regiment. We have Regimental drill every morning and dress parade and drill every evening—besides many company and squad drills during the day."[8] Of course, there was some down time, which many of the soldiers took full advantage of to write letters home. There are few existing letters, however, from Curtis Pollock during the regiment's six-week stay at Fortress Monroe. The first was written on September 28, just two days after the regiment's arrival. In it, he described the journey from Harrisburg to Baltimore and the trip down the Chesapeake to Fortress Monroe. Feeling that he was deserving of a higher rank, Pollock also expressed his displeasure at being appointed third corporal of Company G, setting the stage for what would become a many months' long quest for promotion, one that would eventually come to cause much controversy in camp but which would ultimately lead to his May 1862 commissioning as First Lieutenant. Pollock's other two letters from Fortress Monroe document more of the regiment's doings around camp, the arrival of a vast fleet in mid-October, as well as the rumors that all-too freely circulated around camp about impending attacks and approaching dangers.

———————

Fortress Monroe
September 28 1861

Dear Ma
    I had intended to have my letter [written] to you before but I have been pretty busy fixing up around camp. We left Camp Curtin about 7 o'clock Tuesday morning but did not get fairly off from Harrisburg until one o'clock. The cars were very full and we had hardly room to move around so I got in the car with the luggage and had it quite comfortable. I slept in the car and got awake about 4 o'clock and the train was stopped. I then got out and went to see what was the matter when I found the engine and the first two cars off the track (I was in the third car) the switch being turned by some "secesh." I then went back and lay down until morning and by that time they had the two horse cars back on the track and were working at

---

8. Oliver Bosbyshell to Editors, *Miners' Journal*, printed in *Miners' Journal*, October 12, 1861.

the engine. He [the engineer] did not get it on until about 11:00 o'clock A.M. We then started for Baltimore and after tramping around through the streets for some time we found ourselves at the wharf instead of the depot and we for the first time learned that we were to go to Fortress Monroe. They at last got us all on the boat and we started, the band playing "Hail Columbia." We passed Fort McHenry and Fort Carroll, a new fort that is not finished yet. We had a pleasant ride down the bay, and at night I slept on one of the seats in the ladies' cabin.

[I] got up in the morning and saw the sun rise out of the sea. We arrived here about 6:00 o'clock in the morning and saw any quantity of "contrabands" running around and some fishing for crabs others loafing around and looking at us. We waited about a half hour until Col. Nagle reported to Gen. Wool and then got off and were marched about a mile back and inspected the camp. He [General Wool] is a small man not much taller than Uncle Robert or Joseph and not near so stout.[9] I have been appointed corporal. Capt. [Philip] Nagle appointed some sergeants and corporals over me who were never out before and are almost as dumb as they can be. We have commenced drilling and have about six drills a day. I have just come in from a regimental drill and in about half an hour will have to go out on a company drill. We are kept busy pretty much all the time and have not much chance to run around. I have not been down to the fort yet but think I will go down to church tomorrow if I can get off. No more at present—

Your Affectionate Son
C.C. Pollock

Camp Hamilton
Oct. 27th 1861

*D*ear Ma
I received your letter this morning and as is my usual custom I will answer it immediately. We did not get off the other day though we were all ready to start. We were to have gone

9. At age 77, General John Wool (1784-1869) was the oldest general on either side during the Civil War. He served with distinction in the War of 1812 and during the Mexican-American War and was highly revered by superiors and subordinates alike. He resigned from the army in 1863 after more than fifty years in the service of the United States. He died in Troy, New York, six years later at the age of 85.

to Newport News as they were expecting to be attacked and we were to go over by way of Hampton and attack them in the rear but as it commenced raining in the evening no attack was made. Yesterday we had a grand review. The troops reviewed consisted of the 20th New York, Col. Max Weber, the 16th Massachusetts Col. [Powell] Wyman, also [the] 48th, Col. Nagle and the Naval Brigade. We made quite a long string. Major-General Wool and staff reviewed us, he looked at us very sharp. When we were marching past him in review just as our company marched past him he turned to General Mansfield[10] and said, they are all fine looking young men. And the vessels belonging to this expedition are lying off the fort but are expected to leave in a few days.[11] On Friday last they unloaded them (16,000 in all) on the beach for the purpose of getting them in the way of getting ashore in surfboats.[12] I heard the Capt. say yesterday that we would not leave here before April so that you can send the box here as soon as you please. Send a little molasses in the box and have a lock and key to it and you can put the key on the top with a piece of tin tacked over it.

John Clemens[13] got quite well again for awhile he was pretty bad but I think it was more homesickness than anything else.

I hope I will see Rob before he goes to Hatteras; the troops that are going there generally lay over here for a week or so, so I think it is likely I will see him.[14] There is nothing going on

10. General Joseph King Fenno Mansfield (1803-1862) was eighteen years old when he graduated from West Point, ranked second in the Class of 1822. A gifted engineer, Mansfield had forty years' experience in the army by the time the Civil War broke out. As commander of the 12th Army Corps, Mansfield was mortally wounded at the Battle of Antietam on September 17, 1862. Oliver Bosbyshell reflected the sentiment of most when writing about Mansfield: "His mild disposition and benevolent heart, that caused him to ever be on the lookout for the welfare of his soldiers, combined, however, with firm, just discipline, endeared him to all with whom he came in contact."

11. In mid-October, hundreds of vessels and thousands of troops began arriving in the area around Hampton Roads and Fortress Monroe, constituting a joint army-navy expedition under the command of Flag Officer Samuel duPont and General Thomas W. Sherman. The fleet, totaling 77 vessels including warships and troops transports set sail on October 28-29, heading for the South Carolina coast. Several days later in an amphibious operation , the expedition succeeded in capturing Port Royal, South Carolina.

12. Of particular interest to the soldiers of the 48th Pennsylvania was the fact that the 50th Pennsylvania Regiment was present, as part of the force gathering for the Port Royal Expedition. Companies A and C of the 50th were recruited from Schuylkill County and the regiment was commanded by Colonel Benjamin Christ of Minersville. It is unlikely, however, that the Schuylkill County soldiers in these two regiments had much time to interact while at Fortress Monroe.

13. Private John Clemens, Company G: Mustered into service on October 1, 1861, age 18, a resident of Pottsville. He was mustered out of service upon the expiration of his term of service on October 1, 1864.

14. At the end of August, a joint army-navy force succeeded in capturing Hatteras Inlet, North Carolina. Despite the rumors that they would remain at Fortress Monroe until the following April, the soldiers of the 48th would soon be receiving orders to proceed to Hatteras.

here just now. I have only been on guard twice since I have
been here once on picket and once on camp guard. I have
nothing more to say so I will close with much love to all.

I remain
Your Affectionate Son
C.C. Pollock

⎯⎯⎯•◦•⎯⎯⎯

Camp Hamilton
Oct. 30th 1861

*D*ear Ma

I received your letter this morning and as I am not busy
this afternoon I will write you a few lines. We had another
grand review this morning. It lasted about two hours and a
half but was not so tiresome as the other because we had no
knapsacks on. There were more troops in line today than there
was on Saturday. It consisted of the N.Y. 20th, (Germans) 10th
Mass., 10th N.Y., 48th P.V., 1st Del., and the Naval Brigade.
It was quite a long line and took us about ½ an hour to walk
around. On Monday afternoon, the Captain told us he wanted
us all to go to the funeral; we wondered who was to be buried
as no one in our camp had died. The Captain marched us
down to the fort and we found out that one of Col. [Benjamin]
Christ's men [of the 50th PA] had died on board of one of the
vessels but they would not let any of his comrades come on
shore to bury him so we were called on to do it. There were
eight of us [who] shot over his grave, [and] the first time for me.
I wonder who raises such ridiculous reports about us being
sick? John Clemens was sick for awhile but is now perfectly
well and doing his regular duty; neither of the other two have
been sick at all. If you ever hear anything about me don't believe it until you hear from me because such reports are often
raised about here just to frighten persons at home. We had a
little frost here [the other] night but I generally manage to keep
warm. The only thing that bothers me is my feet but when it is
cold I wrap my feet up in my overcoat and put the blanket over
that and I am as warm as you please. I would like very much if
you would send me a pictorial paper once in a while as we do
not get much to read here except now and then a Phila. Daily.
I saw an account of a fight at Balls Bluff in the Inquirer and

think that whoever ordered that movement without furnishing the necessary arrangements to recross the river in case of defeat should be court-martialed or severely dealt with.[15] These fellows make too many mistakes and it will soon be time to put a stop to them. I am sorry that Dewees had such a time of it the other night give my best respects to all of them. Please send some tobacco and a pipe when you send the things on.

From Your Affectionate Son
Curtis C. Pollock

Camp Hamilton
Sunday Morning
Nov. [October] 30th 1861

ear Ma

    I received your letter and watch yesterday and was very much pleased to get them. The box will be here this afternoon or tomorrow morning and will be very acceptable. We had a general inspection this morning. The whole Regiment paraded and was inspected by the Colonel. We expect to be paid in about a week or so but I do not know how much we will get. I was over to see the 1st Delaware Regt. this morning. They are encamped on the same ground that we were when we first came here but we left it because of it being so low and muddy and it is not any better now than it was then. We have had a great deal of rain here lately and one of those havelocks[16] would come in very nicely. When you get one try and get one that has cap attached to the cape so that I can wear it without another cap. There are several of that kind in the Regiment and I like them very much. On Thursday evening (Hallow eve) the Naval Brigade had quite a spree, they had their street all decked off with branches of trees and as much lager as they could drink and they were all drunk, officers and all; several of our fellows were over and came home drunk. The great naval expedition has gone off at last and has thinned out the number of vessels here considerably. There is nothing new going on

---

15. Fought on October 21, 1861, in Loudoun County, Virginia, the Battle of Ball's Bluff resulted in a rout of Federal forces and a humiliating defeat for the Union.
16. A havelock was a piece of cloth designed to be attached to a cap that would protect the neck and ears from the sun or the rain.

here and I have scarcely been out of camp for a week except for water. There is very little sickness in camp at present; not one being sick in our company that I know of. John Clemens is entirely well again and doing duty. We got five new recruits the other day which makes seventy-eight men all told and we only want five more men to make the company full. Dinner is ready and I will finish it [the letter] after dinner. I have just finished dinner we had bean soup and a piece of fresh beef, boiled. It is just twelve o'clock and I am thinking about you sitting down to a nice Sunday dinner, pies and rice pudding or something like that. You must send that cold roast turkey for my Christmas dinner and some mince pies with plenty of mince meat and plenty of brandy in them. I have nothing more to say at present, so I will close with much love to all.

From Your Affectionate Son
C.C. Pollock

Has Cake's Regt. gone yet?[17] Have they stopped work at the Lumber yard? I heard that Tom Corby was on the fleet off here.

C.C. Pollock

❄ ❄ ❄

DESPITE THE GRUMBLINGS about the seemingly endless drills and monotonous review, generally, Corporal Pollock and the soldiers of the 48th came to enjoy their six-week stay at Camp Hamilton; their next camp, as it turned out, would not nearly be so pleasant, nor their commanding general so kind. The 48th Pennsylvania would return to the familiar tramping grounds of Fortress Monroe several more times before war's end but their first stint there ended in early November 1861 when orders arrived directing the regiment to report to Hatteras Island, North Carolina.

---

17. After commanding the three-month 25th Pennsylvania Infantry, Colonel Henry Cake was authorized by Governor Curtin to raise a three-year regiment. Recruited largely from Pottsville and Schuylkill County, this regiment would be designated the 96th Pennsylvania Infantry when it was mustered into Federal service in November 1861.

CHAPTER THREE

"Here We Are Away Down on The Coast of North Carolina"

November 1861–July 1862

———•◦•———

REGIMENTAL HISTORIAN JOSEPH Gould declared that the soldiers of the 48th Pennsylvania "enjoyed every minute" of their six-week stay at Fortress Monroe. "We were pleasantly situated," wrote Gould in 1908, "having plenty of army rations and luxuries in lavish abundance. Fish, oysters, clams, and crabs could be had with little effort, and despite a few rain storms, accompanied by the wind . . . we were comfortable and happy." But these comfortable and happy days could not last forever. On November 10, 1861, orders arrived for the regiment to depart Fortress Monroe and proceed to Hatteras Island, North Carolina, where they were to relieve the 20th Indiana Infantry, which had been stationed there. "[I]t cannot be said that a very large degree of enthusiasm was manifested over this assignment," wrote Oliver Bosbyshell, wryly, but orders being orders, the men struck their tents, packed their gear, and readied themselves for the next chapter in the regiment's history, one that would be written on the sandy shores of North Carolina.[1]

From the outset of the war there were many—both North and South—who recognized the strategic importance of Hatteras, for whomever controlled the inlet there would also control many of sounds, rivers, and seaports of coastal North Carolina. Soon after North Carolina severed its ties with the Union in May 1861, work began on several coastal fortifications, including Forts Clark and Hatteras on Hatteras Island, which were forcefully constructed by slave labor to protect the inlet. For the first three months of the war and while Confederate troops

---

1. Gould, 37; Bosbyshell, 21.

Famed Civil War artist Alfred Waud's depiction of Fort Hatteras, Hatteras Island, North Carolina. (From Battles and Leaders of the Civil War, *Vol. I)*

garrisoned these forts, privateers used the inlet to launch raids against Northern maritime commerce, disrupting trade and capturing a good number of ships that were laden with goods from South America, the Caribbean, and New England. In an effort to curb this widespread privateering emanating from Hatteras Inlet and as part of the larger effort to tighten up the blockade of the vast Southern coastline, Union authorities approved a joint army-navy expedition against Forts Hatteras and Clark. Led by Flag Officer Silas Stringham, commander of the Atlantic Blockading Squadron, and General Benjamin Butler, this operation was a complete success, with both forts falling into U.S. hands on August 28-29, 1861. Confederate losses totaled four men killed, twenty wounded, and nearly 700 taken prisoner, while Union casualties totaled just one man killed and two wounded. The victories at Forts Clark and Hatteras may have been small compared to later engagements of the war but they were significant in that they provided a morale boost to the North following the disastrous defeat at 1st Bull Run and in securing a foothold on the North Carolina Sounds, which would later be used to

Waud's depiction of Fort Clark, Hatteras Island, North Carolina. (From Battles and Leaders of the Civil War, Vol. I)

launch attacks against other strategic points, such as Roanoke Island and New Bern.[2]

Following the victory at Hatteras, Stringham left a few of his ships behind to guard the inlet while a number of Butler's men remained to garrison the two forts. In late September, the 20th Indiana Infantry arrived to help garrison the forts but theirs was an unhappy experience and in early November, the 48th Pennsylvania was ordered to relieve the gloomy Hoosiers. Setting sail aboard the steamer *S.R. Spaulding* on the evening of November 11, Curtis Pollock and the soldiers of the 48th reached Hatteras the following morning. It was not an easy transition for Pollock and his Schuylkill County comrades who had grown accustomed to life at Fortress Monroe and the sight of the ragged and forlorn soldiers of the 20th Indiana did little to ease their concerns about their new assignment. "Our first impressions of Hatteras were not favorable," said Gould, "When we relieved the 20th Indiana Regiment . . . and saw their deplorable condition, heard their tales of woe and had some experience with the troops—of bugs and things they left to our care—we certainly felt despondent, and 'many a time and oft' wondered 'why we came for a soldier.'" One-by-one, the soldiers of the 48th disembarked from the *S.R. Spaulding*, carefully walking down a narrow, wooden plank that had been placed on the side of the ship to a temporary, makeshift

2. Downs, Gregory. "The Union Finally Lands a Victory," *Disunion: A Blog of the New York Times*, published August 28, 2011 http://opinionator.blogs.nytimes.com/2011/08/28/the-union-finally-lands-a-victory/?_r=0 Accessed: November 26, 2014.

An 1837 graduate of the U.S. Military Academy at West Point, General Thomas Williams was a tough, no-nonsense career army man. While quite strict, the soldiers of the 48th came to respect Williams and his discipline was critical in helping to mould the 48th into an effective unit. Williams was killed in action in August 1862 at the battle of Baton Rouge. (Courtesy of the Library of Congress)

wharf where the soldiers regained their land-legs and gathered. Oliver Bosbyshell captured the sentiment of the men as they arrived and saw, for the first time, their new homes, writing that as they "rattled down" that plank, the men "missed the lovely wooded hills and grassy valleys of their charming mountain homes. No trees here, no bushes to relieve the dull monotony, not a spear of the sickliest looking shrub even, no green grass to gladden the eye, naught save sand and sea!" Having completely debarked from the *Spaulding*, the regiment formed into line of march and proceeded to Forts Clark and Hatteras, where they would spend their first "dreary" night on the island.[3]

3. Gould, 40-42; Bosbyshell, 22-23.

The 48th Pennsylvania was not the only regiment stationed at Hatteras. The colorful "Hawkins's Zouaves" of the 9th New York had been encamped there since late August and throughout the ensuing winter of 1861 additional regiments from New York, Connecticut, Maryland, and New Hampshire trickled ashore. In overall command at Hatteras was Brigadier General Thomas Williams, an 1837 graduate of West Point and a tough old soldier who was only there, believed Gould, "to make our lives miserable." Oliver Bosbyshell remembered that "There was probably no one man ever more heartily hated. . .by the members of the Forty-Eighth," than Williams. A veteran of the Black Hawk and Mexican-American Wars, Williams was a strict and severe disciplinarian who drilled the men unmercifully, or at least so thought many of the soldiers. "He was abused roundly every day for his tyrannical orders, rigid discipline, frequent calls for duty, severe guard regulations, excessive drills, thorough inspections, and the like." The men cursed Williams—his "constant vigilance" at camp and the constant drilling in the ankle-deep sand. But this strict discipline helped to transform the 48th into a body of well-trained soldiers and it was officers like Williams, admitted Bosbyshell, who sculpted the raw volunteers, "gathered from all over the North, into shape for such stern work as war." In time, the soldiers came to grudgingly respect Williams and as the weeks went by they began to realize "that beneath the rough exterior and austere demeanor, beat a heart of true devotion to the old flag, a heart overflowing with love and regard for his soldiers." It was a tough love, to be sure, but one that paid great dividends later in the regiment's history, during its more severe campaigns and trials under fire. General Williams was killed at the Battle of Baton Rouge in August 1862 and, recorded Gould, "many were the expressions of sorrow from the boys [of the 48th] when news came of his death."[4]

Just as General Williams took some getting used to, so too would life on Hatteras. And no matter how unfavorable their first impressions may have been—and no matter how great the difficulties the soldiers were forced to overcome while encamped along Carolina's sandy shores—they would eventually grow accustomed to life there too and would come, said Gould, "to love the old place in time." When not drilling, or improving their camps, the men found the time to take in some of the beautiful

---

4. Gould, 43-44; Bosbyshell, 30-31.

scenes the island had to offer. For most of the soldiers from the anthracite-laden coal fields of Schuylkill County, this would be their first experience walking the sandy beaches of the Atlantic coastline. The men gazed at the waves crashing ashore and at the early morning sunrises over the waters of the Atlantic while every now and then schools of porpoises could be seen swimming past. For souvenirs, the men picked the beach clean of its sea shells, sending them home to their families for safekeeping and as reminders of their time spent at Hatteras. The soldiers spent time getting acquainted with the locals. Most of the residents of Hatteras—at least those who remained in their homes during Union occupation—were loyal Unionists in sympathy or perhaps indifferent, simply desiring to be left alone. They would sometimes prepare food for the men and, in some cases, help to care for the sick within camp. The Hatteras Lighthouse was the source of much interest and, during their stay, many of the soldiers climbed the 130 steps to the top to stare out across the sea and down the islands, awestruck by the scenic beauty of it all.

More than thirty years later, when looking back at the time the 48th spent at Hatteras, an aging Oliver Bosbyshell wrote that "The regiment's sojourn there was a fortunate circumstance; it became its school-house. Little versed in war, here, under the able command of that veteran disciplinarian, General Thomas Williams, it became well-drilled and well-disciplined, fitted for the stern career it was destined to pursue."[5]

Of course, in addition to everything else that occupied their time while stationed in North Carolina—first at Hatteras and later at New Bern—many of the 48th's soldiers found the time to write home, including Curtis Pollock whose letters from North Carolina are many. In his first letter, written just three days after the regiment arrived at Fort Clark, he described the journey from Fortress Monroe and recorded his first impressions of life at Hatteras. Subsequent letters recount life at Fort Clark and at nearby Camp Winfield, Curtis's not so favorable thoughts of General Williams, how he spent his first Christmas and New Year's away from home, as well as some of the things the men did to occupy their time, including collecting sea shells and gambling. Curtis also spoke of the deaths of several of his comrades in the 48th and of his desire for a higher rank, whether within the 48th or in another command. Throughout the regiment's stay in North Carolina Pollock began to lobby for promotion, asking

---

5. Bosbyshell, 37.

his father to exert whatever influence he could on U.S. House Representative James Campbell and on Pennsylvania Governor Andrew Curtin. Young Curtis Pollock was hardly alone in his yearning for promotion; however, and as will be seen, his ambition for a higher rank would ultimately create a considerable controversy within the company when, in May 1862, his efforts paid off and a commission arrived, signed by Governor Curtin, appointing him to the rank of 2nd Lieutenant.

———— ·•·•· ————

Fort Clark
Hatteras Inlet
Nov. 15th 1861

Dear Ma
Here we are away down on the coast of North Carolina in the most dreary place in the world. We received orders to get ready to march for Hatteras Inlet on Sunday evening and about two o'clock on Monday afternoon we got into line ready to march for the boat and after waiting about half an hour, we started for the wharf, as we passed [General] Mansfield's house each company gave him three cheers. After we got to the boat we had to wait until dark before we started. We got off at last and had quite a pleasant ride. About 9 o'clock I began to feel a little sick so I went and laid down and went to sleep and slept it off and when I got awoke I felt as well as ever. We arrived here all safe and sound about 10 o'clock and it took about two hours for us all to get off the boat.

When we all got landed we were formed into line and were marched up to Fort Clark, about half way between the two forts there is a small channel washed by the sea waist deep which we had to wade. After we got up we take off our things and go down and carry up all our baggage which took us until evening and the tide having risen the channel was nearly up to our necks. Some of the men are in small wooden barracks which were built by the rebels and the others are in their tents. I am in one of the houses with ten others and we are fixed very comfortably. We have been eating hard crackers since we have been here but they do very well.

It is [an] awful hard place here, nothing but sand, though there are some very pretty shells to be found on the beach. I suppose you received that shell I sent you in the letter I gave to Capt. [Philip] Nagle. We have but two drills a day and dress parade in the evening. Two of the companies here are drilling on the guns in Fort Clark and they are getting along very well.

Nov. 16th

It is quite cold here this morning. The wind is from the north and the waves are very high. It is quite comfortable in the houses but the men that were in the tents say it was very cold. I do not think much of General Williams; he seems to think we ought to be drilling all the time in the sand up to our ankles.

The sand here is much like snow at home and you sink quite as deep into either. The water is very bad, some of it so salty that you can hardly drink it though in some places you can get some that is pretty good. The mail is very irregular, only coming when a boat happens to come down from Fortress Monroe so you will not hear from me so often, but I will write you a letter once a week and hope you will do the same. The direction is Co. G 48th Regt. P.V. Fort Clark Hatteras Inlet N.C. No more at present.

From Your Affectionate Son
C.C. Pollock

Fort Clark
Tuesday, Nov., 1861

*D*ear Ma

I received your letter last Sunday a week and I do not remember whether I answered it or not so I will write again for fear I have not answered it. We have not had a mail since last Sunday week but the *Spaulding* is expected today and it always brings the mail. There is nothing new of any importance going on here at present but we expect to move about four or five miles up the Island the latter end of this week or the beginning of the next. One of the men in Co. A died yesterday of Typhoid Fever and is to be buried today, he comes from Port Clinton.[6] There are four men out of each company up at

6. Private William Miller, Company A, was a nineteen-year-old yeoman from Port Clinton. He was one of at least thirteen 48th Pennsylvania soldiers who succumbed to disease during the regiment's eight-month stay in North Carolina.

the place we are going to, putting up barracks for us to live in as long as we stay here. The weather is very cold here now but we sleep very warm at night. I would like to have a pair of those mitts you were speaking about and a pair of those socks to sleep in as my feet suffer more than any other part of my body. I do not want them to go over my boots but to go over my stockings as I always sleep with my boots off. We get along very comfortably here although it is such a hard place and I am as well satisfied here as any place else. The two Regiments that were here were reviewed by Gen. Williams with knapsacks on and he marched them around twice in review and then drilled them in the loading and firing until they were nearly tired to death; lucky for me I was on guard and thus got clear of it all. I believe that if some of the men had got a chance they would have murdered him they were so mad at him. I always [try to respond to] every letter you write to me. Is Bob Hill in town now? If he is I would like to know as I owe him a letter and tell him that I would have answered it but that I heard that he was out of town and did not know whether he would get it. I am writing this on the head of a drum and it's not very handy so you must excuse the mistakes &c.

No more at present
Your Affectionate Son
C.C. Pollock

———•◆•———

Fort Clark
Near Hatteras Inlet
Dec. 5th 1861

*D*ear Ma

The mail came yesterday but I received no letter. The mail leaves Fortress Monroe on Sunday or Monday evening and if you would write so that the letter would reach there by Saturday morning I would always be sure of getting it. This morning two rebel steamers came up the sound and fired a few shots and shells at our gun boats lieing off Fort Hatteras but none of them took effect. We returned their fire but with no better success but one shot came very near. Frank Farquhar is now here superintending the building of a fort about six

miles up the island near our new barracks.[7] There are three
companies gone up already and they are sending the others
up as fast as the buildings are ready for them. One of our men
died night before last and the captain is trying to have him
sent home; he lives in St Clair and his name is Philip Diehl. I
do not know what was the matter with him and I do not think
the Doctors did either.[8] He is the third one that has died since
we have been here and there are several others very low in the
hospital. Have you heard anything from Mr. Campbell[9] since
he has been in Washington respecting his doing something for
me? I would like to get out of this place as soon as possible as
it is not very healthy. I will try and send with this boat a small
box of shells that I have gathered along shore since I have been
here and as [the regimental sutler Isaac] Lippman[10] is going up
in this boat I think I can get him to put them in the express
office for me. I suppose you received the money I sent you
by express last week. We get the *Miners Journal* pretty much

7. Born near Pottsville on October 30, 1838, Francis Ulrich Farquhar was a West Point-educated engineer. He graduated ranked second in the distinguished June Class of 1861, alongside such other notable graduates as Patrick O'Rorke (who ranked first in the Class), Alonzo Cushing, George Woodruff, Peter Hains, and George Armstrong Custer (who graduated last in the Class). Farquhar served with distinction during the Civil War, first as an Aide-de-Camp on the staff of Colonel Samuel Heintzelman during the Battle of 1st Bull Run, then as an Assistant Engineer with the Army of the Potomac. He later served as Chief Engineer of the Department of North Carolina and as Chief Engineer of the 18th Army Corps. He remained in the army after the Civil War eventually rising to the rank of Major in the Corps of Engineers. He died on July 3, 1883, in Detroit, Michigan, at the age of 45.
8. Philip Diehl, a teamster from Mill Creek (just outside St. Clair), enlisted as a private in Company G, 48th Pennsylvania, on September 20, 1861. At age 38, he was among the oldest soldiers in the entire regiment. The records reveal that Diehl "Died of Disease" at Fort Clark on December 3, 1861. Diehl was the first soldier of Pollock's Company G to die in the war, and his death seems to have shaken young Curtis, along with the sickness that was taking its toll on the regiment in North Carolina. In his regimental history, Oliver Bosbyshell, who, at the time was serving as 2nd Lt. of Company G, wrote that the "authorities refused permission to send [Diehl's] body home," and thus Private Diehl was buried in the graveyard of an old Methodist meeting house on Hatteras Island. This would be Company G's first funeral for one of their own and it left a deep impression on Bosbyshell who wrote: "It is not the mere burying that makes the soldier's funeral so inexpressibly solemn, it is the thought that there is no one near to mourn for him; none but the moaning wind and the ever roaring surf. It was a doleful funeral, tramping through the sand, up the island to this old graveyard. Digging the grave was difficult. It was tedious to make it as deep as it should be. Two feet below the surface developed water, and the balance of the depth attained was through a constantly increasing volume of water. The coffin was lowered into the grave, and by the aid of sticks was pushed down under the water and held there until a sufficient quantity of the wet, sandy soil had been thrown upon it to prevent it from floating." The remains of Philip Diehl remained buried at Hatteras until May 1862, when they were, at last, sent back home to Schuylkill County, where, today, they rest at the Presbyterian Cemetery in Pottsville. (Bosbyshell, 26).
9. James Hepburn Campbell (1820-1895) was a Pottsville lawyer who served the people of Schuylkill County as their U.S. Representative in the 34th, 36th, and 37th Congresses. He served as Major of the 25th Pennsylvania Infantry during the first three months of the war and, in 1864, was appointed by President Lincoln to served as Minister to Sweden. Curtis was hoping to gain Campbell's influence in securing either a promotion or new assignment, or both.
10. Isaac Lippman was the very popular sutler who traveled along with the regiment, selling his goods.

regularly, but I wish you would send me a daily now and then as I do not see one very often.

We have had some very cold weather here but no frost. To-day is very pleasant but the wind blows cold. I have no more to say at present so I will close with love to all.

I remain Your Affectionate Son
C.C. Pollock

———————◆◆———————

Camp Winfield Sunday
Dec. 22nd 1861

Dear Ma
I have just received four letters from you today dated the 8th 9th 12th & 18th and was much pleased to hear from you. The *Spaulding* came down this morning and brought the mail and Lippman. His store has been closed up for two or three days on account of his not having anything to sell but he has brought a large stock with him. I received the socks and like them very much for on a cold night a person feels the need of them very much. It has now been fourteen days since we had a mail and I have only written one letter in that time and that was to Mary. I had intended to write another to you to go in the same mail but the *Spaulding* came in from Beaufort so suddenly that I had no time to write. I received a letter from Harry and Col. Dewees and the latter one was very unexpected. Tell Mary I have written to Sallie Bright since I have been down here but once. There are several of our fellows sick but I have remained perfectly well and hope I will continue to do the same. I think the box is on this boat but I cannot say yet as we are so far above the fort that there is not much com-munication. There is a working party out every day working on the fort and I think they will have it done before a great while. We also have two drills a day one company and one Regimental and dress parade in the evening and as the sand is much more firm here than down below we do not have it very hard. The corporals and sergeants always have command of the squads that work and so we do not have much to do as our turn does not come very often. I would have sent more money home but I owed three or four dollars to Isaac [Lippman] and one to Lieut. Bosbyshell that I borrowed in Harrisburg before I came home

and I wanted to keep some to buy little things and to pay for washing for they will not take tickets and I do not want to deal in the Jews tickets any more. I only get a private's pay and Sam Ruch[11] is a sergeant and gets four Dollars a month more than I do, and as for gambling, I could not do it if I wanted to and I have made up my mind never to play for even a cent and the Col. has made a special order against playing cards for money and anyone caught is to be put in the guard house and be tried by a Court Martial.

Monday Morning [December 23, 1861]

It has been raining since last night slowly. I had not time to finish my letter last night on account of us being out of candles; in fact we are out of everything; the quartermaster at the fort having no provisions on hand at all and if the *Spaulding* had not arrived when she did we should [have] been in a fair way of trying how it was to go without food for a day or two but thank fortune we are all right now. We had been expecting the *Spaulding* for [a] couple of days and yesterday when she was so far off that you could only see the smoke from her stack nearly half the Regt. were out looking at her. The boat that we have here to bring up the provisions has gone down to the fort and I think it likely that the box will be aboard but I am not sure. The mail closes at 2 o'clock and I will have to hurry as I want to answer Harry Dewees's letter. The barracks are quite lively to day; all the men are either engaged in writing letters or reading their papers of which a large [number] came in this mail. I would like you to take these five dollars and make the youngsters a New Years present and what is left over you might buy some little things that you want for your own self. I think I will be able to send $20 home next pay, that is if we get our two months pay while amt. to $26 but at any rate I will send as much as I can.

No more at present.

Your Affectionate Son
C.C.P.

---

11. Sgt. Samuel Ruch, Company H, 48th Pennsylvania, was a twenty-five-year-old moulder from Pottsville who must have been a family acquaintance of the Pollock's. He enlisted in September 1861, was captured at 2nd Bull Run on August 29, 1862, exchanged, and then discharged from the army in late December 1862.

———••◆••———

Camp Winfield Dec. 27th/61

*D*ear Ma

Christmas has passed and a very dull one it was to me though some of the men seemed to enjoy themselves very much. The *Spaulding* came in on Sunday the 21st inst. and brought over one hundred and fifty boxes but none for me. The Quartermaster was very tardy about bringing up the commissary stores and boxes and they did not get here until Christmas Morning and I was down at the wharf almost all day looking for my box but it did not come and I think it must be lieing at Fortress Monroe and I will very likely get it on the next boat which is expected in on Sunday next and I guess the box will taste as good on New Year's as on Christmas. (I mean what is in the box). Gen. Williams is now quartered up here and is not at all liked, he is very pompous and struts around as if he was a king. The boxes that came for the men mostly had whiskey in them and there were a good many drunken men in camp by evening and of course a couple of fights but not serious ones. There is a good deal of difficulty in getting provisions up to this camp as the only place that the *Spaulding* can land is at Fort Hatteras and we have to bring the provisions up in small boats inside the sound and the only boat we have had was an iron surf boat which is very heavy and it gets aground with anything of a load on it, but this time they hired a small schooner from one of the islanders to bring it up the sound and then we got an old flat boat which laid on the island and bring it in from the schooner. I have not looked for many shells since I sent those home but I have one much prettier than those I sent home and will send it the first chance. I commenced this letter this afternoon but had to stop to go out on dress parade and it is now after supper and I am setting in my bunk writing this and the men have a fiddle and are dancing and seem to be enjoying themselves very much. Frank Farquhar left here in the last steamer and Capt. [Henry] Pleasants has charge of the building of the forts, one of them is nearly done and the other has just been commenced and is to be but a small one. They took all the sick up to Ft. Monroe on the *Spaulding* as they have more advantages there than here and it is nearer for their friends to reach them. Our barracks are livelier to night than

they have been for some time. Some are singing, others dancing and fiddling and everybody seems to be in a good humor.
The weather still continues quite warm with now and then a
cold blow but generally it is very comfortable. Hoping you are
all well I remain

Your Affectionate son
C.C.P.

Sunday Dec. 29th 1861

There is nothing much going on today and there has been
no church since we have been up at this camp. Yesterday two
gunboats came down and one today, they are getting quite a
small fleet at Fort Hatteras but what they are going to do with
it I do not know. There is a good deal of talk about an attack
here but I do not think it at all likely that the Rebels will molest
us here, even if they do they will meet with a warm reception
and the only thing the men seem to fear is that Genl. Williams
will surrender without showing fight. The Genl. has given orders for guard to turn out a Guard Mount with knapsacks but
what this order is for I cannot imagine nor do I suppose he
knows himself, but only does it to make the men think as bad
of him as possible. Tuesday next is Muster day and we will be
mustered for pay and will very likely be paid about the middle
of January. There are five or six of our company now sick but
not very bad.

Monday [December] 30th

Nothing of any importance going on today. The working
[party] only worked this morning to give the men an opportunity to clean up for inspection and muster to-morrow. We had
new orders to night on dress parade in the morning instead
of evening and we get up in the morning at 6 o'clock and turn
out with muskets to roll call what this is for I do not know.
The *Spaulding* did not come in to day but I guess it will be in
tomorrow.

[Tuesday] December] 31st

Today is the last day of the year and it is quite a fine day the
sun is shining brightly and it seems more like Spring than the
middle of winter. The *Spaulding* did not come in to day after
all though she was looked for very anxiously this morning.
We had an eclipse of the sun this morning and we could see it

One of the most recognizable figures of the Civil War, Ambrose Burnside commanded the expedition that secured much of the North Carolina coastline in 1862. He would later command the Ninth Army Corps, the Army of the Potomac, and the Department of the Ohio. The 48th Pennsylvania would serve for most of the war under Burnside's command, in North Carolina, Virginia, Maryland, Kentucky, and Tennessee. (Courtesy of the Library of Congress)

very plain through a smoked glass; about a quarter of it was eclipsed. This morning we had a grand review, inspection and muster which took us about four hours; we went [out] about 10 o'clock and did not get in until sometime after two. We were the last company and it kept us standing a long time before it came to our turn. The Hospital has been removed to Fort Clark where they intend to build the General Hospital but there will be a doctor to remain with the Regt. to attend to those who are not very sick. And so ends this sheet and the year.

C.C.P.

Camp Winfield
Saturday eve. Jan. 4th 1862

*D*ear Ma

I have not had time to write for the last few days but will try and write a few lines this evening. To-morrow morning will be two weeks since the *Spaulding* has been here but I think it will be down tomorrow for sure. Yesterday I was on picket just above us on the island but did not have a very pleasant time as it was quite cold and we had a short shower about four in the morning. It was quite dark at night and in taking the relief around I sometimes had hard work to find the sentinels and other times they would get off their posts & be wandering around fifty or a hundred yards from their posts and I always had to call out to them before I could find them. The pickets have a small hut made out of small trees and the sides and roof are made out of long-stiff grass that grows around here on the swamps and is not very good protection from either wind or rain. About 5 o'clock last night we spied two steamers just coming in sight from the north and as we had to report all boats that come in sight, I went over to camp and reported them to the officer of the day and when I went back the boats had stopped up near the light house, which is about fifteen miles above here, and laid there all night. About the time the boats were first seen in the ocean another boat was seen in the sound and they both being seen about the same time and those two stopping above us, it began to look suspicious and a great many thought they were going to try and shell us out. In the morning however the two boats started and came down and when they got opposite we could their names with a small glass and we found out they were the *Pautuxet* and *Pilot Boy* both coming from Ft. Monroe. They have both lieing down at Ft. Hatteras all day but where they are going I do not know for they do not appear to have any load on them. Some of the boys say that they came to take one of the Regiments away from here but I do not know anything about it. We have to wear our overcoats pretty much all the time just now as it is pretty cold. There has been no sign of snow here though in . . .

[LETTER ENDS HERE; INCOMPLETE]

———— •◆• ————

Camp Winfield
Tuesday Jan 7th 1862

*D*ear Ma
The *Spaulding* arrived here at last. It came this morning while we were out drilling. Lt. [Cyrus] Sheets[12] came with it and brought two letters for me and papers and mittens and I wore them this afternoon while I was drilling and they are very comfortable; tell Mary I am very much obliged to her for them and that she for-got to finish the ends off and left the strings hanging but I fixed it all right. I received three letters [with] this boat one on the papers, another on the gloves, and the other by Mail and it was dated the 24th Nov. over a month on the road. We have a great deal of drilling to do now and are occupied most of the time.

Wednesday [January] 8th
I have not time to delay finishing this letter until the express arrives as the mail is to leave at noon so I will bring this letter to a close hoping it will do you instead of two or three. With much love to all and hoping you are all well I remain

Your Affectionate Son
C.C. Pollock

The boys are sending home a great many shells [with] this boat and I am sorry I have none to send but will have some more before long. It is quite cold this morning but very fine weather.

C.C.P.

✷ ✷ ✷

IN MID-JANUARY 1862, the normal, day-to-day routine of life on Hatteras, which the soldiers of the 48th had by then grown accustomed to, was disrupted by the arrival of an immense fleet, nearly 100 ships strong. Joseph Gould recalled that "on or about the 12th of January, 1862, [the soldiers of the 48th] were surprised, on answering the Reveille Call, to see, far out upon the

---

12. Cyrus Sheetz, a thirty-three-year-old hotel keeper from Pottsville, was Third Sergeant in the Washington Artillerists and was thus a First Defender. In September 1861, he was mustered into service as 1st Lieutenant of Company G. He resigned in early May 1862, though he would later serve as a captain in the 173rd Pennsylvania.

The steamer J.H. Spaulding was a welcome sight to many in the 48th, for it oftentimes would deliver letters from home. (Courtesy of the Library of Congress)

broad Atlantic, first one ship, then another and another, until the ocean seemed full of ships." There were gunboats and other armed vessels, ships carrying provisions, steamers, schooners, and dozens of other transport vessels, bearing, in all, some 15,000 Union soldiers all under the overall command of thirty-seven-year-old Brigadier General Ambrose Everett Burnside.

Throughout the fall and winter of 1861 and by direction of General George B. McClellan, Burnside had organized this vast force—initially designated as the Coast Division—in preparation for the capture and occupation of the North Carolina coast. Burnside's instructions were to expand the area of Union control beyond just its toehold on Hatteras by first capturing Roanoke Island, then moving inland to Newbern and Fort Macon. This primarily amphibious, joint army-navy expedition along the Carolina coast and inlets would prove successful and its commander, Ambrose Burnside, would emerge from it a Major General and a national hero, whose string of victories at Roanoke, Newbern, Fort Macon and other places went far in boosting Northern morale.[13]

Yet no matter how successful its conclusion, Burnside's North Carolina Campaign got off to a very rough start. Unfortunately for Burnside and especially for his 15,000 men on board the various vessels, the fleet's arrival off the shores of Hatteras

---

13. Gould, 48; Richard A. Sauers, "Laurels For Burnside: The Invasion of North Carolina: January-July 1862," *Blue & Gray Magazine*, Vol. 5, Issue 5 (May 1988): 9-10.

in mid-January 1862 just happened to coincide with the arrival with a powerful storm that rocked the coast. The heavy rain, the powerful winds, and the violent sea all combined to delay the fleet's passage through Hatteras Inlet and into Pamlico Sound. From their safety on shore, the soldiers of the 48th watched as the ships "were tossed about like toys." Three vessels—the *City of New York*, the gunboat *Zouave*, and the *Pocahontas*—were wrecked, though all on board these three doomed ships were rescued. Two of Burnside's officers, however—Colonel Joseph Allen and Chief Surgeon Frederick Weller, both of the 9th New Jersey—lost their lives when the surfboat they were riding in overturned. After a few harrowing days, the storm finally abated and Burnside's armada, after deftly navigating the "Swash," continued on its way, sailing up Pamlico Sound and toward its first victory against the Confederate stronghold on Roanoke Island, which fell to Burnside's forces on February 7-8, 1862.[14]

In his letters home, Corporal Pollock discussed the arrival of Burnside's fleet and shared his elation over the capture of Roanoke Island and his thoughts about whether he and the boys of the 48th would be home by the 4th of July. Clearly, though, the young soldier's principal focus was on far more practical and personal concerns: the quality of his food, the sturdiness of his clothing, and the sending home of his pay, while his desire for promotion remained strong.

Camp Winfield
Jan 14th/1862

Dear Ma

I received your letter of the 8th inst. and was very glad to hear from you. I received the box by the last boat and everything was as good as when it was put in except the Turkey which was a little moldy on the outside but I washed and scraped it off and it was as good as ever. Ed Silliman's[15] [box of food from home] was spoiled entirely and was musty all through so I invited him to come and help eat mine and we made a very good supper of

14. Augustus Woodbury, *Major General Ambrose Burnside and the Ninth Army Corps* (Providence, Rhode Island: Sidney S. Rider & Brother, 1867), pgs. 24-27.
15. Edward H. Sillyman, Corporal, Company G, was a thirty-seven-year old machinist from Pottsville when he was mustered into service in September 1861. Later promoted to sergeant, he served throughout the duration of the war, being mustered out with the regiment of July 17, 1865.

it and the rest of the things. Everybody that I gave any of the
Ginger cakes to all said that they were the best they ever ate.
The pies too were particularly good and I soon made way with
them. The butter was also as good and as sweet as the day it
was put in. I am very much obliged to Mrs. Dewees, Frank &
Harry for the things they sent me and the cucumber sauce was
very good. It has been quite cold here for the last couple of days
but not cold enough to freeze and we have had no snow yet
though it rains every once in a while. The forts are progressing
quite rapidly and will soon be finished but I hear that Gen. Williams has plenty more work for us to do after we finish them.
We have received several guns from Ft. Monroe but have not
got them all up here yet. Yesterday morning the boats began to
come down here; first one came in sight and then another and
another and so on until you could count twelve in sight as far
as you could see toward Ft. Monroe until they got behind the
sand banks along the island and they continued to come all
day. In the morning I commenced to count them and counted
up to twenty-seven but after that I lost the run of them. The
Spaulding came down along and brought the Mail and I hear
that she is to go down to Beaufort with about one hundred and
fifty men who were left at Ft. Monroe sick before the Expedition
sailed and I suppose it will not be back before Saturday. The
fleet that came down yesterday is Burnside's and is to go to
Roanoke Island but I am not positive. I have charge of the cook
house this week dealing out the rations and superintending
the cooking. It is a good deal of bother as crackers have to be
dealt out every day and it takes up a good deal of time to deal
out crackers and meat to eighty-five men. I forgot to mention
that none of the boats could land owing to the roughness of the
weather and they are lieing all around from here to the Inlet.
It is so cold and windy to day that we are not drilling any and
most of the men are writing this afternoon. When you write I
would like you to tell me always whether there is any sleighing
or skating about town.

No more at present.

Your Affectionate Son
C.C.P.

I am getting along first rate and hope you are the same. Write
soon.

With much love to everybody. I remain you affectionate Son
C.C.P.

Camp Winfield Jan. 17th/62

*D*ear Ma

It is almost time for tattoo[16] and I have only a small piece of candle so I will only write a few lines this evening. It is raining quite hard now and has been nearly all day so we have not had much drilling to do. The fleet is still lieing here and I do not know how soon it is going to leave but I suppose as soon as the weather is good enough. I heard today that one of the steamers that was lieing down at Fort Hatteras broke her cable and drifted across the inlet and was lost, and that a Colonel, Doctor, and a couple of others were drowned in trying to come back in a small boat but I do not know how true it is about the person being drowned as some say it is not so. We received our new clothes to day, a dress coat cap and shoes. The other things are to come the next boat. My things fit me very well but I do not think the coat I have is quite as good as the one I have at home. I lent my Havelock to one of our fellows who is out on guard to night.

Jan. 18th—The candle went out last night before I could finish this letter but as there is nothing new this morning I will close for the mail will be likely to leave today.

With much love to all I remain
Your Affectionate Son
C.C. Pollock

Camp Winfield
Jan. 19th 1862

*D*ear Ma

I have just heard that the mail is to leave at 10 o clock this morning and as I have something to tell you I will write a few lines. I believe the Governor appoints all vacancies that occur in the army, not giving the companies power to elect them and Dory Patterson is trying to get the 2nd Lieutenancy in Co.

---

16. "Tattoo" was a bugle call for the men to prepare for bed.

D. this Regt[17]. If that is the case, you might get Uncle James to speak a word for me and I might be able to get one as there are very often vacancies in all Regts. We had an inspection this morning in our new dress coats and it looked quite fine. The fleet has not left yet but is expected to go in a day or so. The New York 9th is to go with it and the 6th New Hampshire is here in its place.[18] Yesterday all the pilots of the Island were ordered down to Ft. Hatteras and those that would not report were to be arrested and sent off [to] Ft. Warren.[19] A great many went down but they did it very unwillingly. The Colonel that was drowned was Col. [Joseph] Allen of the [9th] New Jersey Regt. but they say he was a very poor one. His Adjutant and one of the Drs. [Chief Surgeon Frederick Weller] was also drowned with him. There were nine in the boat and the three that could not swim were washed ashore the next morning and are now buried on the beach.[20] It looks very much like rain this morning but it is not cold. I had intended to go and look for some shells this morning but I am afraid it will rain. I am going to get some pretty little shells and put them in that bottle that Mrs. Dewees sent and will try and get it home as soon as possible. I am writing this in the Captain's quarters and it is the first letter I have written on a table since I left home.

No more at present.

With Much love to all
I remain
Your Affectionate Son
C.C. Pollock

Write Soon.

---

17. Theodore Frelinghuysen Patterson was an eighteen-year-old clerk from Pottsville who served alongside Curtis Pollock as a private in the Washington Artillerists as a "First Defender," and in Company G, 48th. Patterson was mustered into Company G, 48th, as the Fourth Sergeant. As Pollock mentioned, Patterson was seeking promotion of his own, in this case, to fill the vacancy caused by the December 1861 death of 1st Lieutenant Alexander Fox. Patterson succeeded in securing higher rank, though not in the 48th Pennsylvania. In late February 1862, he was discharged from the regiment to accept a First Lieutenant's commission in the 67th Pennsylvania Infantry. He later served with the U.S. Signal Corps before his discharge from the service in September 1864. He died in 1906 at Valley Forge, Pennsylvania.
18. The 48th had been stationed alongside the colorful 9th New York at Hatteras since their arrival in mid-November.
19. Fort Warren, located on Georges Island at the entrance of Boston Harbor, was constructed as a defensive measure to help protect Boston. It construction completed by 1861, it served throughout the Civil War as a prison for Confederate officers and government officials.
20. Only two of the party—Allen and Weller—perished.

———◆•●•◆———

Camp Winfield
Jan 23rd 1862

*D*ear Ma

It is raining quite hard to day and we are not doing anything and as I forgot to tell you something that I wanted to say
if you get a chance to send me some smoked sausage I would
like to have it very much send smoked as fresh would spoil.

No more at present.

Your Affectionate Son
C.C. Pollock

I wrote two letters this mail but I am not sure that this letter
will go this boat.

C.C.P.

———◆•●•◆———

Camp Winfield
Feb. 1st 1862

*D*ear Ma

I received your letter dated Jan 22nd and was much
pleased to hear from you. I also received one from Rob Hill and
Will Pollock. All the Mail has not come in yet and I think it is
likely that I will get another letter from you. The mail came
down day before yesterday and was taken over to the *Spaulding*, which is [the] flagship for the fleet, by mistake. The fleet
has left here but where it has gone to I do not know but I
think we will hear of it before long. There is some talk of us
going with it but it is not very certain. Yesterday being the
last day of the month we had a grand review and inspection
which lasted from ten o'clock A.M. until two P.M. and we were
complimented very highly by the General who said he was very
much surprised to see how much we had improved since the
last review. There were about four thousand men in line. The
New York 9th, 48th [PA], 6th New Hampshire and detachments
from the 6th Conn., 89th N.Y., and Battery F. Rhode Island
Vols. and we all presented quite an imposing appearance. The
remainder of the Mail has just come in and I received another

letter from you dated Jan. 16 but I have not had the paper yet. I also received one from Aunt Annie and I will now have four letters to answer by the time the next boat leaves but it is not probable that the mail will leave here very soon. The turkey and pies were very good but the buckwheat cakes were all moldy. Nobody ate with me but Ed Sillyman whose turkey was moldy all through. I sent home a bottle of shells in a box that Jim Niece[21] sent home and directed it to Pa at the Lumber Yard. The shells are getting rather scarce as there are so many [men] picking them up and then we have so much drilling to do that the only time you have to pick them is on Sunday. However I will try to get another box full. We drill from 8 A.M. until 9 ½ and at 11 we have Guard Mounting and immediately after Guard Mounting we have another drill until 12 ¼ and dinner at 12 ½ and 2 o'clock drill until 4 and dress parade at 4 ½ and supper at 5. I am getting along first rate and never enjoyed better health. We have pretty much the same food we always had and sometimes it is not very well cooked but we have pea soup made out of dried peas which is about the best thing we get. Yesterday was a very fine day for the review it being not too warm but today it is raining quite hard and we have not been doing anything to day.

Your Affectionate Son,
C.C.P.

[Monday, February 3, 1862]

Dear Ma
        I enclose with this letter my certificate authorizing Pa to draw the $10 per month I have reserved for my pay from the Commissioners. He can draw it at the end of every month.[22] The fleet started to day and the New York 9th went with it; also the R.I. Battery, and I think there will be a mail to start tomorrow. It has been raining all day and we have not been drilling today. The General has ordered that there is to be a non-commissioned officers school to be taught by the Major

---

21. James C. Niece, a thirty-year-old machinist from Pottsville, served in Company G first as a corporal, then as a sergeant. Wounded at the Battle of Fredericksburg in December 1862, Niece was discharged on September 30, 1864, upon the expiration of his term of service.
22. Instead of waiting for pay while in the field, soldiers were presented with the opportunity of authorizing family members or trusted friends to draw pay from various commissioners throughout the North. There were several such commissioners in Pottsville.

and we meet every day and have quite a serious time of it but I think it will soon fizzle out as it puts the Major to so <u>much</u> more trouble than he has been used to having.[23] Most of the men are engaged in writing this evening as they are all sending their certificates home. I have commenced filling another box of shells but have not got very many yet. I was out on Sunday afternoon but I could not find but very few. Lewis Bright is detached from the Company and is helping Dr. Reber down at Ft. Clark where the General Hospital is situated.[24] I did not receive the paper you mentioned in your letter. We have not had our pay for Nov. & Dec. & I think it is not likely that we will receive it until next month when we will get four months pay at one time.

No more at present. Write soon.

Your Affectionate Son
C.C.P.

Camp Winfield
Feb. 11th 1862

*D*ear Ma

I received yours and Mary's long and welcome letter yesterday and was very much pleased to hear from you. The letter had a full account of the party, and that it was at the Town Hall. I found out from Mary's mentioning that picture of Washington. The other letter that Mary wrote I have not received and I do not know when I will. We were paid this morning $26. and $15. of which I send home with Isaac Lippman and also my watch, which needs some repairing and I would like you to get Elliot to give it a good overhauling as I think he is a better watchmaker than Green. It is a splendid day to day the sun is shining brightly and it is quite warm, though for some days back we have had very bad weather and have hardly seen the sun before today for over a week. The company are

23. Daniel Nagle, a younger brother of Colonel James Nagle, was promoted from Captain of Company D to Major in November 1861.
24. Louis A. Bright, a twenty-seven-year-old telegraph operator from Pottsville, served as a private in Company G until being discharged on a surgeon's certificate in November 1862. Dr. Charles T. Reber (1836-1889) was serving, at the time, as an Assistant Surgeon in the 48th PA. He would soon be promoted to Chief Surgeon following the death Dr. David D. Minis at Roanoke Island. He resigned on February 23, 1863.

now out drilling. I have been excused by the Doctor on account of having a bad cold. The Paymaster came down on the same boat that brought us the mail and has been lieing at Fortress Monroe for about two or three weeks and he commenced paying off yesterday and is not through yet. He is not the same one that paid us last time. His name is Major Haskin but not the one that was at Ft. Washington. I see by the papers that Major Haskin and the same company D that was at Ft. Washington with him when we were there has been ordered down to Fort Pickens and had already started. I have signed my name to the allotment roll to send home $10 per month and Pa can draw it from the Commissioners or someone appointed by them to pay it out. He can either draw $10 at the end of every month or $20 every two months. This morning the General had the whole Brigade drawn up in line with knapsacks and I believe it is his intention to have a Brigade drill after this in the morning. We have to drill now with our knapsacks on to get used to the load on our backs and when we get marching we will not feel it so much. I think after this the Mail will not be so unregular as it has been before and if you could get up a small box and send it on with some Smoked sausage and little corn meal so that I could have some fried mush once in a while I think it would go first rate. I would also like to have a good razor and brush. I like the drawers very much but did not need them very much as I have three or four pairs besides them. We only received dress coats, caps and shoes and the dear [Lord] only knows when we will get the rest but I do not want anything particular except undershirts. My pants are in a good condition yet and I have not worn out the first pair of shoes that I got at Harrisburg. My boots are all right and I could get along with them very well if only I had something to grease them with. We drew some fresh meat to day from the Quarter Master, the first we have had in a month but the way they cook it I would almost rather have pork for after we get pork boiled we always fry it before eating it. The butter you sent in the last box kept very well & a loaf of bread would not spoil if sent. Mince Pies &c. In speaking of vacancies, I meant the Governor of the State fills vacancies that occur. The bottle of Shells will go in this boat and you can lookout for it I wrapped it up very carefully and it was packed very tight the box was marked James C. Neis in care of Mrs. J.H. Kalbach Minersville St. I am getting up another collection of shells and will send them home as soon as I have enough to fill a good-sized box. Send my watch back with Isaac Lippman. Tell Mary she may expect an answer to her letter next . . .

From Your Affectionate Son
C.C. Pollock

I have written Harry two letters and have not had an answer from him yet Why does he not write?

C.C.P.

———————•◦•———————

Camp Winfield
Feb 11th 1862

*D*ear Pa
Enclosed find $15 which I send with Isaac Lippman; he also has my watch which I would like you to get fixed at Elliot's as I believe he is a better watch maker than Green and send it back with Isaac when he comes back again. We were paid this morning and I would send more but I owe about $5 and I want the rest to nic-nax that we need here sometimes. I have signed my name to the allotment rolls to send $10 per month home which you can draw from the Commissioners or some persons appointed by them to pay it out and you can draw $10 at the end of every month or $20 every two months just as you please. I have sent a letter this mail giving you all the news.

Your Affectionate Son
C.C. Pollock

[Wednesday, February 12, 1862]
Last night about 10 o'clock we received news from the fleet. I was down at the Captain's quarters and someone rushed in and told us the fleet had taken Roanoke Island and Elisabeth City and Three Thousand Prisoners, a thousand Stacks of arms, forty-one guns, horses ammunition wagons etc. This is the most decisive victory we have yet gained and I think it will strike terror into the hearts of the Rebels.[25] Elizabeth City

———

25. Union losses at Roanoke Island (February 7-8, 1862) were 37 killed, 214 wounded, and 13 missing-in-action. Confederate casualties were 22 killed and 58 wounded, but over 2,500 were taken prisoner in this decisive victory for Burnside and the Union war effort. Elizabeth City, North Carolina, fell to Union forces two days later, on February 10, following a lopsided naval

lies at the upper end of Albemarle Sound and directly behind Norfolk. I think the next time you hear from us we will be in the heart of the enemy's country and I hope doing our duty. The *Stars and Stripes* brought the news down last evening and the *Spaulding* is to be down to day with the prisoners aboard. I have not heard where they are going to send them to but I suppose to one of the Northern forts. We have not had the list of killed and wounded but I understand it is not a great deal. I have just heard that Bosbyshell has said that twenty seven killed and two hundred wounded but it is not certain

No more at present.

Your Affectionate Son
Curtis C. Pollock

Write Soon.
I am in very good health excepting a slight cold.

Camp Winfield
Feb. 22nd 1862

Dear Ma

Today is [George] Washington's birthday and I have just heard there is mail going to day and I will take this opportunity of writing you a few lines. We had a mail day before yesterday but I did not get any. I have never rec'd that paper that you sent. I wish you would send me papers sometimes as they are rather scarce about here. I have a box of shells almost ready to send off and you can look out for them in a couple of weeks. There is a small bottle in it for Aunt Sarah and a small box you will see the direction on it and I would like you to send it to place directed.

Gen. Williams is to leave here today with his brigade, leaving us here to guard the Island for two or three days when we are to follow him to Roanoke and from there start on an expedition which is fitting out there to go to. . . . [illegible]. I received the news last night from Lt. Bosbyshell and he got it from Lt.

---

affair between thirteen gunboats of the North Atlantic Blockading Squadron and the Confederates' ad hoc "Mosquito Fleet." Morale soared within the Union ranks and on the home front in the aftermath of these victories.

[James] Biddle of Gen. Williams's staff. [26] Col. Nagle will have command of the post. It is not a very nice day for moving as it is raining quite hard. The news that we have rec'd here is glorious and I think it will not be a great while before we will get home. There are a good many bets up about going home some say 4th July and others not until Christmas. We have been having Brigade drill every morning with knapsacks on to get us accustomed to marching with them and I can get along with mine first rate now and do not mind it at all. There are four Regiments in our Brigade and one Battery of Artillery: 48 P.V. 6th N.H. 11th Conn. 89th N.Y. We are to wait here until we are relieved by a Regiment from Ft. Monroe but until it comes we stay here. It is supposed that the expedition that leaves Roanoke is to go to Newbern and in your next [letter] tell me where the house is you lived in.[27] Do not forget to send my watch back with Isaac. I sent it home with him and $15. I was very much disappointed at not getting a letter in the last mail but there was a small mail come in yesterday but [it was] so mixed up that it has not been assorted yet and as the mail leaves here this morning I have no time to wait until it comes in. I have written two letters to Harry Dewees and have not had an answer to them yet. We received pants, undershirts and drawers & stockings. I will send some of the clothes that I do not want home in the box of shells and you can give them to Pa or keep them until I get home. The under shirts are very fine and I will only send one home. There are three pair of drawers also.

No more at present.

Your Affectionate Son
Curtis C. Pollock

------•◦•------

Camp Winfield
Feb. 27th 1862

ear Ma
I received your two letters dated Feb. 12 & 20 yesterday and was much pleased to hear from you. I also rec'd several

---

26. This turned out to be a false report, since Pollock's Company G, 48th, would remain at Hatteras until the middle of May 1862.
27. Curtis Pollock's mother, Emily, was born in New Bern, North Carolina, when her father, the Reverend Jehu Curtis Clay was rector of the Christ Church there. As Pollock noted, New Bern was, indeed, the next target for General Burnside and his expeditionary force.

papers, some from you and some from Will Pollock, who is now one of my regular correspondents. Dory Patterson rec'd his discharge yesterday and goes home in the next boat and I will send this letter with him. The box of shells that I mentioned in my last letter has not left here yet but I think will go the next boat. I am getting along first rate and am in good health and (plenty of clothes) we have just received new underclothes, stockings, and pants from the Government and are very well clothed at present; in fact, I have almost too many and if we have to march I think I will have to get rid of some of them. From all accounts the Soldiers around Washington are in a pretty bad way and I think we are about as well off as most any Regiment in the field and as for health I think we are better off than a great many. The New Hampshire 6th which is in our Brigade but has left here for Roanoke have buried forty-seven in [the] six weeks they have been here and have five hundred on the sick list every morning. I suppose you heard of the death of Dr. Minis the Surgeon of this Regt. He died from over exertion and fatigue at Roanoke Island. He was detailed to go with the 9th N.J. whose Surgeon was drowned with Col. Allen on the night of the storm when that boat was washed ashore opposite Fort Hatteras.[28] That picture in Harpers Weekly is not a very good one; they make it out a great deal worse than it really was. The boat was washed ashore and it remains there yet lieing on shore opposite Ft. Hatteras. I was down the other day and saw it. Those other pictures where the contrabands are, are the ones we were in when we first came here and are very good. The Hawkins Zouaves are some of New York city scamps though there are a few very respectable young men in the Regt. As an illustration of what some of them are I will relate an incident that occurred at Newport News when they were there. They had not been paid for some four months and refused to do duty until they were paid. Gen. Butler ordered a Review and

28. Dr. David Minis, Jr., was born in Beaver County, Pennsylvania, in 1831 and was a gradu-ate of Jefferson College and the University of Pennsylvania. He was a practicing physician who volunteered his services upon the outbreak of war and who was appointed Chief Surgeon of the 48th Pennsylvania Infantry on October 1, 1861. Because of the drowning death of Surgeon Frederick Weller of the 9th New Jersey, Dr. Minis was chosen to accompany Burnside's fleet to Roanoke Island and it was there that he died, overcome by sickness and in overexertion in tending to the wounded. General Burnside, in his General Orders No. 10, paid tribute to Dr. Minis of the 48th, writing that "He lost his life by disease brought on by his untiring devotion to the wounded. . . . To the forgetfulness of self which kept him at his post at the Hospital, regard-less of rest, the Department owes a debt of gratitude." Joseph Gould remembered Minis as "an efficient officer, courteous and affable, and well-beloved by all." Dr. Minis was thirty years old at the time of his death.

after all the other regiments were marched away the captains of each company asked them which were willing to do duty and about four hundred refused, and they were marched out by themselves and a battery wheeled around and faced them and loaded the guns, and Butler asked them whether they would return to their companies or be fired at, about a hundred of them stood, the rest slunk back to their companies. Butler than put them on the Rip-Raps[29] but afterwards released them. They are nearly as bad as [the] Billy Wilson crowd. While here [at Hatteras] they used to live on the Islanders' porkers and chickens. We all begin to think that we will be home by the Fourth of July and I hope so as I am beginning to get tired of soldiering again. Col. Nagle now has command of Hatteras but says we will not be here long. Gen. Williams received orders yesterday to report at Ship Island and when he got them he remarked to someone standing by his side "What! Go and leave these noble fellows!" It seems he thought a great deal of our regiment. You must excuse my bad writing as we have very poor facilities for writing here and I am now standing on the floor and have to lean over my bunk with the paper on the floor of my bunk and not in a very good position for writing. I will try and send you a glass globe that come from the light house if Patterson will take it. No more at present.

From Your Affectionate Son
C.C. Pollock

I see by the papers that the <u>Strange Story</u> is printed in pamphlet form. I wish you would send it to me as I am very much interested in it and have only read a little here and there.[30] You can send it by mail I think

C.C.P.

�֍ �֍ ✖

BURNSIDE AND HIS men had succeeded handily in achieving the first goal of his North Carolina Expedition with the capture of Roanoke Island. Afterward, and as Pollock reported in his letter of February 22, the heavily whiskered general next turned

---

29. The Rip Raps was an artificial island of some fifteen acres constructed largely of jagged rock and stones at the entrance to the Hampton Roads harbor. Soldiers were sent and confined on the Rip Raps as a means of punishment.
30. Pollock may very well be referring to *A Strange Story*, a tale of the supernatural which was authored by the popular English novelist Edward Bulwer-Lytton.

his attention on Newbern, a seaport town located at the conflu-
ence of the Neuse and Trent Rivers. Newbern was an important
target for Burnside's forces because the Atlantic & North Carolina Railroad, an important supply line for Confederate forces,
passed directly through the town. On March 11, Burnside's
fleet sailed away from Roanoke Island and, after rendezvousing
with a fleet of gunboats off the shores of Hatteras, proceeded
up the Neuse River, heading for Newbern. As opposed to the
campaign against Roanoke, however, this time a part of the
48th Pennsylvania would be accompanying Burnside's forces.
Before heading off from Roanoke, Burnside directed Colonel
James Nagle to designate six companies of the 48th to join in.
Nagle selected Companies A, B, C, D, H, & I for the assignment.
For the soldiers of these six companies, this would be their first
opportunity to participate in a significant military engagement;
for the soldiers of the other four companies, however—including
Curtis Pollock of Company G—it would simply be more of the
same: guard and garrison duties at Hatteras.[31]

On March 12, after having packed up their gear, the six
chosen companies of the 48th left Hatteras Island behind and
marched to the wharf where they were to board the steamer
George Peabody for the journey up the Neuse River to Newbern.
When they arrived, however, they found that the vessel had run
aground and they would thus have to wait for the tide to rise
before they could continue to their destination. Because of this,
the soldiers were forced to go into bivouac near the wharf. Many
local peddlers soon began selling whiskey and, unfortunately,
a number of the 48th's men imbibed too freely, with tragic con-
sequences. Oliver Bosbyshell, whom Nagle had plucked from
Company G to serve as his Acting Quartermaster, recalled that
"The orgies almost created a riot," with the officers simply unable to control their men. Around midnight, a few of the disor-
derly and inebriated soldiers broke into the wooden barracks of
the Hotel D'Afrique, which had been constructed on Hatteras
Island as a safe haven for runaway slaves. Once inside, they began attacking the black men who had fled slavery and who had
sought refuge there, and at least one man, "poor, inoffensive old
Galloway," was mortally injured after being stabbed by an unknown, unidentified knife-yielding soldier of the 48th. For some
time, past, Galloway had been acting as a servant to Colonel

31. Sauers, 44-45; Gould, 52.

Pollock and the soldiers of the 48th Pennsylvania spent eight months campaigning in coastal North Carolina, specifically on Hatteras and at New Bern. (From Battles and Leaders of the Civil War, Vol. I)

Nagle, who was furious with his men. Next morning, he publicly reprimanded the regiment but the murderer of Galloway was never identified. The actions on the night of March 12-13 were, concluded Bosbyshell, "a sad page of the regiment's history."[32]

With this shameful incident behind them, the six companies boarded the *George Peabody* on the morning of March 13 and soon began steaming up the Neuse. As it turned out, they would

---

32. Bosbyshell, 38-39.

arrive a little too late and would not participate in any of the major battle action. The greater part of Burnside's fleet had a substantial head-start on the *George Peabody* and as the 48th sailed toward Newbern, most of Burnside's men had already disembarked from their own vessels, preparing for the battle that occurred the following day, March 14. Burnside's three brigades—under Generals John Foster, Jesse Reno, and John Parke—pushed directly against the Confederate forces tasked with defending Newbern while Union gunboats pummeled them from the water. The result was yet another decisive victory for Burnside and his forces. His men captured Newbern and the Confederate forces were put to flight. Burnside's losses totaled 90 men killed, 380 wounded, and 1 man missing; Confederate casualties included some 64 men killed, 101 wounded, and 413 reported as either missing or taken prisoner. The six companies of the 48th did not remain entirely out of the action that day, however; they did play a largely supportive role.[33]

With the sounds of battle echoing in the distance, the six selected companies of the 48th disembarked from the *George Peabody* and formed into line on shore, several miles away from the escalating conflict. While they were forming, an aide to General Foster arrived with an urgent message: ammunition was needed as quickly as possible. It was not long before the soldiers of the 48th began to carry that much-needed ammunition to the front, some 40,000 rounds in all. Said Bosbyshell: "To accomplish this task the men took off their musket straps, and with them tied, or rather swung, the boxes [of ammunition] on fence rails, two men to one box. This was no light load. A heavy knapsack, old Harper's Ferry musket, cartridge box containing sixty rounds, and the box containing one thousand rounds of ball cartridges swung on the rail, made many of the fellow's groan." The groaning soldiers of the 48th had to carry the ammunition at least three miles to the front, much of the way through ankle-deep mud. When they arrived, exhausted, panting, out of breath, the battle had already been decided and their efforts were largely all for naught. Regardless, when he learned of what the 48th had done, Ambrose Burnside directed that the regiment inscribe the word "Newbern" upon their flag; it would be their first battle honor.[34]

---

33. Sauers, 45; 48-49.
34. Bosbyshell, 42-43.

Of course, while all this action and activity was going on at Newbern, Corporal Pollock and the other men who had been left behind on Hatteras continued to do what they had been doing for the past four months: mundane guard duty and drilling. They were chagrined at not having been selected for the expedition to Newbern but they did keep themselves updated on all the events that were taking place both there, with Burnside's forces in North Carolina, and those taking shape further away in Virginia. But with not much else to occupy their time, many of the men at Hatteras continued to write their letters home.

Camp Winfield
March 11th 1862

Dear Ma

I received your letter dated Feb. 27th yesterday but no papers but I expect to get them in the next mail. The *Spaulding* came down this morning but brought no mail; the paymaster came down and we will be paid tomorrow. I suppose you draw my money at home now. You did not say anything about it in your last [letter]. Six companies of the Regt. are going to leave today but where they are going I do not know; we are going to stay here. Co. A.B.C.D.H & I are going. Lt. Col. Sigfried is to have command of Hatteras. I received a letter from Harry Dewees and Will Pollock yesterday. The mail is to leave in ten minutes and I have very little time to write but will write another in a day or two. Paper is very scarce and envelopes and I only have one more sheet. I think it will be very safe to send in a box. Lew Bright[35] sleeps with me now. I have had a very bad cold for the last few days but am getting better fast now. It has been quite cold and unpleasant for the last few days.

I have time to say no more.

From Your Affectionate Son
C.C. Pollock

---

35. This was the same Private Louis Bright who Pollock mentioned in an earlier letter as having been detached from the company to help Dr. Reber at the Fort Clark hospital.

Camp Winfield
March 13 1862

ear Ma

I received your letter from Isaac and also the watch. I have not been very well lately having quite a bad cold but I hope I will soon be over it. If you have not sent the box I guess there will not be any use in sending it as it is likely we will move before long; however, if you have sent it I guess I will get it. Send some Cough Mixture if you can. When I commenced to write that letter yesterday I had only ten minutes' time and the Mail was just leaving when I got there and I had put a stamp on it to get it off. The Regiment started this morning about 7 o'clock we had Reveille at 4 o'clock Breakfast at 5 and the Regt was to have moved but they did not get off until sometime after. The *Geo. Peabody*, which is to take our Regt after the expedition, dragged her anchor last night and [had] run aground in the sound and they will not be able to get off until the tide rises. The expedition arrived off here last night and left today about 10 o'clock and is to go to Newbern. The four companies that are here will be relieved in a few days and we will immediately follow the Regt. Lt. Bosbyshell has gone with the Regt. on Col. Nagle's staff as Act. Qr. Master for the Detachment. We were very much disappointed at not getting along but it was our lot and we had to abide by it. It is a very fine day here today. I will try and get this letter off today although the Mail has gone down to the fort and the boat leaves this afternoon the only one that will leave until we received news from the fleet. No more at present.

From You Affectionate Son
C.C. Pollock

Head Quarters
48th Regt. P.V.
Camp Winfield
Mar 16/62

ear Ma

I received your letter dated March 5th & 9th and was much pleased to hear from you again. We have had two mails this week and I received nine letters with both mails. I received one from Mary dated Jan 29th & I just rec'd it yesterday. The papers I get very regularly now and in very good time. That was quite an exciting time they had at Ft. Monroe but I guess the *Merrimack* has run her race and done all the injury she ever will do.[36] We are still on Hatteras as you perceive and do not expect to leave until we start for home. I would like very much for Pa to come down here but there is no regular boat yet between here and Ft. Monroe and if he was to be detained any time there he would have to pay very high for his board. I think he had better wait until the regular line, which has been spoken of for some time back, is started and then he can get here without any trouble. I think I would rather go to West Point than get a Lieutenancy in the army. We rec'd the news yesterday of the evacuation of Manassas and it created a good deal of excitement in our little camp.[37] The latest papers we have up to this time is the 13th which was brought down by a gentleman who has come down here to see the Light House and the Government are going to have all the Light Houses fixed up and new lamps put in them. It is just 8 ½ o'clock by my watch, which is going again as well as ever, and I guess you are just about eating your breakfast. And don't I wish I was eating it with you. I have had mine long ago and the company has been inspected already. I have not rec'd the box yet but as there is some express down at the Fort that has not brought up yet I guess I will get it to day. We had quite a thunder storm on Hatteras last night the first one since we have been here. Have you not rec'd the box of shells I sent you with some of my clothes in it? It has had plenty of time to get home and you ought to have it [by now]. It is a splendid day the sun is shining brightly and it is very comfortable out. We have not seen one single snow flake all this winter and while we have been nearly freezing some days it has been just like spring here all the time. I often see in the papers <u>great storms at Hatteras</u> and am very much surprised as I have not seen one real hard

---

36. The much celebrated March 9, 1862, battle between the *Monitor* and *Merrimack* in Hampton Roads, Virginia, captured the attention of most everyone in the field and on the home front. Although an indecisive engagement, the battle marked the first fight between ironclad warships and signaled the beginning of a new era in naval warfare.
37. General Joseph E. Johnston, commander of the principal Confederate army in Virginia, evacuated Manassas, which they had held since the spring of 1861, and fell back to Richmond where his men took up positions to guard against an expected advance from General George McClellan's massive Army of the Potomac, which, having been transported by ship down the Chesapeake Bay, was just then preparing to make landfall on the Virginia peninsula formed between the York and James Rivers.

storm any how they never trouble us much. Our muskets were condemned by the officers of the Regt and so were our tents but that is all the good it will do and as for getting new ones we have not got good enough shakers to do anything like that. The six companies who have gone away. . . .
[LETTER ENDS HERE; INCOMPLETE]

———————◆•◆•◆———————

Head Qrs. 48th Regt P.V.
Camp Winfield
Mar 17th 1862

ear Mary
    Although I wrote a letter home yesterday we have received some very interesting news since and as there is a mail going to leave this morning and I have time to write a few lines I thought I would do so. I did not receive your letter until last Saturday and you cannot blame me for not answering it before now. Last night about 5 o'clock two steamers were seen coming in from Newbern. Lt. Sheetz got a horse and went down to hear the news. He got back about seven o'clock and told [us] Newbern was taken with about 1000 prisoners. We had about 200 killed wounded and missing. The 48th was not in the fight; they arrived about a half an hour after the fight was over did not hear much of the particulars. Last night, [we] had a Scrimmage on the Island. Some dozen Islanders fired into a Patrol Party that were out to arrest stragglers who were out of camp. The islanders fired small shot and the Lieut. had his cap riddled and one of our company had his cheek scratched by another. The Patrol fired into them but as it was rather dark and they were in the bushes none took effect. Today is St. Patrick's Day I believe but I do not think it will be celebrated here. My box did not come down with the *Spaulding* as she brought no express. Hatteras is to be abandoned and the Military Seaport of the Department of North Carolina is to be at Beaufort. Ft. Macon has been blown up.[38] The Rebels set fire to Newbern but our men laid down their muskets to one side,

---

38. This rumor was a bit premature. After capturing Newbern Burnside did, indeed, set his sights next on Fort Macon, a Confederate stronghold defending the port city of Beaufort, but this campaign would not begin until March 23 and Fort Macon would not fall to Burnside's forces until April 26, 1862.

got out the fire engines and had it out in less than no time. No time to say more.

From You Affectionate Brother
C.C. Pollock

Write Soon.

I was too late for the mail so I will write a few more lines. It is a splendid morning the sun is shining brightly and it is very warm. The companies have just come in from drill. Capt. Nagle was drilling them. I think I will get a chance to send this letter down today but if I do not get it off this Mail it will got out next. I am going to frank it myself. I am sitting in the guard house writing this the first part I wrote in the Capt. Quarters. We expect to leave here in less than two weeks and very likely we will get to see Norfolk.

From Your Affectionate Brother
C.C. Pollock

————————•◦•————————

Camp Winfield
Mar 21st/62

Dear Ma

I have just heard of the Capt. going home this afternoon and as he is going directly & I thought I would write a few lines or you might be disappointed. Enclosed are two photographs of Gen. Burnside; send one to Aunt Sarah & keep the other one. No news, we have not heard from the Regt. since it started. Very foggy today. Have not had a Mail since the 12th. We have not been paid yet. We are expecting a boat down every day with Mail & express. The Major has not arrived yet. The boat came in from Newbern to day but we have not had the news. Isaac Lippman has sent a branch of his store to Newbern. Some of the officers think we will not get off this Island until we start for home. I would like very much to hear the news [about how General George] McClellan is getting along. I will have to close,

With much love to all; Your Affectionate Son
C.C. Pollock

I have quite a bad cold.

Head Qrs. 48th Regt. P.I.
March 25th 1862

*D*ear Ma

I was on guard Sunday when the Mail arrived and was very glad to receive two letters from you and the medicine and some papers. One bottle of the medicine was broken but the other was safe and I have commenced taking it. My cough is getting better and I scarcely ever have to cough now and I hope you will not be worried about me. Dr. Reber has gone with the Regt [to Newbern] and we have had no Dr since he has gone. I do not know where the other Dr. of ours is. The Major has not arrived yet but is expected every day & I suppose he is lieing at Fort Monroe waiting for a boat. The *Spaulding* & *[George] Peabody* went up on Sunday to Fort Monroe & Capt. [Philip] Nagle went along. I received several papers from Will on Sunday and the latest was the 20th March. I generally have the latest papers that come in the Mail. There is very little going on today. Col. [James] Nagle sent word for the band to come over to Newbern and they will go as soon as they [can arrange] transportation. He also sent word to us that he had seen Gen. Burnside and he said he would have us relieved before long but I think we will be very likely to stay here some time yet. There is a good deal of talk about here about us being home on the 4th of July but I hardly think we will. Isaac Lippman bet a keg of Lager that he would have his shanty up in Market Street [in Pottsville] selling Lager to the 48th on the 4th of July. I would like to hear of McClellan's army having a fight with the rebels and whip them. I heard a rumor yesterday that they were concentrating troops at Fort Monroe and had some 60 thousand there now.[39] We are getting very tired of this place now since the Regt. has left and now when the Band goes it will be worse yet. There was a boat went up this morning but I do not know whether she took a mail or not if she did I had none in it so I thought I would write this morning in case another mail went before long. I sent a letter and four round shells

---

39. McClellan's army of over 100,000 men had landed near Fortress Monroe and, by the beginning of April, began advancing up the peninsula, toward the Confederate capital at Richmond. Much of the nation—and much of the world—was paying attention to this campaign with many in the North believing it would bring an end to the conflict.

by Capt Nagle, which I hope you will receive safe and sound. I have commenced reading the new story by Curtis but have not got through the first paper quite, only commenced it last evening. No more at present.

Your Affectionate Son
C.C. Pollock

Hoping you are all well.

——————•◦•◦•——————

Hd. Qrs. 48th Regt
Camp Winfield Mar. 28 1862

ear Ma

The Major has not arrived yet though we expect him every day. The Col. is going home on a furlough and is now down aboard the boat expects to go in the morning. I will try and get this letter off in this mail if I possibly can. I am nearly rid of my cold and have been on duty since Sunday. I have taken that bottle of medicine and think it has done me a good deal of good. I intend making application for a furlough as soon as the Major comes and will get home for a short time if I possibly can. It is a splendid morning and we had a very good drill of about an hour. There are no signs of a boat and if one does not come this morning I do not believe there will be one until Sunday and then I think the *Spaulding* will be here. The Regt at Newbern have been paid and I think we will be paid tomorrow. Lt. Sheetz received a letter from Bosbyshell yesterday and he says he is kept very busy as Act. Qr Master and hardly has time to write; he says they are encamped just outside of Newbern. The band left here on Tuesday after-noon and we miss them very much. I do not think it is likely we will get away from here before the Col. comes back and likely not [before] then; Somebody has to be here to take care of the Government property and it is not likely they will take the trouble to land troops here and then take us away. So I think it is likely we will have to stay here for some time to come. We received news yesterday of the capture of Washington [North Carolina][40] it was taken without opposition and they seem to be very good Union people. It was rumored here last evening

———————————————

40. Elements of Burnside's force secured Washington, North Carolina, on March 20-21, 1862.

that Island No. 10 had been taken with 15,000 prisoners but it is not known how true it is.[41] I heard there was a great deal of talk in town about Patterson's not going to see Clara Wolff when he was at home. I have nothing more to say at present so I will close hoping you are all well, with much love I remain

Your Affectionate Son

C.C. Pollock

Camp Winfield
Mar 31st 1862

ear Ma

The Major and Bill Mason[42] did not arrive until this morning and I received your letter dated Mar. 15th. I am on guard today and am writing this in the Guard House, time 4 o'clock P.M. I have gotten over my cold entirely and am now as well as ever. There is no Dr. here now but we get along very well without one and there are very few sick. Lt. Col. Sigfried is a very fine man but I do not think he knows a great deal about military matters.[43] We expect a boat down to-morrow with the mail and express and then I will get my box. I received the paper and envelopes I have not had occasion to take any of the flax-seed but will keep it as I may want it some other time. I wrote to Aunt Sarah a couple of weeks ago and I expect an answer the next mail. I received the letter from Isaac Lippman when I received the watch it does not run very well now what did the watch maker say was the matter with it last time it was home? Isaac is still here but sent his two clerks over with part of the goods. I would like to stay here until I get my box and eat all that is in it and then leave the next day. The Chaplain[44] is not

41. Once again, this proved to be a premature rumor, for Island No. 10, an important Confederate position in the Mississippi River, would not fall to Union forces until early April.
42. William Mason: Private, Company G, 48th Pennsylvania, mustered into service on October 1, 1861, at age 29. He was discharged due to disability in June 1862.
43. Born on July 4, 1832, in Orwigsburg, Pennsylvania, Joshua K. Sigfried found work as a coal shipper in Port Carbon prior to the outbreak of civil war. Active in the local militia, Sigfried led the Marion Rifles during the first three months of the conflict then helped Colonel James Nagle organize what became the 48th Pennsylvania Infantry. He entered the regiment as its major, but in late 1861 was advanced to the rank of lieutenant colonel. Despite Pollock's low opinion of his military capabilities, Sigfried would assume command of the 48th upon Nagle's promotion to brigade command and would capably and bravely lead the regiment until the spring of 1864. As will be seen, Sigfried and Pollock's relationship was a sometimes strained one.
44. The regimental chaplain during this time was Samuel Augustus Holman, who studied theology at Pennsylvania (now Gettysburg) College. After becoming a licensed clergyman in 1859, he served as a pastor in Pottsville. He resigned his commission in the 48th on January 2, 1863.

at all liked in the Regt.; he is too lazy. He has charge of the mail and sometimes he leaves off franking them so long that he does not get them all off. I always go to hear him when he preaches but that is not very often lately. He has a furlough and expects to go home next boat. The boots I bought from Cranshaw were to [be] $5 and I suppose his executors want to make the extra twenty-five cents. I guess it will hardly [be] worthwhile to put my out at interest but still if you think I had better do it, I am willing. The Col. did not take Clemens with him and he is now doing duty in the Co. He does not like it at all but will have to stick to it until the Col. comes back. I suppose the Col. is in Pottsville by this time as he left here the beginning of last week for New York. Four boatloads of men for Burnside came down yesterday but could not be unloaded until today on account of it being very stormy yesterday but today the weather is very fine and I have a very pleasant day for guard duty. I have had your letter before me and have answered every question you have asked me. Several of the recruits that come today are for our company and they seem to be very fine fellows. I made out the guard report this morning for the Sergeant and I think it is very well done. Lt. Sheetz is officer of the day to day. The drum has just beaten for dress parade ¼ 5 o'clock. As the Chaplain is going home I will try and get him to take it for me.

Your Affectionate Son
C.C. Pollock

❊ ❊ ❊

IT APPEARS CORPORAL Pollock did, indeed, succeed in securing a short furlough home for there is a nearly three-week gap between his letter of March 31, penned from Hatteras, and his next one, written from Fortress Monroe, Virginia, on April 17. In the latter, Pollock wrote that he had arrived at Fortress Monroe via Baltimore and in his letter of May 1, he does mention having been home. As his correspondence of the prior three months reveal, furloughs were granted quite frequently in the regiment, for a host of reasons. Of course, having not seen home since the previous summer, the short two weeks Pollock spent with his family in Pottsville were no doubt a welcome respite and a happy relief to life on the sandy beaches of Hatteras. There is little to indicate what he did while there, but it is clear that the young soldier did take advantage of his time to again press his father—this time face-to-face—about calling upon Governor

Andrew Curtin in his quest for a lieutenant's commission, for this would become a dominant theme in Pollock's letters upon his return to the regiment in North Carolina. And for Pollock, the timing was right, for there would soon be a great deal of organizational and structural changes taking place in the regiment as a whole and in Company G in particular.

The day after the fight at Newbern, Colonel James Nagle sent his acting quartermaster, Oliver Bosbyshell, to General Burnside's headquarters, seeking orders. Nagle was unsure what he and the 48th were to do next, especially since the regiment did not formally, as of yet, belong to any of Burnside's commands. After tracking down the general, however, Bosbyshell returned with the news that Burnside had immediately assigned the 48th Pennsylvania to his Second Brigade under the direct command of General Jesse Reno—a man whom, like Burnside, the soldiers of the 48th would soon come to love and greatly admire. Nagle was further directed to join Reno's command near Newbern with the six companies he had on hand; the other four companies, including Pollock's Company G, would remain on Hatteras until May 23 when they, too, were ordered up to Newbern to rejoin the regiment. By then, however, even more changes had taken place.[45]

On April 23, Ambrose Burnside restructured his three-brigade Coast Division into a three-division corps. Upon this reorganization, Burnside's three brigadier generals—Foster, Reno, and Parke—were elevated to the command of these three divisions, each containing two brigades. Reno's elevation to command of Burnside's Second Division created a vacancy at the head of his First Brigade—a vacancy that was soon filled by Colonel James Nagle of the 48th Pennsylvania. Of course, with Nagle's promotion, command of the 48th itself devolved upon its second-in-command, Lieutenant-Colonel Joshua K. Sigfried, who would continue to command the regiment for the next two years.[46]

While all of this was going on at the corps, divisional, brigade, and regimental level, there was also a shake-up occurring in the command of Company G, one that directly impacted Curtis Pollock and one that would create quite a controversy. It began with the resignation of 1st Lieutenant Cyrus Sheetz on May 2.

45. Bosbyshell, 43-45.
46. Woodbury, 84-85.

To fill the position of 1st Lieutenant, there seemed to have been no question that it would go to Oliver Bosbyshell who had, up until then, been the company's 2nd Lieutenant. The great point of contention, however, now became who would secure the position of 2nd Lieutenant. Typically, it went to the next senior officer, in this case, Company G's First Sergeant who was, at this time, Henry Clay Jackson from St. Clair. If a position was not filled by seniority, then sometimes elections were held within a company; other times, the regimental commander simply appointed someone to fill the position or, perhaps, the slot was filled from a commission directly from a state's governor.

Curtis Pollock, who like so many ambitious young soldiers had coveted promotion, believed his time had finally arrived. Yet there was a major problem. As the company's Third Corporal, there were at least seven other non-commissioned officers in line for promotion ahead of him. This helps to explain why he leaned so heavily upon whatever influence his father had. At the same time, the 48th's new commander—Lt. Col. Sigfried—believed it was his prerogative to appoint whomever he wanted for the 2nd Lieutenancy in Company G, and the man he wanted was twenty-five-year-old Charles Loeser, Jr., a soldier who entered the company the previous October as a *private*, a rank lower than that of corporal. But Loeser seemed to have been a particular favorite of Sigfried's. Whatever his reasoning, Sigfried was determined to appoint Charlie Loeser for the position Pollock had so yearned for, and Sigfried believed it was his right—and not Governor Curtin's—to fill vacancies in the regiment. Thus, when a commission finally did arrive from Harrisburg in late May, signed by the governor and appointing Pollock as 2nd Lieutenant in Company G, Sigfried not only refused to accept it but also, in a move that provoked Pollock's ire, sent the commission back to Governor Curtin. This triggered a controversy and set off an increased frequency in the letters Pollock wrote to his father—and to his mother—complaining about Sigfried and seeking guidance on what to do next. For the next uneasy month, until the issue was finally resolved with Pollock's eventual commissioning as 2nd Lieutenant, there was much debate in the camp of Company G as to who should have the spot as well as a palpable tension between Sigfried and young Curtis Pollock.

Following Pollock's short furlough home and upon his arrival back with Company G, first at Hatteras and then at Newbern, it was this controversy over his promotion that would come to dominate the subject of his letters home.

———•⋅◆⋅•———

Fortress Monroe
April 17th 1862

*D*ear Ma

  Here I am safe and sound. We arrived here about 8 o'clock this morning after a very pleasant ride down the bay. Col. Nagle is here and there is a boat going down to Hatteras this afternoon and we will not be loafing around here long. I got into Baltimore about 3 o'clock yesterday and the boat did not leave until 6 ½ o'clock but I had no time to go around much. The boat brought down a very large mail, about 30 large bags full. It is very warm today. No Signs of the *Merrimack*. The Steamer *Highland Lights* I believe is going down this afternoon. Nothing more of importance.

Affectionate Son
Curtis C. Pollock

P.S. No signs of the Merrimack; <u>all quiet along the lines</u>. I have seen Frank Farquhar but not to speak to him but will see him before I leave.

———•⋅◆⋅•———

Camp Winfield
Apr. 21st/62

*D*ear Pa

  As there is a Mail going this morning and as I have time to write a few lines I will take this opportunity to tell you I arrived here safely and am getting along very well. I am now almost entirely well of my cold but still take Some of the Medicine Ma sent. There are a good many of the men have bad colds and as I have more [medicine] than I want, I give some of it to them. I wrote a few lines the other day to you and gave the letter to Dick Jones who went to Port Carbon by the last boat. I asked you to give him five dollars as I had not quite enough to pay Isaac [Lippman] and had to borrow five from one of the men. It has been very warm since I have been here but we

have two drills a day just about enough exercise to keep us
alive. I have not had an opportunity to speak to the Captain
alone since I arrived but will the first chance I get. I wrote a
letter to Ma from Fortress Monroe which I suppose she sent
home. I was very lucky in hitting the boat at Ft. Monroe and
not lieing there for a day or so. I met the Colonel there and also
Col. Hartranft[47] of the 51st Pennsylvania; they all came down
on the same boat with us. I am beginning to think it will be
some time before we will get off of this place but I do not care
much. Will Pollock is not here now but with the company at Ft.
Macon. Lt. Hook is also there and Capt. [Joseph] Hoskings[48] of
Co. F has command of Ft. Hatteras and Co. E is at Fort Clark
so we only have two companies up here at present but we get
along very well. I have not been on guard yet but expect to go
on tomorrow. The guard duty is rather heavy now. If you get a
chance to send me a light slouch hat I would like you to send
it as I will need it very much when summer comes on, and also
pay Oliver Dobson the $2 ½ I owe him. I have twenty Dollars at
home now I believe and you can take it out of that I will have
to close now to get this off in the Mail.

With much love to all.
I remain Your
Affectionate Son
C.C. Pollock

———•◆•———

Camp Winfield
May 1st/62

ear Ma
I have not received a letter since I have come from home
but am expecting one every day. The mail always goes over to
Newbern and has to be assorted there and then sent back to
us, so we have to wait a good while always before we get it.
Ed. Sillyman arrived from Newbern yesterday where he was on

47. John F. Hartranft (1830-1889), a native of Montgomery County, Pennsylvania, commanded the 51st Pennsylvania Infantry. He would serve with the Ninth Corps, alongside the 48th,
throughout the entirety of the conflict and, by war's end, he was a major general and division
commander. After the war, he oversaw the execution of the Lincoln conspirators, headed the
Grand Army of the Republic, and served two terms as governor of Pennsylvania.
48. In the summer of 1861, Joseph H. Hoskings (1833-1913), a twenty-eight-year-old carpenter, organized what became Company F, 48th Pennsylvania, from his native Minersville. He
served as Company F's captain from August 1861 until his discharge on September 30, 1864,
proving himself one of the regiment's bravest and most capable officers.

furlough. He says that we will be over there in then days but I do not think we will get off for some time yet.

Friday May 2nd

I had to stop last night to go to dress parade and did not feel like writing last evening We had a Company drill this morning and it is just after Guard Mounting. I have not received any letters since I have been here except those that were here when I came back. I wrote a letter to Pa about a week ago and the captain wrote a few lines stating that I was competent and recommended me to the Governor as fit to fill the office of 2nd Lieut. in his company and if Pa can get enough influence with the Governor there will be no difficulty in getting my commission. I do not think the letter has left here yet and very likely you will get this with the other. There has been several boats come down within the last few days but the mail always goes over to Newbern before we get it here. We had a very heavy thunder Shower yesterday evening but this morning it is clear and very warm. I was on guard day before yesterday and had a very pleasant day for guard duty, in the evening we got some coffee and crackers and about 12 o'clock we had some hot coffee and fried crackers and it tasted very good. I suppose you heard that Col. Nagle is acting Brigadier General and Bosbyshell is Adjutant of the Regt. The Capt has sent over to the Col. to have Bosbyshell sent back which I do not think he will like very much as he is pretty comfortably fixed over there now but as Sheetz has resigned he will have to come back but I think Bosbyshell will be made Adjutant of the Regt as [John D.] Bertolette[49] will [be] the General's Adjt. General and then if I get the second Lieutenancy I will be the 1st Lieut when he is appointed and then if we ever get to marching the captain cannot stand it and who knows but what I may be Capt so there is a great deal lieing in my getting this and Pa will exert himself I think there is no trouble no more at present.

From Your Affectionate Son
C.C. Pollock

---

49. Born in Reading, Pennsylvania, John D. Bertolette (1839-1881) was studying law in Mauch Chunk (modern-day Jim Thorpe) when the Civil War began. He volunteered and became a lieutenant in the 6th Pennsylvania, where he impressed Colonel James Nagle. Bertolette later served as Nagle's adjutant general and was wounded at 2nd Bull Run. When he was mustered out of service in 1866, Bertolette was a colonel by brevet.

Camp Winfield
May 8th 1862

Dear Ma
    I received your letter yesterday and was much pleased
to hear from you and it is but the second letter I have received
since I have come back. I also received some papers from Will
as late as the second of May. I hope Pa can make that little
arrangement all right with the Governor as I am now certain I
stand a very poor show of getting elected in the company. I am
getting along as well as usual and have entirely gotten over my
cold. The bottle of medicine has been used up some time, since
for when I came back there were a great many in the company
had bad colds and I gave nearly all of it away. I am glad to hear
you enjoyed your visit to the city and that you were pleased
with your visit to the Hospital but I think you would find considerably different if you was to see some of the Hospitals that
are in the field, not quite so comfortable by a great deal. I have
never been in the hospital at Fort Clark but once and the poor
fellows there looked so bad that it made me feel bad to look
at them. My appetite is very good and I think you would have
said so if you would have seen me walking into the pot pie we
had to day for dinner but I could not each much more than two
tin cups full, so you see we have pretty good cooks at present
and I have nothing to complain of in respect to our eatables. I
expect to go on guard the day after tomorrow (Saturday) and
hope it will be a pleasant day. James Neis is now at home and
he will bring anything along for me that you send. If it would
be convenient and he would bring it I would not mind having
something in the eating line. We have had very encouraging
news within the last week or so and I think if we can only keep
on a little while longer driving them back until we can have one
open battle that it will wind up, and who knows but what we
will be at home by the 4th of July yet.[50] I am sorry to hear that
Aunt Maria is dead for I always thought a great deal of her but
she has left this world of trouble and care to go to a far happier

---

50. Here, Curtis is most likely referring to McClellan's campaign in Virginia. On May 5, McClellan declared victory at the Battle of Williamsburg, which was the first major engagement of the
Peninsula Campaign. Confederate forces fell back toward Richmond, with McClellan in pursuit.

and better place. The weather has not quite settled yet here as sometimes we have it quite cold. As soon as it gets right warm I am going to have my hair cut off as close as possible without shaving it and then it will be cool and easy kept clean. No more at present.

From Your Affectionate Son
C.C. Pollock

----●-●-----

Camp Winfield
May 10th 1862

*D*ear Pa

We have received our new clothes to day: light blue pants and a blouse. The Capt. heard from Newbern and told me that Col. Sigfried has recommended Chas. Loeser as 2nd Lieut in our company but he [the captain] says if you try you can get ahead of him. The Capt does not want Charley as he does not like him and I will try to get the Capt to write a letter to the Governor saying so. As I wrote a letter home yesterday and nothing new has transpired of any account since I will close with much love to all.

I remain Your Affectionate Son
C.C. Pollock

The Sunset or evening gun has just fired from Fort Hatteras, I suppose Will Pollock was in the fight at Fort Macon and I see by the papers that his company did very good service.

Your
C.C. Pollock

----●-●-----

Camp Winfield
May 12th 1862

*D*ear Pa

I wrote a letter to you the day before yesterday but as Lieutenant Sheetz and Clem Evans are going today I thought I would write you a few lines. If you only received my letter in time to get a head of Charley Loeser who received a recommendation from Col. Sigfried. The Capt. told me to tell you to say nothing about this in case I do not get the commission as it might create a bad feeling toward him. There is a great deal of dissatisfaction in the company in regard to Charley and he is by no means liked and the men talk very hard against him. If I could get the commission this would all be quieted down and everything go on as usual. I have no time to write more at present.

From Your Affectionate Son
C.C. Pollock

Camp near Newbern
May 25th 1862

ear Ma

We have left old Hatteras at last and are now encamped just outside of Newbern in a very pleasant place. We received orders on the evening of the 21st to start the next day but I being on guard had no time to pack up until the next morning but we were dismissed about 8 o'clock and I soon got ready to leave. I went down in a boat with some of the knapsacks belonging to the company; we had a very pleasant ride down and with but little trouble. I was down about an hour before the company came down and [the] poor fellows looked nearly done out as it was very warm. We bid good bye to Hatteras about 6 o'clock on the evening of the 22nd and started for Newbern. We were relieved by three companies of the 105th N.Y. who said they were only to stay two weeks but I guess they will have the chance to stay there for three years or during the war unless sooner discharged The boat only ran until 10 o'clock that night when we anchored somewhere in the middle of the Sound as the Captain said it was impossible to go when he could not see the buoys and the light houses have not got going yet, but as soon as it was daylight we started again and arrived here about 1 o'clock P.M. We found our tents already pitched and all we had to do was to lay the floors and fix up the street and now we are very comfortable.[51] I was down town yesterday but it was raining nearly all the time and I could not get around much but I will

---

51. In his regimental history, Oliver Bosbyshell wrote that when "the boys of E, F, G, and K" companies rejoined the regiment at Newbern, "there was a great hand-shaking" as the 48th was now entirely reunited.

go down again in a day or so and will go all around. I have not asked Col. Nagle for a recommendation as I do not think it is worthwhile for if Charley Loeser does not get the commission (which I think he will if Pa has not got it for me yet) the one the Captain sent will be sufficient. The Captain sent a letter to Pa which I suppose he has received by this time but I do not know what he said in it. It has been raining nearly all day and we had no inspection this morning and I did not go to church as it was very wet, though almost all the churches are open every Sunday, I think. Newbern is a very beautiful place and if our rela-

Colonel Joshua Sigfried assumed command of the 48th Pennsylvania following James Nagle's elevation to brigade command. At once, he and Pollock butted heads over the issue of Pollock's promotion. (From Oliver Bosbyshell, The 48th in the War)

tions were here I might have a pleasant time and think I was down on a visit. I was talking with a couple of young fellows yesterday who were in the 2nd N.C. Regt. the same one that Col. Hode and Wayne are in, they [say] that Col. is Adjutant, Jimmy Hode, Quartermaster and Wayne Quartermaster Sergeant and they were all in the battle of Newbern. These two fellows were in the battle also but were taken prisoner and took the oath of allegiance. Hoping you are all well,

I Remain Your Affectionate Son
C.C. Pollock

Direct your letters by way of Newbern. I have forgotten the place where you said you were born let me know and I will find it out.

C.C.P.

———◆•◆•———

Newbern May 27th 1862

*D*ear Pa

My commission arrived this morning but Col. Sigfried who is now in command of the Regt. will not recognize it. If you can see the Governor at once I think it will be all right as it is all spite on the Lt. Col.'s side as he is angry that he knew nothing about it and he wants Charley Loeser. I received Ma's letter this morning dated 19th but no papers. There is nothing new here and I am getting along very well and like Newbern very much, what I have seen of it. I do not feel like writing more to night.

From Your Affectionate Son
C.C. Pollock

Newbern May 28th 1862

Dear Pa

I was over to see the Lt. Col. this morning to see why he would not recognize me and he says that he recommended Chas. Loeser and he does not think that the Governor has any right to appoint anybody but him, especially if they are not recommended by some person in higher rank, and he also thinks that I have no right to go above all the sergeants in the company so he has written to the Governor to ask him what he means so I will soon find out and I hope it will turn out all right. If you can see the Governor after you get this and get him not to make another appointment in my place the Lt. Col. will have to recognize me. I am going down to see Col. Nagle this morning and see what he says about it. Sigfried says he has nothing against me but in the Governor's appointing he goes against his own orders. I have seen Col. Nagle and he says that the letter which came with the commissions (for mine and Bosbyshell's 1st Lt. came together) says "Enclosed are two commissions which were recommended by you" and as the Col. did not recommend me he thought there was something wrong but you can easily fix that up so the sooner you go to Harrisburg the better it will be for me. I was told that Sigfried had sent my commission back to Governor again which he had no right to do, but I shall demand it from him this evening and will see if he has it for it was sent for me & I have the only right to it.

No More At Present.

From Your Affectionate
C.C. Pollock

Enclosed is an express rect. for a box I have sent home.

Camp near Newbern
May 30th/62

*D*ear Pa

I have written several letters to you within the last few days and hope you have rec'd them by this time. In my last [letter] I told you that I had seen Col. Nagle and he said I had a right to demand my commission from Sigfried but when I asked him for it he told me he had sent it back to the Governor. It was rather a mean trick as he could have given it to me under a protest until he had heard from the Governor but I can see he is doing his very best to get me out of it altogether. Do you think if I were to resign and come home that [I] could raise a company for the new regiment about to form in Penna.[?] as I do not care about going to West Point I can get a commission in the State Vols. but if that is impossible why, then, I will go there. You can tell Mr. Campbell after you find out whether this thing is sure or not. You must try and see me get justice in getting my commission for this Co. The Capt. was very angry when he found out that Sigfried would not give it to me and he went and told him to give it to me as he and Bosbyshell were both satisfied but he would not give it to me nor did he even notify me of his having rec'd it and Bosbyshell (who is Acting Adjutant) asked him if he should put my name in the order to be read out at Dress Parade, he said he would be Court Martialed first. I have seen several officers and they all think [it] is a great outrage in him sending it back. I do not think that I could hardly raise a company around Schuylkill Co. but I want your opinion of it. We moved our Camp on the 29th inst to the other side of the Trent River and are now camped in a very pleasant situation on the bank of the river just opposite Newbern. I was down town the other day and went to see Cousin Isaac's house and was inside looking around; there are two Dr's living in it and I was invited to take dinner there yesterday but on account of our moving I could not go but will go on Sunday I think. We are to have a grand review tomorrow (Saturday) in Newbern of the whole Division which will be quite an imposing spectacle I believe. I have not been doing duty in the company since my commission but have not bought any

Shoulder Straps yet. The day we came here they had a Rebel flag with the Union down hanging from Dr Hughes's house.

No more at present.

From Your Affectionate Son
C.C. Pollock

P.S. I received a letter from Ma dated the 20th and she did not know anything about my commission which was dated the 16th of May.

❄ ❄ ❄

POLLOCK DID, INDEED, have his supporters in the developing showdown with Lt. Col. Sigfried over this controversial issue of promotion and commissions. Among them was Captain James Wren, commander of Company B. A native of Scotland, Wren had arrived in Pottsville in the early 1840s where he took an early and active interest in the city's budding militia. He was with a young James Nagle when the Washington Artillery was organized in 1842 and had served with the company in Mexico. And it was Wren who, as captain, led the Washington Artillery into the capital in April 1861. In his diary, Wren recorded that on the afternoon of June 1, 1862, he was visited by Curtis Pollock who sounded out Wren's thoughts on whether he was entitled to the position and Wren replied in the affirmative, stating that Pollock's commission had come directly from the governor. Apparently, Wren and Colonel James Nagle, now commanding the brigade, had discussed this whole affair a short time earlier. During their conversation, Nagle asked Wren why he felt Pollock should have the spot since he was not next in line for the promotion. Wren was quick to remind the colonel that his own brother—Daniel Nagle—had been promoted to the rank of major over the heads of the regiment's more senior captains—including himself— and that Pollock simply could

Major James Wren, 48th Pennsylvania Infantry. (From Bosbyshell, The Forty-Eighth in the War)

not be "laid aside." Wren advised Pollock to outfit and equip himself as the 2nd Lieutenant. When Pollock told him he had no money, Wren gave him a coat and sword and loaned him money to purchase 2nd Lieutenant shoulder bars. Wren noted that Pollock took his advice, "rigged himself up & appeared in uniform," which set off "quite a talk in Camp." But Wren also knew that Pollock had to do more than just simply look the part. In his diary entry of June 2, Wren wrote that "Thear was nothing of note in Camp today, except Drilling & the Chatring [chattering] of Lieut. Pollock's appearance. I told Pollock, 'It is your duty to study that tackticks [tactics] & get Booked up or you might be reduced to the Ranks again.'"[52]

Pollock never mentioned his conversations with Wren in any of his letters home but it is clear he did seek counsel from numerous other officers, especially those in his own Company G, including Oliver Bosbyshell and Captain Philip Nagle, who had both supported Pollock's claims. The issue remained unresolved throughout much of the month of June; however, on June 2, Captain Philip Nagle tendered his resignation from the service on account of poor health. His resignation opened a vacancy, one soon filled by Oliver Bosbyshell who was promoted to captain. Bosbyshell's promotion thus created an opening for 1st Lieutenant. By month's end, Curtis Pollock would, at last and after much drama and controversy, hold that position and rank, having been commissioned by Governor Andrew Curtin. Charles Loeser would eventually also be promoted, first to sergeant-major and then, in September 1862, to 2nd lieutenant in Company C. By the time of his discharge in October 1864, he was Company C's 1st lieutenant.

----------•◦•◦•----------

Camp near Newbern
June 6th 1862

*D*ear Ma
    As the Capt. is going to leave today I will send a few lines with him. I have not been doing any duty since my commission arrived here and am now waiting to hear from the Governor

52. James Wren, *Captain James Wren's Diary: From New Bern to Fredericksburg*, edited by John Michael Priest. (Shippensburg, Pennsylvania: White Mane Publishing Company, 1990), pgs. 34-36.

which I think I will by the next mail and if the Governor returned my commission, which I have every reason to believe he will do, I will be all right. What do you think of Sigfried's behavior? I only hope the Governor will give him what he deserves and Court Martial him. He is very unpopular and all the men I have spoken to about myself say I must not let a stone unturned until I get righted again. We have had a great many reports in camp which if true I think the war will soon be over. One is that Jackson was captured with 9000 prisoners, another that McClellan has taken Richmond with 10000 prisoners and that Halleck had taken Corinth with 20000 prisoners.[53] If all this is true there [will] not be much more work for the army. I am getting along very well at present and have no sort of a disease at all. We have had very wet weather for the last few days and it is raining quite hard now. There is to be a Brigade drill this morning but if it rains as hard as it does now I do not think it will come off. Each man in the company has had his likeness taken give it to Captain Nagle and he is to buy a handsome frame in Philadelphia and take it home as a present from the company. The First Division was reviewed on Monday last by Governor Stanly[54] and Gen. Burnside and all looked very well. General Foster commands the 1st Division Gen. Reno the 2nd and Gen. Parke the 3rd. Col. Nagle commands the 1st Brigade of the 2nd Division consequently we are on the right of the 2nd Division which is the post of honor. Geo. Gowen[55] returned from Beaufort on Tuesday and is now acting Adjt., Lt. Bosbyshell being ordered to return to his company. I have not had a letter from any of my friends since I have been here and I think it is very strange that Bob Hill and Harry do not write. I have nothing more to say at present, So With Much love to all.

I Remain Your Affectionate Son

C.C. Pollock

---

53. As was the case with many other rumors, the reports about Stonewall Jackson being captured and that George McClellan had conquered the Confederate proved to be untrue. And while General Henry Halleck had, indeed, taken Corinth, Mississippi, the Confederate force there had simply withdrawn to Tupelo and thus, no 20,000 men were captured.

54. A native of Newbern, North Carolina, David Stanly was an attorney and politician who served for a time in the U.S. House of Representatives and North Carolina State Legislature. A strong advocate of Union over States' Rights, Stanly was appointed by President Lincoln to serve as the military governor of North Carolina in late May 1862.

55. George Washington Gowen entered the 48th Pennsylvania as a lieutenant in Company C. A civil engineer, Gowen would rise to the rank of colonel and following the departure of Henry Pleasants in the Fall of 1864, took command of the regiment. Gowen was killed during the regiment's final battle, on April 2, 1865, at Petersburg, Virginia.

Camp near Newbern
June 10th 1862

*D*ear Ma

I received three letters yesterday from home, two from Clem Evans, and one by mail. I have not heard anything about my commission since I last wrote, but I heard yesterday that the Col. received an official letter from Harrisburg, and I will likely hear something about it today. I suppose you received the letter I wrote you when I first heard of Sigfried's doings, as I wrote several. Even now if the commission does come back I do not know whether he will recognize me, but I think the Governor will finish him pretty soon if he does not. Some persons say that they heard him say, "he would be Court Martialed and resign before he would recognize me" but I would consider that I had done a favor to the Regt. if it was on my account that he resigned, as he is not at all liked by the men. If I can get the commission, and get recognized by the Col. I will have no difficulty in getting along with the men, as they all seem to want me to remain and not resign, so if Pa can fix it all right with the Governor there will be no trouble on that point, and as for my resigning you need not fear, as I will hold on as long as I can. I have the good will of nearly all the men in the company, and there is very [many] but what say they would rather have me than either Chas. Loeser, or the Orderly Sergeant. Yesterday the Colonel had Brigade drill; he has five Regiments in the Brigade, and all are here except the 9th New Jersey, which is guarding [the] Rail Road between here and

One of the five "Fighting Nagle" brothers in the 48th Pennsylvania, Philip Nagle helped to raise Pollock's Company G and was the company's first commander until his resignation from the army in June 1862. Philip Nagle passed away in March 1891 at age 58. (From Gould, The Story of the Forty-Eighth)

Beaufort. They maneuvered very well under the guidance of Col. Nagle, who I think makes a very efficient and able commander. By the way, I suppose you will ask, "why do you not go to Col. Nagle"? The reason why is that I was there once and could get not the least satisfaction out of him, and I know, it will be the same way if I go again, and he says, he has given up the command of the Regt. to Lt. Col. Sigfried, and does not want to interfere with him. So you see how I am situated: Sigfried goes down town, and has a consultation with Col. Nagle and they are both doing their best to wrangle me out. You need not be in a hurry about sending me any clothes yet, until I know something more about what I am to do. I can buy everything I want here but at a much greater cost than it would be at home. Capt. [Philip] Nagle left here for home yesterday but the boat came back this morning on account of a storm that came while entering the sound but I suppose it will start again this morning.
[LETTER ENDS HERE; INCOMPLETE]

Camp near Newbern June 17, 62

Dear Ma

I have not received a letter from you for some time, and think it very strange that I do not receive your letters more regularly. I have not received any [from] Harry Dewees, or Bob Hill since I have been in Newbern. I have not heard anything about my commission yet, and do not know what has become of it; Col. Sigfried has had time to receive an answer from the Governor. General Burnside has been up to Fortress Monroe to have a chat with General McClellan and returned day before yesterday. Yesterday afternoon he went down to Beaufort with the train but I think he will be up again this morning. I suppose you receive the Weekly Progress[56] which I subscribed to for three months and you can get more news out of it than I can tell you. I have not been down town for about a week, I would have gone to church on Sunday but it was the hottest day we have had this summer and I did not feel very well. We had a very heavy storm on Sunday evening and since then it has

---

56. The *Weekly Progress* was a Newbern-based newspaper that Pollock had subscribed to and apparently sent home on a regular basis.

been quite cool. That pair of drawers you gave me when I was at home are nearly worn out, and if I send home for anything it is not probable that I will for should we move before I would get my things from home I would be in a pretty [bad] fix. I can get everything I want in town but will have to pay a little more than I would at home anyhow you could not get pants and coat made to fit me without my measure. I am getting very tired of this war business and often wish I was at home again. I wonder how long it will take McClellan to take Richmond or will he lay around there until he compels them to evacuate again? We have papers here of the 13th which are the latest. I received some papers from Will and two from you—the Evening Bulletin and the Press—but they were rather old. There are two engines running now between here and Beaufort making two trips a day. I would like to go down and see Will Pollock but do not think I could get down without a furlough and that's too much trouble. I had a saucer of Ice cream the other day and paid the small sum of 25 cents a saucer I did not ask him how he sold it until after I was done eating or he would not have imposed upon me so. I heard that there was a boat came in last night but did not hear where it came from, and if there had been a mail aboard we should have had it by this time. Hoping that you are all well and that the war will soon be over.

I Remain Your Affectionate Son

C.C. Pollock

Write soon.

Camp near Newbern
June 22nd 1862

*D*ear Ma

I received two letters from you yesterday, one with the telegraph message in it. About 5 O'clock John Clemens came up to see me as I was sitting in front of the tent and said that Col. Nagle wished to see me. I went down and he handed me my commission and told me to report to Lt. Col. Sigfried as soon as he would come back (he had gone up to 51st PA camp). After Dress Parade I went up and reported to him, he very politely told me he would not assign me to duty with the Company. He also told me he had nothing against me but it was the way the Governor treated his recommendation, never letting him know anything about it, whether he had received it or not. I am going to borrow $25 from Isaac tomorrow and buy myself an officer's blouse. Lt. Bosbyshell has given me his old shoulder straps and by tomorrow I will be out in style. I am going to buy very little until I get ordered to duty. There is very little of any importance going on around here at present, the only excitement we had around here was the sword presentation to Gen. Burnside; all the troops in the department that are about here were present and made quite a fine appearance, the 48th marching particularly well. There was a little shower came up but did not do any damage as it soon passed over. I was a little unwell for the last few days with a slight touch of fever and ague but the Dr. soon brought me around and I am now as well as ever with the exception of being a little weak yet. I wrote to you about that dinner John Clemens and I were at and if you did not receive the letter I am sure, I wrote it. I think there are several other of my letters that you have never received. Will Pollock was up here the other day, and I saw him, he looks very well and is getting along very well in his new situation and is liked very well. I believe he left Beaufort again on Friday evening. The Company received new Enfield Rifles yesterday and we like them very much. The whole Regt. are now provided with them and look very well. I did not go to church this morning on account of not having anything to wear and did not want to go in my uniform as I would have to have a pass. The Regt. was down with muskets and generally go every Sunday; it is the custom here for the Regiments to go church with muskets and stack them in the street with a guard over them. I think I shall write to the Governor myself telling him that Sigfried refuses to assign me to duty and Pa can write to him too. The Governor said he wrote to Col. Sigfried a peremptory order, ordering me to be mustered in but Col. Sigfried never received a line from Gov. Curtin though Col. Nagle might have received it with the Commission and I will go down and see him tomorrow and let you know immediately how everything is.

From Your Affectionate Son
C.C. Pollock

P.S. I shall not write to the Gov. until I see Col. Nagle.

C.C.P.

Newbern June 24th 1862

*D*ear Ma

I have been ordered on duty by Col. Nagle and will commence to day. I have been talking with Bosbyshell this morning and we have come to the conclusion that I ought to resign as there is a great deal of bad feeling toward me around the non-commissioned officers who were above me and Bosbyshell thinks I can make a great many more friends by resigning then if I were to stay here; so I think you may expect me home before a great many weeks are over. There is nothing going on here. I was down town this morning and bought a blouse for $9 and a cap which purchases are all I intend to make. I will receive about $200 for my pay as Lt.

From Your Affectionate Son
C.C. Pollock

Newbern June 25th 1862

*D*ear Ma

I do not know whether you know it but I am at present 1st Lieutenant of Co. G. and am on duty. I was out on Regt. drill today and Dress Parade and am going on guard tomorrow. I wrote you the other day that I thought I would resign but I have given up that notion for the present, until further developments. The mail has been very irregular lately and I have not had any letters since the one you sent the Telegraph message in. I was up to see Capt Merrill Sinn today and he says "do not resign on any account" and says that I have as much right to it as anyone in the company, that I was recommended by the Capt. and if he were in my place he would stay just because Colonel Sigfried treated me so badly, that if I would resign I would be doing just what he tried to do, and could not. So I think I will stay for a little while anyhow. There is an expedition fitting out here and is expected to leave to-morrow or next day to go to Wilmington, so you can expect to hear some good news before long. The expedition is composed principally of Regiments of the First Division. Will Pollock left here for Fort

Macon on Tuesday afternoon. I was down town and saw him
off; he looks very well and says he likes it pretty well. They are
garrisoning Fort Macon now and Will says he has a great deal
to do there only being two officers in the Company and one of
them commander of the Fort. The 51st Penna. Vols. are encamped about two miles above us in a very pleasant situation
and I borrowed the Major's pony and had a very agreeable ride
all alone by myself. I have been sleeping on the floor for the last
few nights but this afternoon we fixed up a very comfortable
bed and all three are sleeping in one tent. I will get my uniform
here and guess I can get it nearly as cheap as if it was made
at home. I will send one hundred dollars or as much as I can
spare and you can take what I have at home. I do not know
how much I will draw this pay but will send $100 if I can pos-
sibly do it. You seem to have had quite a storm in Schuylkill
County and there seems to have been a good deal of damage
down in Saint-Clare; more in fact, I think, than any other place
in the County. I am now entirely well of the slight touch of the
fever and ague and am going around as usual. I was over in
town this morning but there is very little to be seen in Newbern
now a days. I went over principally to see Colonel Nagle about
resigning but he told me he would not advise me to resign but
should use my own judgment and that I knew more about
what I ought to do than he did. We very often have quite heavy
thunderstorms but it does not affect us much as we tie up
tight and enjoy ourselves amazingly while it is raining. Nothing
more at present.

From Your Affectionate Son
C.C. Pollock

P.S. Direct to Lieut. Pollock next time you write.

C.C.P.

Camp near Newbern
June 28th 1862

Dear Ma
I received your letter this evening dated June 23rd 1862
and was very glad to hear from you. I wrote to you the other
day telling you I was 1st Lieut. of Co. G and suppose you have

received it by this time. I have no idea of resigning at present
but if anything should turn up I may come home. I was on
guard on the day before yesterday and was very highly complimented for doing so well at Guard Mounting as it was my first
attempt. I got along very well all through and had no trouble,
though I had to put two of the guards in the Guard house
for sitting down on their post but I soon let them out again.
To-day I was on Police and had to superintend the cleaning
of the camp. I was out on Dress Parade this evening and got
along very well. To-morrow we have inspection and I expect to
be out. On Monday we have Muster for Pay and will be paid in
a week or so from date, and you can expect a hundred Dollars
or so home before long. I will get a receipt from the Express
Agent and send it home in a letter. I have only been on drill
once since I have been on duty as I have been on some other
duty all the time. It is now some time after Tattoo and Capt.
Bosbyshell has just made a pitcher of lemonade and we are
all enjoying it (ice cold lemonade) we get ice here occasionally
and whenever we get it we always have ice water on hand. Lt.
[Henry] Jackson is on Guard today and I will have the bed
all to myself tonight. We had a Mail today and I received one
letter from you and one from Will. I did receive a letter from
Harry but had an idea that I had answered but I guess I have
not and I will answer it tonight. Capt. Bosbyshell is very much
liked and there is not one in the Company (except it be Charley
Evans) but what would do anything for him. We live pretty
well here; we have new potatoes and peas with fresh beef etc. I
shall be very happy to hear from Mary anytime she may write
and I do not think she ever answer my letter. How is Augusta
getting along now-a-days and is Bob as attentive as ever? I
have not had a letter from Bob since I returned from home. I
wish you would ask him why he does not write. There is a good
deal of talk about us leaving here but I will not believe it until
I hear the order read out. The regiment were out firing blank
cartridges this morning and were only to fire fifteen rounds but
Col. Nagle came up just before they started and after speaking
to Lt. Col. Sigfried he marched the men down to where the
ammunition is kept and gave out all the blank cartridges they
had on hand, the Major said they wanted to get rid of them.
This looks a little like leaving but it may only be a verbal order
to get ready in case we should have to move. Col. Nagle sent

up orders this evening ordering the commanders of Regiments to muster their commands for Pay on Monday, just the same as if nothing was going on. No person about here has any idea which way we shall move in case we leave here.

From Your Affectionate Son
C.C. Pollock

———◆◆◆———

Camp near Newbern
June 30th 1862

Dear Ma
     I received your letter dated 25th 1862 and take this opportunity answering it. I am now 1st Lieut. of Co. G and have no intention of resigning at present; there is very little or no opposition to me in the Company and that is wearing off very fast. I think it is very strange you do not get my letters as I have written several to you explaining the whole matter and I hope you have or will not write to Col. Nagle as it can do no good now. He ordered me on duty when Lt. Col. Sigfried would not recognize me and I feel very grateful to him for doing so. I was mustered for pay this morning and will be paid in a week or so if we are not on the march. I have just heard that Levi Nagle[57] is going home on a discharge and I will send this letter by him, I am quite surprised to hear that he is going as I have not heard anything about it before. We expect to leave to-morrow but have not received the order yet, though I expect we will receive it this evening. Col. Sigfried has just come around and ordered the men to carry their knapsacks down to the boat, they are not to carry their knapsacks but only their blankets and overcoats, the balance of the baggage is to go aboard a schooner and follow us up. We are allowed to take nothing but what we can carry and our trunks are to go with the balance of the baggage. I will have to hurry and close as Levi is going to start in a few minutes No news here lately so I will close.

Your Affectionate Son
C.C. Pollock

---

57. Levi was the brother of the other Nagles in the 48th: James, Daniel, Philip, and Abraham. Born in 1835, Levi was a printer prior to the war. He was a talented musician and in that capacity he entered the 48th Pennsylvania. Upon resigning from the army, Levi returned to Pottsville and later opened a toy store. He died in 1908 at age 73.

✳✳✳

NEW ORDERS HAD, indeed and at long last, arrived: the 48th Pennsylvania was to proceed immediately to Virginia where, along with two of Burnside's three divisions, it was to reinforce General George McClellan's army that was just then heavily engaged a few miles outside of Richmond. After an eight-month stay at Hatteras and Newbern, Lt. Pollock and the Schuylkill County soldiers of the 48th Pennsylvania were about to bid farewell to North Carolina. With three days' rations in their haversacks, the regiment marched through Newbern on the morning of July 2 and then boarded the steamer *Cossack*. A long journey down the Neuse River ensued and by the following afternoon—July 3—the *Cossack* had reached Hatteras. There, however, the *Cossack* made a sudden halt as another ship—the *Alice Price*—steamed up next to it with the most welcome report that McClellan had taken Richmond! Oliver Bosbyshell later recorded that "Three rousing cheers for the news and three more for Little Mac shook the timbers of the old 'Cossack' from fore to aft." It was quite the celebration and now, since Burnside's men would not be needed after all, the *Cossack* dropped its anchor and the 48th's officers held a spirited meeting to discuss the best way they could celebrate the news of McClellan's victory as well as the nation's Independence Day, now just hours away. The men were boisterous, jubilant. Surely, they thought, the war would soon be over and they would soon be heading back home. First, however, they would be heading back to Newbern. Since his men were no longer needed in Virginia, Ambrose Burnside directed his ships to return the men to their camps. This meant the men of the 48th would spend the Fourth of July on board the *Cossack* as it steamed back up the Neuse. All the plans to celebrate and commemorate the Fourth were thus "greatly interfered with," wrote Bosbyshell. Still, "National salutes were being fired by the gunboats and shore batteries, bells were ringing and flags flying when the regiment arrived at the wharf at Newbern." It was a festive, joyous atmosphere as the men disembarked and proceeded toward their old camps, thinking of their homes and wondering how soon they would all be back, embracing their loved ones with the war over and the nation intact.[58]

Soon after arriving back in Newbern, Lieutenant Pollock wrote a letter home describing the aborted journey; it would be his last letter written from North Carolina.

---

58. Bosbyshell, 49-50.

———•◦•◦•———

Camp near Newbern
July 5th 1862

ear Ma
   Here we are back in Newbern after having a Fourth of July excursion to Hatteras. I will copy what I have written in my diary, which is a full account of all our proceedings.
   Monday June 30th we were mustered for pay this morning at 6 o'clock. We are making active preparations for leaving Newbern, such as packing up all extra baggage.
   Tuesday July 1st Have not received our orders for marching yet but Col. Sigfried told us to be ready to move at eight hours' notice. Was down town this morning trying to get some tin cups but could not get them. The Col. received his orders to day and we are to strike tents to-morrow at day break and be ready to go on board the *Cossack* at 5 ½ A.M. Went to bed early tonight.

Wednesday July 2nd
   Was up this morning about 3 o'clock, and had coffee and crackers for breakfast. We did not strike our tents until 5 o'clock and we formed line about 6. Marched over to town and after waiting there about an hour we got aboard. We were riding until about 4 o'clock getting schooners in tow, each steamer had one or two in tow, the *Cossack* had two. One of the schooners ran into our stern and tore part of it away but did not do much damage. We were to take three days' rations of Coffee and sugar and Capt. Bosbyshell understood that they were to be taken over in the small boat but after we got aboard, he found out that each company was to carry their own rations. So he had to take one of the steamer's small boats and go back for them. In the meantime the steamers moved down stream to get the schooners ready to start just about the time Bosbyshell was appearing in sight and he thinking we were already started got considerably excited and the way he made those poor fellows work was a caution, but when we got down to the place where the schooner was we stopped and then he soon caught up to us, and such a tired and warm looking set you never did see. We had a very good dinner on board, which I walked into with a relish. After dinner I went into the stateroom which we occupied and took a nap. Had supper about

7 o'clock and after supper the band played and we had several songs. Passed the evening very pleasantly. Raining nearly all day. The Col. opened his orders this evening after we had dropped anchor and we were all very much surprised to hear that we were to go to Hampton Roads.

Thursday July 3rd

Got up this morning about 5 o'clock and found the boat had already started. Had a cup of coffee and some crackers and cheese for breakfast, did not get breakfast at the regular table. Still raining every now and then and very foggy. Had a very good dinner about 2 o'clock. Have been running steady all morning and have run out of sight of the balance of the fleet. Arrived off Hatteras about 4 A.M. and anchored inside the swash, we had not been at anchor more than 15 minutes before we saw the *Alice Price* coming in from Newbern. She came up alongside and brought the news that Richmond was taken and our orders were countermanded. She had a rebel prisoner aboard who was taken at Elizzton; he was one of the chief rebel Quartermasters and was after eggs and chickens when captured. After supper the officers held a meeting for the purpose of making arrangement for the proper celebration of the Fourth of July. We adopted resolutions and will have a grand time I expect.

July 4th

Orders came this morning for our return to Newbern before I was up and by the time I arose we were on our road back. The grand celebration did not come off for reasons unknown to myself. We have two schooners in tow that we had with us coming over. It is rather a dry Fourth and we have not been doing anything but laying around loose in a most miserable state of existence. It is quite cool and cloudy today but we have had no rain. We arrived at Newbern after a very short voyage of about ten hours at 4 ½ o'clock and marched at once up to camp, we got our tents off the schooner and have them all up. The boards are still here and we are just as comfortable as we were before we left. Col. Nagle told me he had received the letter from you. I have not got my blankets off the boat yet but will get them to day if we are not to move again before long.

From Your Affectionate Son
C.C. Pollock

CHAPTER FOUR

"Here We Are Once More, On the Sacred Soil of Virginia"
July 1862–August 1862

H ARDLY HAD THE soldiers of the 48th Pennsylvania settled back into their old camps at Newbern before the hard truth hit: the reports and rumors they had been hearing were wrong, the Confederate capital was not taken—not by a long shot—and instead, it was McClellan who had been defeated—driven back from the very doorstep of Richmond to the safety of the gunboats on the James River. During the waning days of June and into the first of July, General Robert E. Lee, the newly-appointed commander of the Army of Northern Virginia, had launched a week-long series of savage attacks in a campaign soon labeled the Seven Days' Battles. While costly, these Confederate attacks did stop McClellan's drive on Richmond and ultimately forced him back. Independence Day, 1862, would thus come and go with the end of the war nowhere in sight. It may have been well that the celebration planned by the officers of the 48th to take place aboard the *Cossack* did not transpire, for there would have been little for them to celebrate that Fourth of July. And now, as word of McClellan's defeat spread throughout camp, the soldiers of the 48th shook their heads in disbelief, especially after they received orders that they were to proceed to Virginia after all. So, once more, the disheartened soldiers struck their tents, packed up their gear, and found themselves climbing back on board the *Cossack*. And at last, on the afternoon of July 6, the regiment steamed away from Newbern—leaving North Carolina forever behind and heading for the Virginia peninsula. The mood aboard the packed vessel this time was more somber. No longer were the soldiers thinking about an imminent return home and the warm and hearty embrace of

119

loved ones in Schuylkill County. The thought now running most through their minds was where the next campaign would find them. Yet no one could have predicted the violent combat and sheer carnage that lay ahead of them later that summer, along an unfinished railroad cut near the Bull Run creek in north-eastern Virginia and at an idyllic three-arched stone bridge that crossed another creek—the Antietam—further north and west, near Sharpsburg, Maryland.

Sailing past the familiar old stomping grounds of Fortress Monroe the *Cossack* steamed up the James River to Newport News where, after a two-day journey, it finally dropped anchor. Oliver Bosbyshell remembered that it was "under the bright light of the moon" on the night of July 8 when the soldiers of the 48th disembarked from the vessel, stretched their cramped legs, and established camp, settling in for what proved to be a three-week stay at Newport News.[1] In his letters home, Lieutenant Curtis Pollock described the journey and the 48th's return to the "sacred soil" of Virginia.

Hampton Roads
July 7th 1862

Dear Ma
Here we are at Old Point Comfort again though it is not very comfortable here just now as it is very warm. We arrived here yesterday morning and are still on board the boat though we expect to go on again today. I think we will go up the James River though it is not known where we will go yet. I was on shore last evening in swimming, a great many of the officers are on shore this morning and I want to go if I can get off. The cooks were sent on shore last night to cook two days provisions. It has been very warm and sultry since we have been here. As soon as we get off the boat I will give you another copy of my diary which I have kept regularly since we have started. Papers which were so scarce at Newberne are floating around here in abundance. I wonder if John McCleery and Thad Bogh escaped without injury; I hope they did. I looked over the list very carefully to see if I could see either of their names but did

---

1. Bosbyshell, 52.

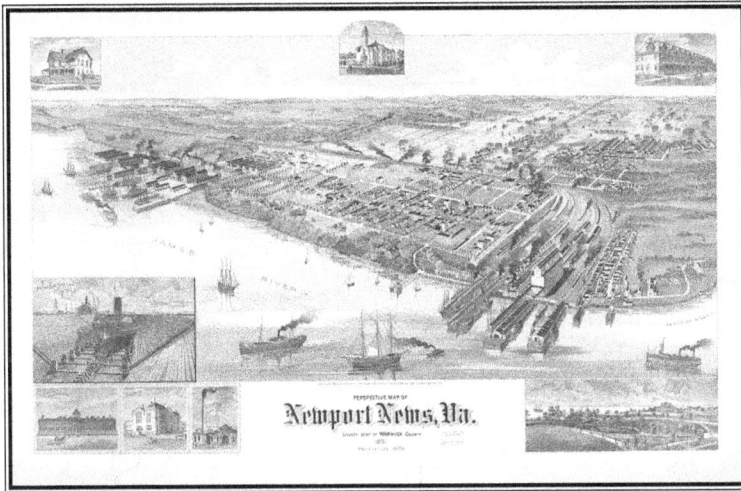

An 1891 Perspective Map of Newport News, Virginia. The 48th Pennsylvania would spend several weeks encamped at Newport News, first in the summer of 1862 and again the next year, in February-March 1863. (Courtesy of the Library of Congress)

not see any name except a J. McCleery but that I am sure was not his as he is a Captain and this name in the paper did not belong to the reserves.[2] We have very poor water on the boat and very little ice and it is almost sickening to drink it without ice. I do not know how to you should direct a letter so that it would reach me but will let you know as soon as possible. I am getting along fine and have no more trouble and am in a very good state of health. We stand a poor chance of being paid very soon now. The President and Sec. of War went up to see McClellan last night they passed by very quietly and it was scarcely known that they were here. I suppose you have heard all the news before this and I will not trouble you with news that you have had long ago. There is hard fighting going on today in front of Richmond but I guess it will not be all over before we get there and then you will see what the <u>48th</u> will do. and I will inform you that they will not disgrace themselves

No more at present.

Your Affectionate Son
C.C. Pollock

---

2. These were no doubt the names of friends or acquaintances who served in other Pennsylvania regiments that participated in the Seven Days' Battles.

Newport News Va.
July 11th 1862

Dear Ma
Here we are once more, on the sacred soil of Virginia. We disembarked on the night before last and slept out without our tents as we had no time to get them off the boat. I slept very well for my first night's sleep in the open air. We got our tents yesterday morning and soon had them up. I think today has been the warmest day I have experienced this summer. It was so hot that you would perspire lieing down. We had quite a shower last evening but we did not get wet any. I had [a] cramp in my stomach last night but a couple of doses of ginger set me all right and I feel as well as ever this morning. I cannot find my diary this morning and I do not feel like writing so I will write again in a day or so.

From Your Affectionate Son
C.C. Pollock

Newport News Va.
July 15th 1862

Dear Ma
We have not received a mail since we left Newbern but are expecting one every day. I have lost my diary and cannot give you the latter part of our journey as I have forgotten where I left off. I was on guard last Saturday and got along very well. Yesterday I was on a board of survey to look at some meat which the Quartermaster reported unfit for issue and it was very bad, it was so strong that you could smell it for some distance off. It is quite warm here now but we do not do much, only having short drills to keep us from getting too lazy. We had a short brigade drill yesterday afternoon and we got along very well. There are only three Regiments in our Brigade at present, the other being left behind at Newbern. [3] I have no

---

3. There were a few changes in the structure of the brigade to which the 48th Pennsylvania belonged. While still commanded by Colonel James Nagle, the brigade now consisted of the 48th Pennsylvania, 2nd Maryland, and 6th New Hampshire Infantry regiments. The 9th New Jersey and 103rd New York had been transferred to other commands.

idea where we shall go to nor how long we will remain here. There is a report around here that 10,000 of Halleck's troops are on the road to join us and that all of us under Burnside are reserved for some special duty. It is also reported that there is a great deal expected of Burnside's corps. One of the 96th was here yesterday, he is a teamster and came down to the White House [Landing] after some provisions just about the time of the Battle of Fair Oaks and could not get back for some reason or the other and is now over at Hampton waiting for a chance to get back.[4] We are moving our camp this morning nearer the river so as to get on higher ground and the men are now busy moving their things out of their tents. We have no boards and I have been sleeping on the ground since we have been here, we have plenty of blankets however and do not mind it much. We get the papers everyday now and are pretty well posted with regard to the news, though there has not been much in lately. There is a mail lieing at Newbern for us which we expect to have in a day or so, as I understand there is a boat went down a few days ago and is expected back shortly. They have commenced taking down the tents and if I do not hurry I will be routed out of here before I am through. Everything is cheaper here than at Newbern and if we were only paid I could fit myself out nicely. Money is very scarce in camp no person hardly having any, and the men are asking every day to borrow ten cents to buy a plug of tobacco. We have a very good view of the Cumberland with her masts sticking up out of the water and about ¼ of a mile from shore.[5] We can get ice cream here and all other sort of luxuries that at Newbern we had to pay 25 cts a saucer get it here for ten. There is nothing going on here but what would occur in any other camp thus it is rather a hard job to write anything of a long letter. Hoping to hear from you soon I remain

Your Affectionate Son

C.C. Pollock

---

4. Raised and recruited in the late summer and early fall of 1861, the 96th Pennsylvania was composed largely of Schuylkill County men. Attached to the Sixth Corps, Army of the Potomac, the 96th witnessed heavy battle action during the Seven Days, especially at the Battle of Gaines's Mill, where it lost 87 men.

5. The *U.S.S. Cumberland*, a fifty-gun frigate in the service of the U.S. Navy since 1842, was rammed and sunk by the *C.S.S. Virginia* in the harbor of Hampton Roads, Virginia on March 8, 1862.

Camp near Newport News
July 16th 1862

*D*ear Ma

I received two letters from you last evening and I will take this opportunity of answering it. I was busy this morning making out the report of the board of Survey I was on and did not get out to Company drill. It has been most uncommon[ly] warm for the last few days and we do not do much of anything but try to keep as cool as possible. Several Regiments came in this morning from South Carolina and among them Col. Christs,[6] they are now landing and if it were not so very warm I would go down and see some of them that I am acquainted with. I was down at the wharf this morning to see some of them but they were not yet landed, but while I was down I saw something that occurs very often in the army. A couple of negroes brought a boat load of apples up to the wharf and they had not sold more than a couple of dollars worth, when the soldiers getting into the boat commenced putting them into their pockets and carrying them off right before his face without paying for them and before 15 minutes there was not an apple left in the boat. Such is war. We had a very good dinner to day; boiled cabbage and potatoes, cold slaw, bread and coffee and then for dessert we had corn starch with milk, quite extravagant, don't you think so? I ate so much cabbage and potatoes that I did not get over it for an hour or so. I hardly think we will have a Regimental drill this afternoon on account of the heat. We received a small mail to day from Pottsville but none for me, but I hope to get one tomorrow, fortune favoring me. I have seen Capt. [illegible] several times since I wrote you, they are now encamped quite near us & I go over to see him quite frequently. I have no idea of resigning at present as it would never do on any account, now that we are likely to be on the eve of a battle, anyhow I think that the dissatisfaction is rapidly wearing away and I do not apprehend any trouble whatever. We get the papers the day after they are published and always have the latest. I do not see why those two regiments surrendered in Tennessee. I do not

6. Colonel Benjamin Christ, a hotel keeper from Minersville, Pennsylvania, commanded the 50th Pennsylvania Infantry. Companies A & C of the 50th were composed largely of Schuylkill County soldiers. The other regiments that arrived with the 50th formed part of what would become the Third Division of the Ninth Army Corps. They were engaged in a successful operation in Port Royal, South Carolina, prior to their arrival in Virginia.

think there was any occasion for it. The Battalion of Wynkoop's Calvary suffered rather severely.[7] I wonder what has become of Reilly and whether he has been in any battles yet. It is hard to tell how soon we will leave here and I am sure I do not care about marching much in this hot weather. We have the bottom of the tent up all around but only catch a breeze every once in a while. We made an advance movement the other day toward the James River. That is to say, we struck tents and moved the camp about 50 paces nearer the river than it was at first. We had a very heavy storm last night and as we occupy one tent and have no boards in it the rain came in and we had about a foot of water in it but the Capt., having a few boards in his tent, we went in there and slept very comfortably. The drum has just rolled for drill and I will have to close With much love to all. Write soon.

Your Affectionate Son
C.C. Pollock

P.S. We had a short drill but it was very warm and I was perspiring even when I was standing still. I think you can buy a trunk cheaper in Pottsville than I can get it here. I want a new one with a canvas cover and on one end I want Lieut. C.C. Pollock Co. "G" 48th Regt. & on the other, C.C.P. You had better buy it at once and send it on as soon as possible. I do not want too small a one. Get it a pretty good size and you can put in it any little thing you might think I would want. A couple of shirts for instance and some drawers as mine are beginning to wear out. Any other little things good to eat or something in the way of corn starch or [illegible], in fact anything nice, that will embrace all. Capt. got a letter from Capt. Nagle but has not said anything to me about it. He did not read it aloud to the Company as he usually does but just said that it was a business letter between him and the Capt. He answered last almost directly after he received it. Write as soon as you receive this and let me know if you can send the trunk. I expect the drum to beat for dress parade in a few minutes so I will close,

Your Affectionate Son
C.C. Pollock

---

7. George Campbell Wynkoop made his home in Pottsville in the years prior to the Civil War. He came from a military family, heavily involved in the state militia and in the summer of 1861 he helped to raise what became the 7th Pennsylvania Cavalry. Some of the regiment's twelve companies were recruited in Pottsville.

Capt wrote to you this morning. I do not know what he said. The Capt told me this evening that the Lt. Col. said that the Governor wrote as if the Col. had recommended me which he knew was not so. They were all very much surprised and the Col. who was up when it came did not know what to make of it.

No more at present
Yours &c
C.C.P.

�֎ ֎ ֎

INCLUDED AMONG THE Pollock letter collection is the one that Captain Oliver Bobsyshell did, indeed, write to Curtis's father, William, on July 16, 1862. Apparently, William had made it known that he was upset with Captain Bosbyshell for his advice that his son resign during the promotion controversy. In this insightful letter, Bosbyshell did his best to explain to Curtis's father why he had suggested and why Curtis's elevation to the rank of lieutenant sparked such a clamor in camp.

———————

Newport News Va. July 16th 1862

*D*ear Sir;

I should have written to you before probably and certainly would have done so had I known that you felt "very much hurt" at my advising Curtis to resign. An explanation is necessary.

There can be no doubt in regard to my friendship for Curtis—at least I feel none & think he will coincide with me. I've had no reason to be other than on the most friendly terms with him and I advised with him as I would desire a friend to do with me. Now, you will recollect, Curtis was 2nd Corporal—between him and a 2nd Lieutenancy in this Company, in regular order of promotion, were five Sergeants & one Corporal, either of whom were & are capable of performing a Lieutenant's duties. It is natural that they should feel aggrieved at a junior in rank being placed over them & also feel sensitive on the subject of obeying & respecting a former junior as a superior. Besides all were led to believe by Gov. Curtin's order that promotions

Oliver Christian Bosbyshell would serve with Curtis Pollock throughout much of the war. A First Defender, Bosbyshell would later take command of Company G, 48th Pennsylvania, before being promoted to major. Bosbyshell considered Pollock a brave and good officer, though did suggest he resign to quell the controversy created by Pollock's promotion to lieutenant. Bosbyshell would later author a history of the 48th Pennsylvania, published in 1895, and would become the fourth Superintendent of the U.S. Mint at Philadelphia. He passed away in August 1921 age 82. (From Bosbyshell, The Forty-Eighth in the War*)*

would be made from the ranks, according to rank—but now there is no hope of such a result, no matter how capable, an Orderly Sergeant is as likely to be superseded by a private as to be promoted, provided said private has influential friends at home. Now these Sergt's & Corporal who were thus discarded have their friends in the Company & of course their friends feel aggrieved also. Do you wonder then at there being dissatisfaction in Co. G? There is no one [who] doubts the ability of Curtis—he has no enemy in his Company socially—but what so keenly cut was the injustice to our Sergts. I am speaking plainly but give you the Company's side of the question. How I knew of this feeling—why men came to me & told me frankly that they would not obey Curtis. Some went so far as to swear they would not. Yet none dislike him as a friend—not one. I told the men he was duly commissioned & ordered on duty & that they would be bound to obey & respect him as their Lieutenant. How knowing the feeling, had I not every reason to believe Curtis' position would be anything but pleasant? I felt also that he did not know of the opposition to his being a Lieutenant—and was I not in duty bound to prepare him, for what I believed would happen, downright refusal of the men to obey? I told him frankly what the men thought of his promotion—and advised him to resign as I thought it would be better for him to do this and become popular at a jump, than to remain & have enemies in the Company. I did what I thought was right, and would do it again under similar circumstances. Had Curtis resigned at that time & told the men why he did so, I'll venture to say every many would have thrown up his hat in admiration of his course. Thus I've stated the position of affairs at this time of Curtis' promotion.

Let me add, before closing, that none rejoice more than I to see Curtis promoted, and I believe the Company is perfectly satisfied now—at all events Curtis is 1st Lieutenant of Co. G and <u>obeyed & respected as such</u>. and so long as such is the case I'll see that he continues to be obeyed & respected.

To assure you of my friendship for Curtis he will tell you that he read every line of this letter before it left.[8]

Please give my kind regards to Mrs. Pollock & the young ladies, and believe me to be with feelings of great respect

Yours &c
Oliver C. Bosbyshell

Newport News Va.
July 18th 1862

ear Ma

I think it is very strange that I do not get a letter from you. I have written several letters to you since we arrived here but have received no answer as yet. We are getting along very well and have not a great deal to do. I have had the Company out drilling several times and get along very well. I wrote a

---

8. This very clearly contradicts Curtis's claim that he had no idea what Bosbyshell had written.

letter to [you] yesterday about sending me a trunk and would like you to send it as soon as possible because I do not know how soon we may leave here and I would like to have it before we start. I have no towels and I would like to have a few white pocket handkerchiefs and you might send me a half a dozen pairs of white gloves. I have not got my sword yet but will buy one as soon as we are paid. I am now using one that I borrowed from one [of] the Lieuts. who has two but it is so nearly used up that I would rather buy a new one than keep the one I am now using. If you do not have money enough why what I send home you can take to make it up.

Sat. July 19

We [were] laughing and cutting up so last night that I had no chance to finish my letter but will do so this morning. I do not know what put us in such a good humor last evening but we certainly had a quite a gay time cracking jokes and telling funny stories that I laughed until I was tired. It was raining nearly all day yesterday but today the sun has come out and I guess we will have a fine warm day. We have a Brigade drill this morning at 7 ½ A.M. which will be all the drilling we will do today. I would like to have a box of cigars and if you could buy a good pistol cheap I would like to have one, if not I will get one the first battle I am in. New troops are coming in almost every day and we are expecting 10,000 of the Army of the West in a few days. Burnside, I believe has gone to Washington. They had quite a time of it in New York at that great Mass Meeting they had but I do not believe it did much good in that city. There was a report in camp the other day that Cousin Francis had been arrested by order of the Sect. of War in Phila. You never told me whether you rec'd that box I sent home soon after we arrived at Newbern I have not been over to Fortress Monroe since I have been here but am going one of these days. We sent our darkey out yesterday to pick some blackberries which abound in this country. He brought back a pitcher full of very nice ones and we had blackberries and milk which did not go bad. I have no time to say more as it is nearly time for drill.

From Your Affectionate Son
C.C. Pollock

Newport News Va.
July 20th 1862

Dear Pa

I have not received any letters from home except those I received by way of Newbern and I think it is very strange you do not write. However that is not what I want to say. I heard today that D.A. Smith[9] was getting up a regiment and I would like you to ask him if he would recommend me for Adjt.[adjutant] of it. This is one of the finest positions in a Regt. and one that I would like to have. I wish you would ask him about it and see what he says. I have written a letter almost every day since I have been here and nothing particular has occurred to day of any importance. Please send me some paper and envelopes in the trunk. The Rev. Mr. Meredith Chaplain of Col. Christ's (50th P.V.) addressed the regiment this evening on dress parade and delivered a very neat and appropriate speech. I do not want to leave the Regt on account of any dissatisfaction as that has all worn off and I think I am very well like in the Co. The only reason why I do not want to leave here is on the account of us being likely to be in a fight before long, but you can see Capt. Smith or not just as you please, do what you think best.

Your Affectionate Son
C.C. Pollock

I only have three pair of white stockings.

Newport News Va.
July 23rd 1862

Dear Ma

I have received two letters; one yesterday dated 18th and another to day dated the 20th. I was getting very anxious about not hearing from you for so long and began to think you did not receive my letters. I hope you received the letter in

---

9. David A. Smith, a thirty-seven-year-old tailor from Pottsville, served as a 1st Lieutenant in the Washington Artillery then as the Lieutenant-Colonel of the 48th Pennsylvania before his resignation in November 1861. In the summer of 1862 and then again in 1863, Smith helped to raise several companies of Pennsylvania Militia. Pollock, after having experienced so much of a struggle and controversy to attain a lieutenant's commission in the 48th was now looking to join up with Smith's company as a staff officer. Nothing came of this request.

which I mentioned about my trunk. There is very little going on here and consequently not much to write about. I have had no return of the cramp and do not care about it; as for drinking ice water you need not trouble yourself about it as ice is very scarce and I do not see it very often. I was out on company drill this morning and got along very well.

July 24th 1862. The mosquitoes were so bad last night that it was almost impossible to write, so I postponed it until this morning. We have school now every day and are getting through with the School of the Battalion quite smart. We had apple dumplings yesterday for dinner and are to have some more today. Our money is running very short and soon we will have to live on Government rations if the Paymaster does not arrive but I heard today that he was to be here the latter part of this week. I hope you have received all the letters I have written as there are a good many things that I want and as I did not think of everything I wanted at once there several things in different letters. The weather is rather pleasant at present the only time it is very warm is between 11 o'clock and 2.

Major D. Nagle has resigned and his resignation has been accepted but is waiting for the Pay Master before he will leave for home. I do not know his reasons for resigning nor do I know who will be our new Major but I suppose it will lie between Capt. Kaufman of Co. A and James Ellis, Qr. Master.[10] I have not been out of camp for several days and there is nothing going on here.

From Your Affectionate Son
C.C. Pollock

———◆———

Newport News Va.
July 29th 1862

ear Ma
Yesterday was my birthday but I did not think of it until towards evening. I came off Guard in the morning and was

---

10. Daniel Nagle, the thirty-four-year-old younger brother of Colonel James Nagle, resigned after having failed to receive a leave of absence in order to return home to take care of his wife and son, who were apparently quite ill at the time. Daniel Nagle, who had previously served as a drummer in his brother's company in the Mexican-American War, would later command the 173rd Pennsylvania Infantry and would be a leading member of the 48th's veteran organizations. He died in 1918 just a few months shy of his 90th birthday.

sleeping nearly all day. I have received but three of your letters
and you say you have written four. I do not see what has become of it. We had a grand dash into the country the other day
but returned without losing a man. On last Friday morning at
7 o'clock we formed line and marched off up the James River.
The sky was cloudy and the sun had not a very good chance
to get at us but nevertheless it [was] warm enough. I took my
blanket, haversack and canteen along. I had our one day's
rations of crackers in my haversack. Capt. [Bosbyshell] had
some biscuits in his and [Lieutenant] Jackson had a couple
of pounds of cheese in his. I perspired very freely and drank
two canteens full of water (about 3 qts.) during the day. We
had a rest every once in a while but I used to get pretty tired
sometimes before it would come. We arrived at a place called
Youngs Mills, where the rebels had several entrenchments
thrown up and they looked pretty strong, about 12 m. [merid-
ian/noon] and stopped to rest, we staid here until about 4
P.M. when we started again and after a march of several miles
reached Warwick Court House. Here we were marched into
a large field and bivouacked for the night. I went over to see
what could be seen about the Court House and found it to be
about the size of one of our Squires offices and two jury rooms
about 5 ft + 8. The building is built of brick and there is a jail
just behind the Court House is another small building used for
keeping the county records in. I was digging around through it
but did not find anything but an old Docket which I send home
as a memento of Warwick C.H. After dark a heavy dew began
falling and I went to bed. There was a lot of wheat stacked up
in the field when we came there and as soon as ranks were
broken they got it and made a very comfortable bed. I slept
with one of the men. In the morning when I got up my blanket
which I had over me was all wet with the dew but it did not get
through. We started again at 5 o'clock and after a very hard
march arrived in camp 11 ½ A.M. very tired, thirsty hungry,
blistered and everything else.[11] We soon had a good dinner
of cabbage & potatoes ready for us and we walked into them

---

11. On July 24, orders arrived for the regiment to prepare one day's rations and to be ready to
move at a moment's notice. But while there was a state of "great excitement" with many of the
men believing they were to make a "dash at some impudent rebels," the purpose of these orders,
as Oliver Bosbyshell later explained, was for "merely a trial march, as frequent moves were
considered beneficial." The 48th marched eleven hours in the heat at arrived at Warwick Court
House greatly fatigued. Next morning, the return march to Newport News commenced and by
noon on July 26, the regiment was once more in their familiar camps.

pretty considerably. After dinner we got a tub of water and I had a good wash and after I got clean clothes on I felt first rate. I have just come off Police this morning and as Major Nagle is going home this afternoon I will send this with him also the Docket I spoke of. No more at present.

Your affectionate Son
C.C. Pollock

I will give you a draft of Warwick C.H. & vicinity

✳ ✳ ✳

THE NEXT LETTER in the Pollock collection is one of the few existing ones written from Emily to her son. She composed this particular one on the final day of July and in it, she informed Curtis about the fates of some of his acquaintances in service in other regiments, told of the news from home, and discussed her hopes about the possibility of a draft. On the same day Emily wrote this letter in Pottsville, Curtis was composing one of his own over 300 miles away in Newport News.

Pottsville
July 31 1862

My Dear Curtis,

I intended to write last night but was not very well. We received your letter yesterday, dated the 24th and are glad to hear you have received <u>some</u> of my letters. I write now that you are at Newport News twice a week, and you ought to hear frequently. I have just had a letter from your Aunt Sarah. John McCleary and Charley Dougal have reached home from Richmond and mighty glad they were to get away from R[ichmond].[12] John was taken to the hospital in Baltimore and his father had considerable difficulty in getting him home, but finally accomplished it. He is wounded in the fleshy part of the <u>thigh</u> and not below the knee as we first heard. Charley Dougal was sick at Savage Station, where he was taken prisoner and

---

12. John McCleary was a twenty-four-year-old Captain from Milton, Pennsylvania—William Pollock's hometown. Serving in the 5th Pennsylvania Reserves, McCleary was badly wounded and captured during the Seven Days' Battles and resigned on account of his injuries. Charley Dougal may have served with McCleary in the 5th Pennsylvania Reserves and was also among the casualties of the Seven Days.

spent his Fourth of July by being summoned to Richmond. He and John met in the Tobacco Warehouse; when they first went there, there were four dead bodies in the [illegible] and the stench was intolerable. They were finally removed. They took everything away from Charley—his money, watch, surgical instruments, even the spurs off his boots and would have taken his boots, in addition but he plead so hard for them that they let him keep them. He met two of his old college mates who are officers in the Rebel Army. One of them sat down & talked to him, as if they were the best of friends; the other merely spoke. John McC. can only remain home twenty days but he will not be fit for service in that time.

Your Aunt Annie and Henry arrived yesterday, Henry & Jimmy have just come home from "the Circus," and it is almost 11 o'clock P.M. You remember last Spring you sent two engravings of Gen. Burnside, one for your Aunt Sarah? I never had an opportunity of sending it and your Aunt Annie is such an admirer of Gen. Burnside, and seemed to want it so much that I gave it to her. You have never sent your Aunt Annie anything, and your Aunt Sarah has received [illegible], and you ought not to show so much partiality. Your Aunt Sarah I think has never heard of it and it don't make much difference. Your Aunt Annie sends you a great deal of love and congratulations on your promotion; she is much pleased that such is the case and hopes that you will continue to do well. Have you received your trunk which we sent off a week ago today? And did I send all you wanted? I hope the Paymaster will be along soon, and how will you dispose of your money? I hope you will try to be economical, and save all you can. Recruiting does not grow as fast as it ought to. The Volunteers are very slow about enlisting and I think the government ought to draft. In the Revolutionary War and the W. of 1812, men were drafted and why not now? Uncle Charles was visiting Pottsville a few days and took tea with us. He says he was drafted in the war of 1812 but his father would not let him go and paid 170 dollars to buy him off. The soldiers then had not as many comforts as now, and in the war of the Revolution it was far worse. It is late and I must close.

> With much love I remain
> Your Affectionate Mother
> E.C.P.

Newport News Va.
July 31st 1862

Dear Ma

I received your letter yesterday, but it is only the fourth one I have received and I think the first one you wrote must be lost. I have not received the trunk yet but it is on account of there being so much express here that they have kept it over at Baltimore until they can get rid of some that they have here. I think I will get it tomorrow however. I think it is likely we will leave here before long but how soon it is hard to tell I have been reading Tom Brown at Oxford[13] and liked them very much. We had a grand inspection and review today it being the last of the month and it all passed off very well. There has been nothing going to day and I have been reading nearly all day. I have not been out of camp for some time and for that matter you can see as much in camp almost as you can out. So I do not run about much. We are very short of money and are anxiously looking for the Paymaster, we have been expecting him every day since we left Newbern but he must have got lost, wounded or strayed. I am getting along fine; never had a better appetite in my life and if I keep on eating the way I have for the last couple of weeks I think I soon be quite fat. How are they getting along recruiting about town? I only wish they would commence and draft as all the able bodied men are wanted at once and if we do not soon get a larger army in the field than we now have the Rebels will commence and whip us out of every place we now hold by their overpowering force. They are now a great deal nearer our lines than is comfortable and I believe they will attack us in our entrenchments on the James before long. I hope Pa will not think of coming out unless he can get some position where he can ride such as quartermaster or something as that. I think the Post of Regt. Qr. Master would suit him first rate, but he must remember he is getting old and would [not] stand long marches & exposure as well as he could have done a few years back, and the rheumatism that he is subject to would have him laid up half the time. I spent

---

13. Published in 1861, *Tom Brown at Oxford* was a popular novel authored by Thomas Hughes.

my birthday very quietly and was not aware of it until evening but I am now out of my teens and in another short year I will be of age. Time flies very fast in the army one day slips by after the other and you hardly notice it. We had a shower this evening which will make the weather quite pleasant tomorrow. You would be surprised to see the quantity of bugs that we have flying around here in the evening they are quite trouble-some but the mosquitoes take down anything I ever saw they are sometimes so thick that you are kept continually slapping at them and it almost impossible to do anything but try and keep them from biting you. The flies too are regular and bite almost as bad as mosquitoes. So Bob is really going to be mar-ried, but he better look out or else he may have to postpone his wedding or else it come off sooner than he intended. I write to him and tell him that he ought to wait until the war is over do that I can be his groomsman. No more at present

With much love to every body
I remain your affectionate son
C.C. Pollock

————◆•◆•◆————

Camp near Falmouth Va.
August 5th 1862

ear Ma
I have no doubt you will be much surprised to learn we have got way up into this part of the country but here we are encamped about a mile outside of Falmouth in a very fine situation on top of a hill and have everything handy except the water which we have to carry some distance. We received orders to move last Friday the 1st and on the 2nd we got on board the Steamer *Cossack* and after fooling all day we started about 6 o'clock P.M. and went as far as Fortress Monroe where we anchored to wait for orders. When I got awoke the next morning we were on our road up the Chesapeake Bay having started about 1 o'clock; we had three schooners in tow. We had a very pleasant ride and were totally ignorant of where we were going, however we turned into the Potomac and then it was rumored we were going to join Banks[14] and thought we

---

14. Brigadier General Nathaniel Banks commanded a corps in the newly-formed Army of Vir-ginia which was just then maneuvering south through Culpeper County, Virginia.

would get to see Washington. The Potomac is a beautiful river and I do not think I ever enjoyed a ride on a boat more than I did that one. We arrived at Aquia Creek and were landed; [then we] got on board the cars and started for Fredericksburg. It is only about 15 [miles] from Aquia Creek to Fredericksburg and the road is very uneven the road runs over two small hills and going up it goes very slow but coming down the cars run just as fast as they can.

Friday Evening
August 8th

I have been kept from finishing this letter by different things; was on Guard day before yesterday and yesterday I went over to see Fredericksburg. It is a very fine town and there are a great many of the inhabitants there still. The stores are all opened but vegetables are very scarce. I bought myself a sword for $15.00 and a belt for $6. There is an express office there & I expressed $100 to you which I hope you will receive. Enclosed I send you the receipt. We were paid on the first of the month and started away the next morning. Our baggage is limited to fifty pounds and I guess if I ever get my trunk I will have to send it back immediately for we are all three going to put our things in the Capt's trunk and take nothing but it and the mess chest. I would like very much to get my trunk more on account of the clothing that is in it than anything else, for one pair of my drawers are nearly worn out. Capt [Bosbyshell] is going over to town tomorrow and very likely it may have got there by this time for we received a mail to day and I received that letter you first wrote after my coming to Newport News. I was out on Brigade drill this afternoon and had command of the company and got along very well. I was down and had a bath this evening with Lt. Jackson. Our watering place is not very extensive it merely consists of a spout made out of bark running over a small descent of about four feet but it is as good as a shower bath, and I assure you I feel much better after it. It is very warm here in the day time but the mornings and evenings are very agreeable. We will send our things home that we do not need in a few days but do not expect to leave here for some time. The trunk will be directed to Jos. E. Jackson the school teacher. He boards at Ligers but you need not go and look for him now as he is at home, but he will send word when the trunk arrived. I received $204.98 for my pay, the largest amount of money I ever owned at one time but it took the best part of one hundred to pay my bills and buy the things that I need. No more at present. Hoping you are all well I remain

Your Affectionate Son

C.C. Pollock

Write soon

❋ ❋ ❋

AFTER A THREE-week-long interlude at Newport News, the soldiers of the 48th Pennsylvania were, indeed, once more on the move, as Lieutenant Pollock explained in his letters of August 5 and 8. What Pollock failed to mention, however, was that just a few days earlier the forces that Ambrose Burnside had gathered at Newport News, including the 48th, had been formally organized and designated as the Ninth Army Corps. Commanded by the hard-fighting Burnside, the new Ninth Corps was composed of the two divisions he had brought with him from North Carolina—commanded respectively by Generals John Parke and Jesse Reno—as well as General Isaac Stevens's division, which had joined Burnside's command at Newport News after participating in several successful battle actions in South Carolina. Having already served under Burnside's command in North Carolina, the 48th Pennsylvania would remain proudly attached to the Ninth Corps for the duration of the conflict.

Burnside had received orders to proceed with his 13,000-man Ninth Corps to Fredericksburg, by way of Aquia Creek, and, as Pollock noted, by 6:00 p.m. on the evening of August 2, the force was steaming away from Newport News, down the James, then up the Chesapeake Bay. The journey aboard the regiment's familiar "old friend" the *Cossack* was a delightful one, at least per regimental historian Oliver Bosbyshell, even if the men were initially unaware of their ultimate destination. All questions were answered early on August 4, however, when the *Cossack* dropped anchor at Aquia Creek. Going ashore, the soldiers bade farewell to life on the waters—at least for the next few months— then headed out immediately by train for Falmouth, where they arrived later that evening. Establishing camp directly across the Rappahannock from Fredericksburg, the 48th Pennsylvania would spend the next week there. As Pollock indicated, many of the regiment's officers took the time to explore the historic city

General John Pope commanded the Union forces at the 2nd Battle of Bull Run. (Courtesy of the Library of Congress)

along the river. Captain Bosbyshell was impressed with Fredericksburg despite the sentiments of the inhabitants who "were decidedly 'secesh.'" Four months later, the regiment would return to Fredericksburg under much different circumstances and, as Bobsyshell recorded, the "picturesque hills" surrounding Fredericksburg were "not nearly so pleasant and delightful" when they bristled with Confederate artillery and infantry.[15]

For the time being, however, the men of the 48th did their best to enjoy their time at Falmouth and at Fredericksburg. It was there, of course, that Pollock found the time to write the above letters home, in which he described the journey from

15. Bosbyshell, 56-57.

Newport News and how he spent his time—and money—at Fredericksburg. But as it turned out, this would be Curtis's last letter home for quite some time. Nearly a month would pass before he could write home again—his next letter being dated September 4. By then, he and his comrades in the 48th had experienced the sheer hell of combat, receiving their true baptism by fire while savagely battling Stonewall Jackson's Confederates along an unfinished railroad cut near Manassas, Virginia, just to the west of the Bull Run Creek.

The tide of the war had changed dramatically that summer. The spring had dawned so bright, so hopeful for the Union. But now, as spring turned to summer, the situation very quickly grew dim. A new star for the Confederacy had emerged in the form of Robert E. Lee and, having driven McClellan back from the gates of Richmond, Lee next set his sights northward and specifically toward a new Union army that was just then gathering and posing a new threat to Richmond. That army, numbering some 60,000 men, was titled the Army of Virginia and it had just recently been organized, being pieced together from three smaller armies that had been mystified, misled, and defeated by Stonewall Jackson earlier that year in the Shenandoah Valley. To command this new force, President Abraham Lincoln called upon the boastful and aggressive John Pope, a general who had achieved some success in the war's Western Theater. Pope came east, assumed his new command, and quickly began driving his army southward, to threaten Richmond, of course, but also to relieve some of the heavy pressure that was just then being placed upon McClellan. Pope made waves soon after his arrival in Virginia by issuing a series of controversial General Orders instructing his men to live off the land, to take what they could from the countryside—to strip it clean, as it were—and by so doing, he was introducing a new kind of war to Virginia. Pope's orders sparked outrage and Lee, who famously labeled Pope a "miscreant," declared that this new general had to be suppressed, and the sooner the better, thought Lee, before Pope's forces could be reinforced by either McClellan's now dormant army or by Burnside's force, which had just arrived from the Carolinas. While leaving a part of his army under James Longstreet behind to keep a close eye on McClellan and guard the capital, Lee ordered Stonewall Jackson north to hunt down and strike at Pope's command.

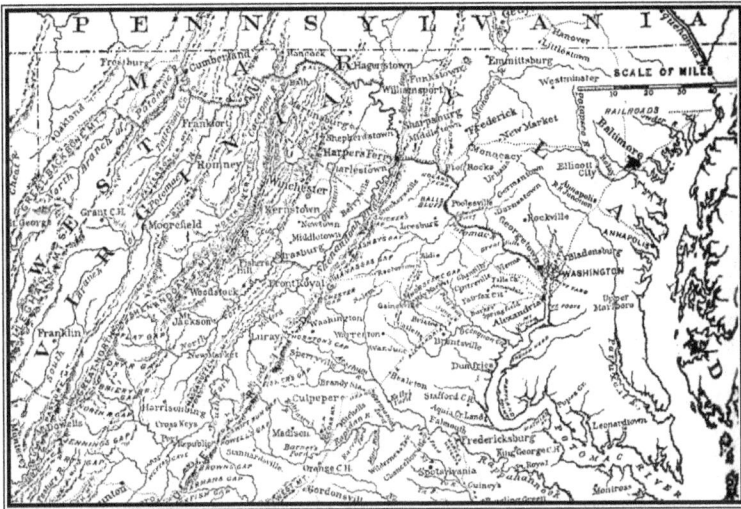

From July 1862 until March 1863, the 48th Pennsylvania campaigned across northern Virginia and western Maryland, seeing action at the Battles of 2nd Bull Run, South Mountain, Antietam, and Fredericksburg. (From Battles and Leaders of the Civil War, Vol. II)

As Jackson set off northward from Richmond, civilian and military authorities in Washington were doing all they could to unite the various Union forces in Virginia. In early August, McClellan received orders to evacuate his army from the peninsula and bring his men north to bolster Pope's command, while Burnside had already received his instructions to shift his force from Newport News to Fredericksburg. An obstinate McClellan, however, not wishing to see his army given over to Pope, made excuses and dragged his feet, and did not put his men in motion for another two weeks. Burnside, on the other hand, moved rapidly and by August 5, his Ninth Corps—the 48th included—had reached the area around Fredericksburg. A few days later but further west, Stonewall Jackson struck at the advance elements of Pope's army under General Nathaniel Banks at Cedar Mountain. After a bloody, day-long fight neither side could claim a great victory but Lee was determined to keep after the blue coats. Convinced McClellan had been entirely neutralized and no longer a threat, he called up Longstreet's men from Richmond and ordered Jackson to sweep around Pope's left flank to cut off reinforcements coming from that direction and to get astride his lines of supply and retreat. But Burnside's presence near Fredericksburg complicated matters as did some heavy rains that raised the waters of the Rappahannock. What was more, on August 18, captured Confederate dispatches revealed to Pope that Lee was fully moving after him. In response, Pope directed his army to begin falling back, northward across the Rappahannock. His prey may have been getting away but Lee would not give up. Instead, on August 24, he embarked upon a new course of action. Instead of swinging around Pope's left flank, Lee now ordered Jackson to move around his right and sever the principal Union supply line along the Orange and Alexandria Railroad. In the meantime, as this great cat-and-mouse game continued to unfold, the first of McClellan's army began to arrive as had Burnside's Ninth Corps.[16]

After their week-long stay at Falmouth, the 48th Pennsylvania would spend the next two weeks marching fast to link up with Pope. Setting off in a heavy rain and along dreadfully muddy roads on the evening of August 12, the regiment marched through the night before finally going into bivouac at 3:00 a.m. After just four hours' rest, however, they were once more on the move. Making their way through the lush Virginia countryside, the soldiers of the 48th had no qualms whatsoever about obeying Pope's orders to live off the land. Indeed, as regimental historian Joseph Gould wrote, the men "took great liberties with" Pope's instructions, while Bosbyshell declared that many of the men "indulged in an exciting chase after calves, sheep, pigs, and the like. Corn and potatoes were plenty; the boys lived well" off the land.[17]

The regiment reached Culpeper Court House on August 14 where they could see the scarred landscape and bloody aftermath of the fight at Cedar Mountain. And as the march continued, so did the pillaging. Fences "melted in an instant," said Bosbyshell, while "great havoc" was played with the fresh meat nearby. "Sheep, hogs, calves and chickens, not alone suffered, but heifers and even steers were brought low. The camps were all slaughter pens," said Bosbyshell, "the number of impromptu butchers immense." Late on the night of August 18, and under Pope's order to withdraw across the Rappahannock, the 48th marched quietly away, with their campfires still burning and their tin cups, canteens, and other "rattling objects" firmly

16. For the best secondary account of the Second Manassas Campaign and Battle, see John J. Hennessy, *Return to Bull Run: The Campaign and Battle of Second Manassas* (New York: Simon & Schuster, 1993).
17. Gould, 62-63; Bosbyshell, 59-60.

secured to prevent the nearby Confederates from becoming wise to the movement. Moving through the night and during much of the next day, the regiment at last crossed the waist-deep waters of the Rappahannock at Kelly's Ford. The men were "pretty well fagged out," admitted Bosbyshell, but there was to be but little rest. By this time, it was becoming very much apparent that a great battle was imminent.[18]

Conditions were miserable as the 48th resumed its march on August 22. "The weather was murky, rainy and clear, by fits and starts, and intensely warm," remembered Bosbyshell, "hence marching was far from agreeable." Arriving at Rappahannock Station, the exhausted soldiers fell asleep during a drenching rain. Over the next six days, the regiment got little in the way of rest and, instead, remained in motion over increasingly mountainous terrain, with the far-off thud of artillery the musical accompaniment to their movements. August 24 witnessed the men arriving at White Sulphur Springs; next day, they reached Warrenton. Continuing to tramp north in the pitch darkness of night, the 48th spent most of August 26 at Warrenton Junction where, that afternoon, the soldiers at last "enjoyed the luxury of a good wash." It was their first bath in the past fourteen days. Feeling refreshed and cleaner, and no doubt smelling better, the regiment moved out again on August 27 and the next day, they arrived at Manassas Junction. There, smoldering train cars and torched wagon trains made it very apparent that Stonewall Jackson's Confederates had just recently passed through. Indeed, following Lee's orders, Jackson slipped around Pope's right and got in his rear; however, Longstreet had yet to catch up and Jackson's men were isolated. Despite seeing his supply depot go up in flames, Pope believed he had Jackson in the bag. In the ranks of the 48th, said Gould the prevailing thought was that "Jackson and his 'ragamuffins' were certainly in a tight place and sure to be captured." But as Gould was quick to point out, "The sequel proved different."[19]

After torching Pope's supply depot at Manassas Junction, Jackson led his men north and took up position in a thick woodlot and along a railroad cut very near the same field where the legendary Confederate general had acquired his famous nickname the previous summer. Pope continued after him, hoping

---

18. Bosbyshell, 60.
19. Bosbyshell, 61-64; Gould, 64.

to catch Jackson while he was still isolated from the rest of the Confederate army. On the evening of August 28, Jackson attacked Pope's passing columns and the two sides—at long last and after much maneuvering—finally locked horns. The Second Battle of Bull Run had commenced and it would rage with a fury for the next two days.

With a rush of nervous adrenaline, Lieutenant Curtis Pollock and the men of the 48th Pennsylvania arrived on the field of battle during the early afternoon hours of Friday, August 29. Taking up position on the top of a hill, a vast panorama of conflict and carnage spread out before them. All morning, Pope had been ordering attacks against Jackson's men, well positioned in the trees and in that railroad cut, and now the soldiers of the 48th could see the wreckage and slaughter of these earlier attacks. No doubt the men's hearts beat a little faster and their palms sweated as they prepared themselves for their first true taste of combat. As they waited, the battle to their front continued in its hellish intensity and for the next two hours the regiment could do nothing but be spectators. Their eagerness—rather, their anxiety—continued to build until, finally, at 3:00 p.m., orders arrived: their turn had come.

Taking deep breaths, the soldiers of the 48th dressed ranks and took up position in their brigade formation: the 2nd Maryland and 6th New Hampshire constituted the front while the 48th would move behind them in support. Colonel James Nagle—the man who had raised the 48th the previous summer in Schuylkill County but who had since risen to brigade command—led his three regiments forward, the soldiers advancing toward a part of Jackson's line known to be well-posted in the distant trees. A rail fence skirted the woods and as the regiment was in the process of climbing up and over the rails, Jackson's men opened fire. "[T]he fight was on," said Bosbyshell, "the beginning being brisk, fiery, and bloody." Under their first hostile fire, it soon became clear that all the training over the past ten months—all the drills, all the parades, all the practice—had paid off, for the regiment never faltered, not even in the face of this tremendous fire; the men, wrote Bosbyshell, proudly marched "with the steadiness of regulars," never quailing "before the first shower of leaden hail."[20]

Nagle's three regiments—including the 48th—moved magnificently forward and, at the point of the bayonet, drove

---

20. Bosbyshell, 65-66.

Jackson's men from the cut; the Confederate line was pierced. As was the hallmark of most Union attacks that day, however, Nagle's men would receive nothing in the way of support. No troops were sent forward to secure their gains and this allowed the Confederates to rally. Men in gray and butternut—with their unnerving rebel yell rising even above the cacophony of mus- kets—soon launched a series of counterattacks. Isolated as they were in those trees with no reinforcements coming their way and with Confederates thick as fleas, the solders of the 48th Pennsylvania soon found themselves cut off. They had taken up position in the corpse-strewn railroad cut from which they had initially driven back Jackson's men. From there they had to first contend with increasing fire coming in from their front; then, suddenly, volleys ripped into the regiment from their left flank and rear. Confederates were closing in on three sides. Their first thought was that they were being fired at mistakenly by sup- porting troops. To put an end to this supposed friendly fire, the men carrying the flags raised them ever higher and waved them swiftly through the thick, sulfurous smoke. Some of the regi- ment's officers—including young Lt. Pollock, in the thickest of the fray for the first time and no doubt determined to prove his worth as an officer—jumped onto the very banks of the cut, flail- ing their arms and waving their caps. These actions, however, only further provoked the counterattacking rebels and when the fire grew hotter and drew nearer the men fully realized what a dire situation they were in. Half the regiment about-faced and returned fire but it was too unequal a contest. As Captain Henry Pleasants of Company C wrote, that Virginia forest was being fast "converted into a slaughter house."[21]

With hostile fire coming in from their front, from their left flank, and from their rear, the regiment was ordered to retreat. The only safe way out was to the right—and the men ran for their lives, seeking to escape the closing Confederate vise. Those who turned left found themselves in Confederate hands and soon marching to the rear as prisoners of war. In the confusion and the chaos, as the two sides mingled in the Virginia trees, some hand-to-hand combat broke out. Eventually, however, those who escaped death or capture reformed. Stained by pow- der, drenched in sweat, panting and out of breath, the survivors gathered while other fresh waves of blue took up the attack.

21. Gould, 69-70.

Lieutenant Pollock made it safely through though the toll taken within the ranks of the 48th that Friday in late August was terrific. Within just a few hellish minutes in those trees and along that railroad cut, the regiment lost more than fifty of its men killed or mortally wounded; more than fifty other soldiers either limped to the rear or were carried back with non-fatal wounds, while another sixty or so were listed among the captured or missing in action. 2nd Bull Run was the regiment's first battle and, as it turned out, it would also prove to be their worst battle of the war, in terms of numbers lost. But while the 48th Pennsylvania may have been driven from the field in great disorder there was no shame in the way they fought. Quite the contrary, despite the great loss, the veterans of the struggle were quite proud of their performance, convinced that had they been properly supported the battle would have resulted in a Union victory.

Next day—August 30—the battle resumed though the 48th spent most of it in reserve providing battery support. All day the men were under cannon fire. "The shells literally plowed up the ground all about," is how Captain Bosbyshell remembered it. Late in the day, Lee launched a massive attack led by General James Longstreet, whose men had at last caught up. In the face of seemingly endless ranks of men in gray, Pope's forces were driven from the field. Further back and in an effort to stave off a rout—a repeat performance of the first battle at Bull Run—the thinned ranks of Reno's division, Ninth Corps, were called forward. The 48th moved to the front while other troops raced to the rear. Going into line of battle directly in rear of an artillery battery that was belching forth its fire, the regiment again "witnessed the full terrors of the battle." Artillery fire helped to dam the oncoming gray tide and by this point, Longstreet's men were running out steam. The Confederate onslaught abated and that night Reno's men were pulled from the front though it still covered the retreat of the army as it fell back toward Washington. Bosbyshell later claimed that the 48th was the last to leave that field of slaughter—where so many of the soldiers' comrades and friends had been left behind to be soon buried as "unknown" under Virginia soil many miles away from their homes and their families. The thought of these fallen comrades no doubt filled the minds of the men as they fell back, their retreat made ever more somber by the drenching rain that fell through the night.[22]

---

22. Bosbyshell, 67-68.

Robert E. Lee had scored yet another win but he in no way rested upon his laurels. Instead, he directed Jackson to move out to the north and east with the hope that he might somehow be able to get in between Pope's retiring columns and the Union capital. But Pope reacted quickly and on September 1 fought the Confederates back at a battle called Ox Hill by some and Chantilly by others. Being near the back of the army and thus closest to the pursuing Confederates, the 48th Pennsylvania was involved in this fight though, admittedly, the battle's opening shots caught the regiment entirely unawares and unprepared. As Oliver Bosbyshell recorded in his regimental history, the men were just then in the midst of foraging when the battle opened, with a good number of the soldiers "up the apple trees of some poor unfortunate's orchard, gathering all the luscious fruit within reach." The first Confederate volley "brought these chaps scampering out of the trees to their places in line, their pockets, shirts and mouths filled with apples." Bosbyshell recalled an amusing incident once the men took up their places in line and even as the bullets flew thickly nearby. He remembered that Lieutenant Pollock asked one of his men if he could have some of his apples; the soldier—who Bosbyshell did not identify by name—was "so excited and scared" that he "eagerly raised his arms and shoulders up, pulling his shirt out of his trousers, and as the fruit rolled down over his legs and feet to the ground, exclaimed: 'Here! Take 'em all!'"[23]

A heavy rain and thunder storm rolled across the field late that afternoon as the two sides traded volleys. The Battle of Chantilly presented "a grand spectacle," a "terrific, horrible, phantasmagoria," wrote Bosbyshell, but the 48th spent much of it in reserve and thereby suffered lightly.[24] When the contest ended, Pope resumed his retreat to Washington while General Robert E. Lee weighed his options. Retaining his hard-won initiative and riding high after a summer's worth of victories, the Confederate army commander looked to the north, across the Potomac River and onto Union soil.

---

23. Ibid., 69-70.
24. Ibid.

CHAPTER FIVE

Campaigning in Maryland
September-October 1862

L ATE ON THE evening of September 2, 1862, and through a heavy rain, the ragged and heavily-thinned ranks of the 48th Pennsylvania Infantry trudged into Alexandria, Virginia, having slogged their way along an almost impassible road, nearly ankle-deep in mud. Once there, Lieutenant Pollock found the time to write a quick letter home, describing the regiment's travails at Bull Run and Chantilly. It was his first letter home in nearly a month.

Camp near Alexandria
Sept 4th 1862

Dear Ma
I do not feel like writing a long letter but as I know you will be anxious about how I have been getting along I will give you a short account of the battles I have been in. On Friday the 29th [of August] we were drawn up in line of battle and marched toward a dense woods in which the rebels were in strong force. We marched into it and [were] hardly in before they opened a brisk fire on us which we immediately returned and soon drove them back. We got into a ditch that ran through the woods and while there the rebels flanked us and got in our rear and our men commenced firing on them when one of the officers commenced calling out "do not fire; there they are our own men," which created some confusion as they did not know what to do. I jumped up on the bank nearest to them and then saw the rebels as thick as could be and when I was sure they were not our own men I got down again and got the men to fire to the

rear. Soon after, the cross fire became too severe and we were ordered to retreat by the right flank along the ditch and from there out of the woods. I caught up to the colors and went out with them. We immediately reformed when out of the woods and as we were entirely fagged out we marched to the rear. We lost 10 wounded & three missing now known to be prisoners of which Lt. [Henry] Jackson is one.[1] On Saturday [August 30] we were again drawn up and marched in rear of a battery which was firing on the rebels and which they were to capture. Here we laid down behind a hill and the shells bursting all around us but no one was wounded. About 6 o'clock they marched us to where the infantry had been fighting all afternoon and in another wood but it soon became dark and the fighting stopped and at 9 o'clock we commenced the retreat toward Centerville. On Monday afternoon [September 1] we left Centerville and after marching three or four miles we suddenly came on the enemy. We were again marched into the wood but they were so thick we could not go far but were under fire here we only had three or four wounded.

No more at present
Your affectionate Son
C.C. Pollock

✳ ✳ ✳

HAVING ARRIVED AT Alexandria, the men were hopeful of getting some much-needed rest but it was not to be. Just a few hours after Pollock wrote this letter home orders arrived for the now battle-tested regiment to fall in and at 9:00 that night, the men were once more on the march, falling back through Washington before finally settling into camp on the northern outskirts of the city. The men were exhausted; their muscles were aching. "Excessive marching, exposure to all kinds of weather, with the Bull Run and Chantilly fights thrown in, left the regiment in a pretty well used up condition," declared Oliver Bosbyshell while Joe Gould remembered that "The condition of the regiment on its arrival [in Washington] was deplorable. Hungry, footsore, and almost famished; dirty and vermized . . . to such a degree that it would seem almost impossible to get into normal condition again."[2]

1. Here, Pollock is noting the losses just in Company G, which amounted to three killed, eight wounded, and two missing.
2. Bosbyshell, 71-72; Gould, 76.

Wishing to maintain the initiative following several notable victories in the summer of 1862, Confederate General Robert E. Lee led his Army of Northern Virginia on an invasion of Union soil in early September 1862. This invasion would culminate along the banks of the Antietam Creek in western Maryland. (Courtesy of the Library of Congress)

Early September 1862 was truly a perilous time for the United States; indeed, thus far in the war, the stakes had never been higher. Just three months earlier, the war was a but a proverbial stone's throw from Richmond; now, it was on the very doorsteps of Washington. Along the way, General Robert E. Lee, the recently appointed commander of the Confederate Army of Northern Virginia, had defeated two different Union armies, the shattered and scattered ranks of which were now falling back, despondent and demoralized, while Lee and his men—though thoroughly exhausted and much reduced in number—remained confident and still very dangerous. For Lieutenant Curtis Pollock and the other former "First Defenders" in the ranks of the 48th, this would be their first visit back to Washington since the previous spring when they arrived immediately in the wake of the war's opening shots at Fort Sumter. And just as they did then, these men once again found the city greatly on edge, fearful of a Confederate strike which many believed would come at any moment. However, and despite the prevailing fears among many in Washington, Lee entertained little thought about attacking the Union capital. Instead he would lead his army north across the Potomac and upon Union soil. Lee really had no other viable option. Unable to successfully attack Washington and unwilling to surrender the initiative by falling back into a defensive position, Lee let the momentum gained that summer carry his army northward and on an invasion of Maryland hopeful that such a movement would draw the Union army out from its defenses before it had time to properly rest and regroup and to ground of Lee's own choosing where he hoped to achieve yet another battlefield victory.

Amid this great crisis that had suddenly befallen the young nation, and even as Lee and his men crossed the waist-high waters of the Potomac near Leesburg, Virginia, President Abraham Lincoln turned once more to George McClellan who quite rightly proclaimed to his wife that he had been again called upon to save the nation, considering the stakes involved. John Pope had been relieved, rather unceremoniously, from command of his army and was sent away to frontier duty in Minnesota while McClellan assumed command of all the Federal forces gathering in Washington, which included his own Army of the Potomac—the troops he had led during the Seven Days' campaign—as well as the army Pope had led to defeat at 2nd Bull Run, including the Ninth Army Corps. For the soldiers of the 48th Pennsylvania, this thus meant that for the first time they would fall under McClellan's command and though they—and most of the soldiers of the Ninth Corps—held no special reverence or awe for him, the reappointment of McClellan to army command went far in revitalizing the spirits of the other army corps. Meeting the crisis head on and with great energy, McClellan fashioned a new army and within just a matter of days was leading it north and west out of Washington and in pursuit of Lee's invading columns.[3]

Of course, McClellan could not know exactly where Lee was ultimately headed but to guard against any contingency and to help expedite the movement, he divided his army into three wings. His Right Wing, commanded by Ambrose Burnside,

---

3. Ethan Rafuse, *McClellan's War: The Failure of Moderation in the Struggle for the Union* (Bloomington: Indiana University Press, 2005), pgs. 273-278.

consisted of the First and Ninth Corps, the former led by General Joseph Hooker and the latter by General Jesse Reno. These men, including the 48th Pennsylvania, would move north then turn westward, to block any movement Lee might make toward Baltimore. At the same time, the other two wings of the army set out in a northwesterly fashion, with the Left Wing hugging the Potomac. All three wings were directed to converge upon the city of Frederick and, as it turned out, Burnside's men were the first to arrive, reaching the city limits on the afternoon of Friday, September 12, even as the last of Lee's army was departing.

Having successfully crossed the Potomac, Lee had halted his army in Frederick for several days while he contemplated his next move. He wanted to keep pushing north but knew that if he continued moving north from Frederick, his lines of supply and communication would be cut by any Union force pursuing from Washington. He would thus have to march west, across the Catoctin and South Mountain ranges. Doing so would enable him to establish a safer line of supply running south through the Shenandoah Valley, and, once across, he could turn north while using the mountains to help shield his movements. There was, however, a considerable problem. At Harpers Ferry, the so-called gateway to the Shenandoah, was a sizable Union garrison, some 10,000 men strong, along with another, smaller Union force at nearby Martinsburg, Virginia. The presence of these Union troops complicated Lee's proposed movements and forced him to alter his campaign plans to deal with these threats. To do so, Lee decided that after crossing South Mountain, he would divide his army. He sent three divisions south, toward Harpers Ferry, while Stonewall Jackson led another three divisions toward Martinsburg. At the same time, General Daniel Harvey Hill was instructed to hold Boonsboro, at the western foot of the mountain, while James Longstreet—after a brief stay in Boonsboro—would ultimately be directed a dozen miles further north, to Hagerstown. Finally, remaining east of the mountain ranges would be General Jeb Stuart with most of the Confederate cavalry, to provide a screen and to keep a close eye on any Union force that may be approaching from Washington. Lee outlined this plan in Special Orders No. 191 and early on the morning of September 10, the Confederate army marched westward from Frederick, its various parts moving in many different directions to carry out Lee's objectives.

The first major battle fought north of the Potomac River, the Battle of South Mountain resulted in a much-needed Union victory. The 48th Pennsylvania was engaged in the struggle for the possession of Fox's Gap, as seen in this 1864 depiction of the fight created by Endicott & Company. (Courtesy of the Library of Congress)

Lee was hopeful—indeed, he had anticipated—that his army would be reunited within just a matter of days. As it happened, however, he had completely miscalculated the time needed and had completely misgauged just how fast George McClellan was advancing from Washington. Lee's invasion—his first campaign north of the Potomac—unraveled rather fast.

As Lee's army divided itself on the western side of South Mountain, the Union army gathered in Frederick, just a few miles east of the mountain range. And it was there, on Saturday, September 13, where some great fortune fell upon General McClellan. That day, one of his men just happened to notice a bulky envelope lying in a meadow. Stuffed inside were three cigars, wrapped together by a piece of paper. That piece of paper turned out to be nothing less than a copy of Lee's Special Orders No. 191, which had been carelessly dropped and lost as the Confederate army marched away from the city. Revealing that Lee's army was split, McClellan decided to act. His plan was to push westward, across South Mountain, to both relieve the besieged Union troops at Harpers Ferry and to destroy Lee's army in detail—piece-by-piece—before it had the chance to reunite. Orders went out and on the morning of September 14, the Union army began moving west toward the South Mountain, with the soldiers of the Ninth Army Corps in the lead. In the meantime,

Lee was scrambling. Late the night before, and responding to reports that the Union army was closing in quick, the Confederate army commander directed Harvey Hill to take his division to the mountain top and guard the gaps at all hazards. James Longstreet's men would be making their way back to the mountain in the morning, and, hopefully, would arrive in time to lend support. At the same time, Lee sent several 'hurry-up' messages to his various commands at Harpers Ferry, which now included Stonewall Jackson and his three divisions. Suddenly, Robert E. Lee had lost the initiative and he was forced on the defensive. Lee knew that the Union army simply could not be allowed to get across the mountain; if so, his divided army would be in very serious jeopardy.

The result of all this maneuvering was the September 14 Battle of South Mountain, the first major battle of the war fought north of the Potomac River. All day the two sides slugged it out, with Confederate forces trying desperately to hold onto the critical mountain passes and the Union troops doggedly clawing and climbing their way up the mountain's steep eastern slopes. Casualties that bloody Sunday exceeded 5,000 men and included Major General Jesse Reno, the beloved commander the Ninth Corps who fell at twilight with a mortal wound. By nightfall, Union troops belonging to the Ninth, First, and Sixth Army Corps wrested control of three of the four major mountain gaps and it was perfectly apparent that Lee and his men—despite their desperate stand on the mountain—had been beaten. McClellan had emerged victorious and within the blue ranks, morale soared. Late that Sunday night, Robert E. Lee ordered a retreat. During the overnight hours and well into Monday morning, September 15, the battered Confederate troops abandoned South Mountain and trudged westward toward the Potomac River, their line of retreat carrying them through the small, western Maryland town of Sharpsburg.

As Longstreet's and D.H. Hill's shattered commands tramped westward away from South Mountain, Lee sent out several orders to his commanders at Harpers Ferry instructing them to move north and meet up with these men at Shepherdstown; his primary, overriding concern was to get his army once more united before any more damage could be done. But he had heard nothing in response and fearing he would be abandoning a good number of his men had he continued across the

The much-beloved General Jesse Reno, commander of the Ninth Army Corps, was fatally wounded during the closing scenes of the Battle of South Mountain. His loss would be deeply felt in the army, and especially in the Ninth Corps. (Courtesy of the Library of Congress)

Potomac, Lee, just before dawn on Monday, September 15, decided that he must halt his retreat near Sharpsburg. A few hours later, his campaign would take another dramatic turn when Stonewall Jackson sent word that the Union garrison at Harpers Ferry had at last raised the white flag of surrender. Encouraged by this news and seeking to somehow wring the initiative back from McClellan, Lee called off the retreat and, examining the great defensive ground immediately to the west of a meandering creek called the Antietam, he decided to make a stand. He ordered Jackson north and placed Longstreet's and Harvey Hill's men in position. Soon, Union troops arrived on the creek's eastern banks and the stage would thus be set for yet another colossal brawl, one that would prove to be the single bloodiest-day battle of the Civil War.

It began just at daybreak on a foggy Wednesday morning, September 17, 1862, and by the time the sun set some thirteen hours later, more than 23,000 men would be counted among the killed, wounded, captured, or missing. Throughout that bloody morning and into the early afternoon hours, McClellan hammered away at the Confederate left flank transforming the once peaceful and idyllic farming fields north of Sharpsburg into vast killing fields. Farmer David Miller's 24-acre cornfield and a narrow, sunken farm lane just to the south of the modest, unassuming meeting house of the local Dunker Congregation became awash with blood and carnage. In the end, Lee's left flank was pushed back but not broken. The Confederate line would ultimately hold and the fighting to the north of town dwindled to a close sometime around 1:00 p.m. To the south, however, Union forces would make one more determined push. These were the men of the Ninth Army Corps and upon their shoulders rested the most difficult assignment of that horrific Wednesday.

Three days earlier, the soldiers of the Ninth Corps--the 48th included--had fought very well atop South Mountain, securing the critical Fox's Gap but losing their much-venerated commander, Jesse Reno, during that battle's closing scenes. Now, at Antietam, they were called upon to force their way across the Antietam and then strike at the Confederate right flank. These were the only Union troops who had to literally fight their way across the creek that day; all the others having crossed without any opposition further to the north. Prior to the battle, the soldiers of the Ninth Corps had taken up position east of the Antietam and on the far-left flank of the Union line. To their front was a picturesque three-arched stone bridge known locally as the Rohrbach Bridge but which would soon become known in history as the Burnside Bridge. Defending that bridge and taking up excellent positions on the steep western banks of the Antietam were several hundred men from Georgia, under orders to delay for as long as possible any Union force attempting to make a crossing. Three-quarters of a mile further west, on the dominating high ground south of Sharpsburg, was Lee's right flank: men from Longstreet's command supported by more than forty cannons. Burnside's objective was to attack that right flank but first he had to carry the bridge.

Receiving his orders sometime just before 10:00 a.m., Burnside launched the first of what would be several assaults upon that infamous bridge, which was quite easily turned back by the well-placed, well-protected Georgians on the Antietam's western bluffs. Sometime near 11:00 a.m. a second effort was made, this one by the men of Colonel James Nagle's brigade. Recognizing the great difficulty of storming the bridge head-on, Nagle directed his two smallest regiments--the 2nd Maryland and 6th New Hampshire--to instead storm the bridge directly up the Rohrersville Road, which ran parallel to the creek for several hundred yards before crossing the creek at the bridge. The 48th Pennsylvania was brought up in support and as the two undersized regiments made their valiant though forlorn assault up that road, four companies of the 48th—including Pollock's Company G—took up position on the high ground just east of the creek, where they provided a covering fire. Although Nagle's attack met with failure and rather high casualties, the soldiers of the four companies of the 48th would hold onto their ground and remain there until after the bridge was finally taken. When that happened, the men rushed forward, swept across, and began climbing those steep bluffs which had been very persistently held by those tenacious Georgians. It had cost Burnside nearly 500 casualties and had taken more than two hours but, finally, the bridge was taken. For Burnside and the men of his Ninth Corps, however, the hard part was only just beginning.

Burnside's true objective—Lee's right flank—still lay some three-quarters of a mile ahead and though fewer in number, the Confederate soldiers were positioned on dominating high ground and were backed up by more than forty cannons. The ground over which the Ninth Corps had to cross was broken, rolling, and uneven—far more difficult ground than what faced any other Union corps that day. And it would take Burnside some time to get his remaining three divisions fully across that twelve-foot-wide, 150-foot long stone bridge. With the fighting to the north against Lee's left having subsided, all eyes—all attention—shifted to the south. Having barely survived the morning brawl, Lee watched nervously as Burnside's men at last stepped forward to the attack—it was 3:00 o'clock and all of Lee's divisions had already been committed and bloodied that day save for one, a division of hard-fighting soldiers under the command of the fiery A.P. Hill. When Stonewall Jackson completed the siege at Harpers Ferry two days earlier, he had left behind the 3,000 men of Hill's division to parole the prisoners and gather

The Charge Across the Burnside Bridge by artist Edwin Forbes. The 48th Pennsylvania participated in the taking of the famed bridge but saw heavier action during the subsequent attack upon the Confederate right flank, west of the Antietam Creek. (Courtesy of the Library of Congress)

the captured supplies. Under orders from Lee, however, A.P. Hill's men had marched away from Harpers Ferry that Wednesday morning and were now moving fast toward the sound of the guns. Lee could only hope that these men would arrive before Burnside had the chance to deliver the knock-out punch.

Having been engaged at the fight for the bridge, the soldiers of the 48th Pennsylvania took up a supporting position on the high ground west of the creek and from this high ground they watched at 3:00 p.m. as two of Burnside's divisions swept forward, amid the bursting shells and rattling musketry. Men in blue fell fast yet they continued onward—up and over the rolling terrain—and up that final hilltop where Lee's men were desperately holding on. In places, the Confederate line broke. Men, horses, and cannon fled rearward and choked the narrow streets of Sharpsburg. Despite the difficult terrain, Burnside's men were somehow on the point of breakthrough. Yet it was at this most dramatic moment, just when things looked the dimmest for Lee—that A.P. Hill's men arrived on the scene, and when they did, they struck hard on Burnside's exposed left flank. Caught unawares and watching as his line was driven in from left-to-right, Burnside ordered his men to fall back. To help cover the retreat, the soldiers of the 48th Pennsylvania were ordered forward. Crawling on their hands and knees to the advanced point, it was there where the regiment suffered its highest losses of the day. Shells burst all around while bullets coursed through the ranks but the men held and the Confederate attack ran out of steam. Expending all sixty rounds, the 48th remained on this high ground until nightfall when darkness brought an end to the engagement. The curtain thus fell across a torn, bloody, and smoldering landscape. America's bloodiest day was over and to the total tally of 23,110 casualties, the 48th contributed 59 men killed or wounded.

Within just three weeks, from late August through mid-September, 1862, the men of the 48th Pennsylvania had proven themselves to be solid, reliable, and hard-fighting soldiers. They held up well at 2nd Bull Run, their first major battle, despite ultimately being driven from the field under the weight of a crushing flank attack. They were next engaged at Chantilly, and just two weeks later at South Mountain and at Antietam where, once more, they performed admirably. James Nagle, the man who had first organized the regiment a year earlier and who—upon the battlefield of Antietam—at last received his much-earned promotion to brigadier general, wrote proudly of his former command, declaring that the men "have done nobly, and marched up to the work like old veterans. . . . The 48th has gained a high reputation for its gallantry," bragged Nagle, "and old Schuylkill need not be ashamed of her representatives in the field."[4] The price the regiment paid for their gallantry, however, was high. Over those three weeks and on battlefields in both Virginia and Maryland, the 48th Pennsylvania lost more than 200 of its men.

Among those who survived the savage combat of these violent storms was Lieutenant Curtis Pollock and in his letters home, the young officer documented well his and his regiment's experiences throughout the crucial campaign in Maryland. He wrote of the warm reception the men received while moving out across Maryland in pursuit of Lee, and described, as best he could, the battle actions at both South Mountain and at Antietam.

4. Gould, 86-87. For a full description of the 48th's actions at Antietam, see Gould, 77-93, and Bosbyshell, 74-83.

———————•◦•———————

Camp near Brookville Md.
Sept. 10th 1862

*D*ear Ma
    I received several letters from you while we laid at Washington and was very much pleased to hear from home once more as it had been some three weeks since we had received a mail. We left Washington on Sunday Morning [September 7] about 11 o'clock and went as far Leesboro where we camped a day and two nights and then left yesterday morning and came to Brookville where we now lay. It is a very small place not more than twenty-five or thirty houses. We passed a great many fine Country seats along the road and all the people were out to see us and the ladies waved their handkerchiefs to us and were very kind giving us water &c. We received marching orders last night to start at daylight this morning but just before we were ready to start the orders were countermanded. I bought myself a gum coat in Alexandria while we were there they are much better than a gum blanket. I had my photograph taken the other day and I enclose one I think they are very good. There is no use in me giving you any more account of the fight as I see there is a very good one in the *[Miners']* *Journal.* We received a mail this morning but I did not receive any letters. I wrote to you from Warrenton Junction and at Alexandria. I suppose you received them. We have been marching so long now that we are all pretty nearly played out but lately they have been marching us one day and resting the next so we manage to get along. Reno now commands the 9th Army Corps and Gen. Sturgis[5] commands our division so you will have to change your direction to me. I have not heard from Harry or Bob for some time; ask them why they do not write. There is a great many of the men sick with diarrhea and I have a slight touch of it but am getting better. We are going to have a good dinner today stewed chickens and potatoes, luxuries we do not often get. We

---

5. Samuel Davis Sturgis (1822-1899) was a native of Shippensburg, Pennsylvania, and an 1846 graduate of West Point. A veteran of the Mexican-American War, Sturgis commanded the Second Division of the Ninth Corps at the battles of Antietam and Fredericksburg and was later appointed as Chief of Cavalry for the Department of the Ohio. He remained in the army following the Civil War and was serving as Colonel of the 7th U,S, Cavalry when his second-in-command, Lieutenant Colonel George Custer, led it to slaughter at the Little Big Horn. At that time, Sturgis was on recruiting duty and detached from the commander though he did lose a son who fell alongside Custer.

received the shelter tents yesterday and like them very well. We have had to reduce our baggage and now only have the one trunk our mess chest we left behind. I saw Mr. Campbell just as we were leaving Washington and he told me of Pa's raising a Company.[6] We have not received the papers this morning yet but there is a report in camp that Stonewall is in Gettysburg but let him go on, he will soon get into Ft. Laffayette or some other sea port.[7]

No More at present
Your Affectionate Son
C.C. Pollock

Co. G 48th Reg.
1st Brigade 2nd Division
9th Army Corps
Washington D.C.

————•◦•◦•————

Camp near Frederick
Sept. 13, 1862

ear Ma

We arrived here last night from Newmarket, the rebels leaving just before we came. There was a slight skirmish at the bridge, which the rebels attempted to blow up, but did not succeed. We left Brookville day before yesterday and marched to Unity where we stayed all night, and yesterday we came through Newmarket and laid there a couple of hours and from there to about two miles from Frederick where we lay now. I think it is likely we will stay here today and wash up our dirty clothes but it is not certain yet. There is some firing going on the other side of Frederick this morning but it is not very heavy. I am on guard this morning and feel very well but rather tired. I sent you my photograph which I had taken in Washington the other day. I suppose you received it. The country we passed through was very fine and the inhabitants treated us very well. Nearly every place we stopped they had water standing out in

6. In response to the Confederate invasion, Governor Curtin of Pennsylvania called upon his state to furnish volunteer troops to meet the anticipated emergency. It seems as though Curtis's father, William, endeavored to raise a company in Pottsville.
7. While preparing to depart Frederick, Stonewall Jackson made it appear as though he would be heading directly north, into Pennsylvania, and specifically to that flourishing market town of Gettysburg, the seat of government for Adams County, and the scene for the war's bloodiest battle the next summer.

buckets for us and they would bring apples, as many as we wanted. There is not much to write about and as I suppose you only care about hearing I am well I only write to let you know I will have to give up writing to so many persons as I cannot carry paper and I do not often see the trunk. I never received the trunk nor heard anything about it, though I believe there is a schooner load of express lieing in Washington, from Fortress Monroe and very likely my trunk is amongst it.

No more at present.

Your Affectionate Son
C.C. Pollock

I will write whenever I get an opportunity.

On the Field of Battle
Near Middleton
Sept. 15th 1862

Dear Ma
We have been in another engagement near Middleton and drove the Rebels from a very strong position in the hills. We fired all our cartridges and then retired in good order to let someone else have a chance. We were marched up the hill about 5 o'clock but were not engaged until about 7 o'clock. We were lieing down behind a fence and peppered the rebels pretty well. I went around over the field this morning and found the rebels lieing very thick.[8] We are now about leaving for some other place. I am told that the rebels are about four miles from here and our troops are following them up.

Sept 16.

I had to stop writing yesterday on account of receiving orders to leave. I received three letters from you this morning dated 5th, 7th & 11th and was very glad to get them. I will now try to answer all your questions. My health is very good at present and I have nothing to complain of. I have not received my trunk nor do I want it; as for clothing I have plenty. I supplied myself at Washington. When I caught up to the colors the

---

8. The regiment's casualties at the Battle of South Mountain were comparatively light, with ten men wounded and one missing.

company was scattered in every direction, some were in other regiments, and I was one of the last to get out of the ditch. We got out of the ditch the best way we could but formed again as soon as we got out of the woods.[9] I have not the same opportunity to write as I had at Newport News as it is only now and then that a mail leaves, but I will write every chance I get. We always have enough to eat and I do not know anything about the rebels capturing our supply trains. I have not lost anything, though the men left their knapsacks lieing at Bull Run and could not get them again but they have now an entire new outfit. I stand marching very well and do not think I have lost much flesh, I think now I have answered all your questions in the three letters. They are cannonadeing this morning. I do not know what the name of this place is. Our wagons have not yet come up and we are nearly out of crackers but we are expecting them every minute. I have no more to say at present

Your Affectionate Son
C.C. Pollock

Sept 20 1862

Dear Ma

We were in another engagement yesterday but I am all right yet. I have not time to say any more as we move in a few minutes.

Your Affectionate Son
C.C. Pollock

———•◦•———

Camp at the mouth of Antietam Creek
Sunday—Sept. 21st 1862

Dear Ma

I wrote to you on Friday but dated in the 20th instead of 19th. On Wednesday we were in another fight at Antietam Bridge. We were first engaged on the other side of the bridge in the morning and afterwards in the afternoon on this side. The heaviest fire was in the afternoon when we were lieing down on the top of a hill firing at the rebs behind a stone fence, and we

---

9. Here, Curtis is answering his mother's more specific questions about 2nd Bull Run.

were under a very heavy fire of artillery and none of our batteries could get into position to return their fire so we received
it all and it was terrible. There we lay; their shells bursting
all around us. The 51st P.V. had gone up ahead of us and we
went to support them—the 9th N.H. a new Regt. had gone up
but broke and ran to the bottom of the hill and as we passed
them, they in disorder, commenced to cheer us (the miserable
cowards).[10] When we got up near the brow of the hill we halted
and laid down until they had expended all their ammunition
when we got ahead of them and commenced firing. The 51st
withdrew about 10 paces to our rear and though they were out
of ammunition they fixed bayonets and stood ready to support
us in case the Rebels charged. We fired all our ammunition
and then [the] Regt. withdrew to the bottom of the hill in good
order, not even going at double quick, though their shells were
bursting all around us. On Thursday [September 18] our Regt
was on [the] same hill all day skirmishing and lost several
men. Our whole loss in the Regt is 58 killed & wounded of
which 8 or 9 only were killed. We lost in our company 1 killed
& 4 wounded. We now lay near where the Antietam empties
into the Potomac and about three miles from the battle field.
I had good wash in the creek yesterday. On Friday Col. Nagle
received his commission as Brigadier [General] and Sigfried
will now be our Colonel, and [Captain Henry] Pleasants will be
Major. We have a report today that Richmond & Charlestown
are captured but we do not know whether to believe it or not.

No more at present
Your Affectionate Son
C.C. Pollock

❋ ❋ ❋

MANY SOLDIERS IN both blue and gray expected the great
bloodletting at Antietam would be continued the next day—September 18—but that Thursday would pass in tense and anxious
anticipation of a battle that never came to fruition. Instead, that
night Robert E. Lee began the retreat; his invasion was over,
his objectives not realized. On Friday, September 19, McClellan
gave chase, sending forward his cavalry and his Fifth Corps to
the Potomac. After a sharp engagement along the river banks,

10. As was the case for ¼ of the Union army at Antietam, the 9th New Hampshire was a brand
new regiment having been recruited and organized during the summer of 1862.

however, McClellan gave up the hunt and opted against any further pursuit. The time had arrived, he believed, to rest, refit, and reorganize. The much-criticized Union army commander had done much within the past three weeks, having assumed command of a demoralized army at a time when things could hardly appear worse, reorganizing and reinvigorating it, and leading it out quickly from Washington in pursuit of Lee's invading columns. Along the way, he had scored two victories—at South Mountain and Antietam—driving the Confederate army off Union soil while keeping Washington protected. In the capital, Abraham Lincoln breathed easier and just a few days after the guns fell silent at Antietam, he moved forward with a proclamation of emancipation, transforming, with one signature, the very meaning—the very purpose—of the war. Lincoln, though, was not entirely satisfied; he wanted more. In the weeks following Antietam, the Commander-in-Chief continually pushed, prodded, and pressured McClellan to go after Lee and strike again but McClellan would not oblige and, instead, kept his army encamped north of the Potomac for the next six weeks.

During this time, the 48th Pennsylvania marched away from the blood-soaked battlefields of Antietam and set up camp, first near the Antietam Iron Works and then a few miles further away, in Pleasant Valley. And while there was much headshaking in the regiment over the fact that McClellan did not continue after Lee, the men certainly enjoyed this break from active campaigning. They scoured the countryside for provisions—for something more edible and palatable than "hard tack and salt horse"—and made many sight-seeing trips to that "battered old town" of Sharpsburg and even down to Harpers Ferry. The soldiers also had occasion to visit with old Schuylkill County friends and acquaintances who were serving in other regiments that happened to be encamped nearby. Being so near to Pennsylvania, it was not long before friends and loved ones from Schuylkill County arrived "and hearty receptions were accorded them." According to Captain Bosbyshell, "The reveille and tattoo never sounded so beautifully, during the [regiment's] whole service, as in Pleasant Valley," while there were few other more picturesque camps. "The mess was greatly improved by the ample supply of good things to be had from the farmers," said Bosbyshell. "Apple dumplings became a staple dish." Making things even more pleasant there in Pleasant Valley was the "charming weather," "the brilliant moonlit nights," and the "lovely sunrises and charming sunsets." There was, of course, some military matters to attend to: drills mainly, with the occasional parades and reviews. One such grand review was held on October 3 when the men polished their weapons of war and appeared at their very best to welcome and impress President Abraham Lincoln, who had traveled out from Washington to see the men, yes, but mostly to urge McClellan to action, but all to no avail. The soldiers of the 48th relished in this six-week repose in Pleasant Valley, particularly after the bloody and brutal action they had experienced near those two creeks: the Bull Run and the Antietam.[11] And as they foraged and did some sight-seeing, and as they greeted old friends and embraced their loved ones, the soldiers of the 48th—Lieutenant Pollock included—also found ample time to write.

------◆◆◆◆------

Camp near Antietam
Oct. 2nd 1862

*D*ear Ma
      We have moved our camp on the other side of the creek and toward Harpers Ferry. We have now been resting for nearly two weeks and feel considerably improved but there is a great deal of diarrhea in the Regt. & I am one of the subjects. We received a small mail last evening and I got but one dated the 22nd. This is the first letter I have written since we changed camp. I would write oftener but there is nothing occurring to write about. We get the papers every day and have some idea of what is going on in the world. Quartermaster [James] Ellis has returned to the Regt. and looks very well. There were a good many promotions in the Regt. as several of the officers have resigned and Col. Nagle have rec'd his commission as Brig. Gen. makes several openings. We are now in Nagle's Brigade, Sturgis's Division of the 9th Army Corps. com'd by Gen. Cox.[12] I was on guard yesterday and just come off this morning. There was a slight shower yesterday but [I] did not get wet. We expect to move our camp again tomorrow but how far I do not know

---

11. Bosbyshell, 83-87.
12. General Jacob Dolson Cox assumed command of the Ninth Corps following the death of Reno but his tenure proved short since he and his division of Ohio troops would be transferred to western Virginia that fall. By the time that happened, McClellan had been replaced with Burnside in army command and Brigadier General Orlando Willcox took up command of the Ninth Corps.

but I believe nearer towards Harpers Ferry. C. Carter & Wm Feger are in camp today; they came from Hagerstown in a private conveyance. We have not been paid yet but are expecting it every day and we need it bad enough too for we are all entirely out of money We received a letter from Lieut. Jackson; he is now at Annapolis, he sent on for his good clothes and says he is boarding at the City Hotel. He was only fifteen days in their hands but they most starved him in that time, he tells the old story of the Richmond prison.[13] I would like to have some gray flannel shirts for this winter and the only way that you can get them to me is by mail several of the men have received them in that way. I want them made long and you had better send them in separate bundles as I think they will come safer. I do not want more than three

Nothing more at present. Hoping to hear from you soon; I remain

Your Affectionate Son

C.C. Pollock

Camp near Antietam

Oct. 4, 1862

ear Ma

Mr. Whitney & Baber are here and as they are going [to leave for home] to day I will send a few lines with them. I am getting along very well and getting over the diarrhea. We expect a mail this morning I hope to get a few letters. We were reviewed yesterday by President Lincoln & Gen. McClellan and the troops looked very well.[14] No more at present.

Your Affectionate Son

C.C. Pollock

I wrote to you the other day.

---

13. Captured at 2nd Bull Run, Lieutenant Henry Jackson of Company G was paroled and directed to proceed to Annapolis where he waited to be exchanged. When that happened, he returned to the regiment.

14. In his regimental history, Oliver Bosbyshell wrote much more about Lincoln's visit and of the review, which, he said, was "of more than usual significance." The men were drawn up and when Lincoln approached, a salute of twenty-one guns was fired "and three rousing cheers given by the men." Regarding the physical appearance of Lincoln himself, Bosbyshell wrote that "The thin, care-worn appearance is distinctly remembered—a marked change from the year before. He was dressed in a suit of black, with a heavy band of crape on his high black hat." He also remembered that Lincoln appeared "lank" and "ungainly" and that while riding on a "small-sized horse" his feet nearly touched the ground. (Bosbyshell, 84)

Camp near Harpers Ferry
Oct. 9th 1862

*D*ear Ma
     I received two letters from you lately, one dated Sept. 29th & Oct. 4th. We received orders last Tuesday evening to be ready to move the next morning at daybreak with one day's rations in haversacks. We got off about 7 o'clock and after a very hard march across the mountains we arrived at Pleasant Valley and are now encamped on the side of the mountain about 2 or 3 miles above Harpers Ferry. I would be very glad to see Pa come on & now he would have a very good chance as it is likely we will stay here for some time—I have nearly gotten over my diarrhea and feel very well. I have a splendid appetite and you ought to have seen me pitching into several apple dumplings at dinner today. We have 51 men present [in Company G] but only 35 privates fit for duty; some are sick and on extra duty and the non-commissioned officers are not counted in the 35. We live very well when we have a chance to buy anything and as there is generally a Sutler about we do not suffer a great deal and then we get bread, potatoes, toma-toes, apples &c. from the farmers. The 51st P.V. is in the 2nd Brig. of our division under the comm'd of Gen. Ferrero.[15] The 1st Lieut. of Capt. Simms's company was killed when cross-ing the bridge. I was acquainted with him and he was a very fine fellow, he comes from Lewisburg. We have preaching now every Sunday afternoon at 4 o'clock and I think our Chaplain is improving as he give us some very good sermons. My trunk is at Washington with a lot of other express goods for the Regt. and I think it will now be sent on to us. I am glad to hear you intend sending Mary to Boarding school as I think she will like it and it will do her good and if she goes she shall hear from me at least once every two months. There is nothing going on here. Capt. Porter's (Co. I) wife arrived here yesterday on a visit

---

15. Edward Ferrero (1831-1899) commanded the Second Brigade of the Second Division, Ninth Corps. Like General Nagle, Ferrero, a former dancing instructor from New York City, received his promotion of brigadier general on the battlefield of Antietam. It was Ferrero's men, specifi-cally those of the 51st Pennsylvania and 51st New York, who captured the Burnside Bridge.

and is still here. We have Brigade drill this afternoon the first one since we left Newport News.

No more at present.

From Your Affectionate Son
C.C. Pollock

Write Soon.

Pleasant Valley Md
Oct. 24th 1862

ear Ma

Knowing you will be anxious to hear from me, I will write you a few lines though I have nothing to communicate. I have been getting along very well since Pa left and we missed them very much after they had gone.[16] We are not doing much of anything except reading Charles O'Malley in which we are all very interested. The commissions for all the new officers came the other day, and night before last we had a jollification up at Lt. Col. Pleasants's tent. I suppose you will see Col. Sigfried who is now at home. There are a great many visitors to the camp now, though I do not know many of them. If my uniform is finished by the time Col. Sigfried returns I think he would bring it on for me. I wrote a letter to Bob Hill the other day; how is he and Augusta getting along? Does August keep house next door? We have fixed our shanty up very nicely and have about twice as much room as before and much warmer and more comfortable in every way. We are going to have apple dumplings for dinner today. Geo. Gowen is now Capt. of Co. C. and Charlie Loeser is 2nd Lieut.; Dan. McGinnes is Adjutant.

I think it is very likely we will not stay here a great while longer, though it is very uncertain when we move. I am very glad the new commissions have come on as there were so few Lieuts that we came on guard every five days. The Capt. is setting alongside of me writing to his <u>duck</u>.

No more at present.

Your Affectionate Son
C.C. Pollock

---

16. Clearly, Curtis's father, William, and perhaps a few of his siblings were among those who visited the camps of the 48th Pennsylvania in Pleasant Valley.

CHAPTER SIX

A Winter of Despair
October 1862–February 1863

———◆•●•◆———

T HE FINAL NIGHT the soldiers of the 48th Pennsylvania spent in Pleasant Valley was anything but pleasant. Temperatures dropped considerably and a cold rain set in, which persisted through the night and made it difficult for the men to get anything in the way of a good night's sleep. Next day, however, the clouds parted, the skies cleared and though still unseasonably cold, the soldiers did their best to dry themselves off, shake of the proverbial rust, and prepare for a new campaign. It was October 27 and nearly forty days had passed since the great bloodletting that was Antietam. But now, finally, that Monday, and after having been hounded for the past six weeks by Lincoln to act, McClellan at last put the army in motion, with the Ninth Corps— screened by cavalry—leading the way. At last breaking camp, Lieutenant Pollock and his fellow soldiers of the 48th spent that October afternoon tramping south through Pleasant Valley. By nightfall, the regiment would bid farewell to Maryland, cross the Potomac, and be back again upon the "sacred soil" of Virginia.[1]

McClellan's plan was to get his army across the Potomac at Harpers Ferry and at nearby Berlin (today, Brunswick), Maryland, then march it south through Loudoun Valley, with the Blue Ridge Mountains to the army's right and Bull Run Mountains on its left. He wanted his army to converge in the area around Warrenton and from there, to continue moving south, along the line of the Orange & Alexandria Railroad. McClellan pursued this strategy in part to mollify President Lincoln. In a letter written in mid-October, it was Lincoln who had urged his general to adopt this course of action with his hope being that McClellan could maneuver the army between Lee and Richmond, thus

---

1. Bosbyshell, 87.

*Confident, charismatic, and controversial, General George Mc-
Clellan led the Union army to victories at South Mountain and
at Antietam, though was relieved of his command in November
1862. (Courtesy of the Library of Congress)*

forcing Lee to attack at disadvantage. McClellan was not so
sure Lincoln's idea would work, believing—rightly as it turned
out—that Lee, whose men had been occupying the Shenandoah
Valley, south of Winchester, since the end of the Maryland Campaign, would not simply sit idly by while the Union army began
moving south. McClellan further believed that winter would set
in before any decisive engagement could take place. Nevertheless, the Union army commander moved forward. Crossing the
Potomac and sweeping south down the Loudoun Valley the advance of the Army of the Potomac reached the Manassas Gap
Railroad by November 5 having covered more than 60 miles in
less than two weeks, oftentimes in poor weather. The next step
in McClellan's plan was to continue moving south to Culpeper.

The problem, however—at least for McClellan—was that no matter how fast his army had moved thus far in the new campaign, Lee was always able to move quicker.[2]

As McClellan had anticipated, Lee did not remain idle in the Shenandoah. Indeed, as early as October 28, just a day after the Union army began crossing the Potomac, the Confederate army commander sent General James Longstreet's Corps south to Culpeper while Stonewall Jackson was directed to remain in the Valley to keep up a menacing threat to McClellan's right flank and rear. If there was a race to Culpeper, then Longstreet won when on November 3 his men began arriving. For McClellan, the way south was now blocked and it was no longer possible for him to wangle his way between Lee and Richmond, at least not by the route Lincoln had suggested. In response, McClellan simply shrugged his shoulders and sought another avenue, one more akin to his own way of thinking and one that would shift the army southeast, perhaps to Fredericksburg or back to the Peninsula, and for an advance on Richmond from there. Lincoln, however, would not grant him that opportunity. Instead, on November 5, he drafted orders relieving McClellan of command, removing the charismatic and controversial general in the very midst of the campaign. Lincoln's patience had finally worn out; Longstreet's arrival in Culpeper was the final straw. It was very late on a cold and snowy November 7when the idolized commander learned that he had been relieved and replaced by Ambrose Burnside. After helping Burnside get situated and caught up on the locations of the army's various corps, McClellan formally bade farewell to his army on November 10. The men were drawn up for one final review and as McClellan rode past the serried ranks, with Burnside galloping alongside, many a battle-hardened soldier in the Army of the Potomac wept openly. At times, it seemed as though the ground shook from the thunderous ovation McClellan received. Some in the ranks—including some general officers—believed McClellan ought to lead the army on a march on Washington to overthrow Lincoln. McClellan dismissed such dangerous talk and urged his men to give their full faith and loyalty to their new commander Burnside. Following these final dramatic scenes of McClellan's tenure with the Army of the Potomac, the deposed general boarded a train car and set off for home, awaiting orders that would never arrive.[3]

2. Rafuse, 364-367.
3. Ibid., 371-380.

Shock and anger, outrage, and downright sadness were the sentiments felt by most of the Union troops in the Army of the Potomac upon hearing news of McClellan's removal but not so by the men of the 48th Pennsylvania and by most of the soldiers in the Ninth Corps for that matter. The time they spent under his command was limited and the reverence that most of the soldiers felt toward McClellan never really took hold in the Ninth Corps. What was more, many in the Ninth Corps believed McClellan had failed to fully support their attack at Antietam and that he had squandered several great opportunities to deliver a more crushing, more decisive blow there to Lee's battered army. They held no special loyalty to McClellan, no great admiration or attachment. Instead, it was Burnside who remained their man and news of his elevation to army command was thus met with feelings of pride and acclamation within the ranks of the 48th.

Curiously, however, there is no mention of any of this in Lieutenant Pollock's letters home. Rather, it was business as usual, it seems, with Curtis commenting on the weather and documenting the regiment's movements and activities as it made its way from Pleasant Valley down Loudoun Valley to White Sulphur Springs during that final week of October and into the unseasonably cold and snowy first two weeks of November. And though Pollock wrote nothing about McClellan's ouster and Burnside's advancement to army command, he was sure to tell of his own temporary promotion. In early November, Colonel Joshua Sigfried ordered Lieutenant Pollock to take command of Company D, 48th Pennsylvania, which at that time had no commissioned officers of its own to lead it. For the upcoming campaign—including at the Battle of Fredericksburg—Pollock would thus serve in the capacity of company commander.

————•◦•————

Camp near Lovettsville Va
Oct. 29th 1862

Dear Ma

We received orders to move on Monday and about 1 o'clock P.M. we started off, came down through Knoxville and crossed the river on a Pontoon bridge at Berlin. We are once more on the sacred soil and it looks as bare as ever. We got into camp on Monday evening at dark and have not moved since.

Col. Sigfried & Gen. Nagle have returned; they made quite a short visit. I think after this movement is over we will be able to get home. We had a very severe storm on Sunday and I was on guard through it all but I did not get wet. I have been taking Blackberry Brandy for my diarrhea and it does me more good than anything I have yet taken. I have ordered a jacket from Helms of Schuylkill Haven and told him you would pay him for it. We will not be paid until next month when we will get four months' pay. I do not know how long we will stay here, for we have not received any orders as yet. Our regt. is losing a good many men by enlisting in the regular army but none have gone out of our company yet. John Hodgson[4] is talking about going but I do not believe his mother would like him to go and Capt. will not let him go without her consent. Flanagan & Humble are getting along well. Humble is one of our prisoners. I have nothing more to say at present.

From Your Affectionate Son
C.C. Pollock

———— ◆•◆ ————

Camp near Wheatland Va.
Nov. 1st 1862

*D*ear Ma
I received your's and Mary's letters the other day and as Capt. [Joseph] Gilmour goes to Harrisburg tomorrow, I will send a few lines with him. I wrote you a letter but a few days ago and there has not much happened since. We have orders to move tomorrow but I do not know where. I would like much to have come home but I did not ask, however I think we will have a chance to get a furlough before long. We had a Brigade drill today and had expected to remain here longer, but orders came to night to move tomorrow morning.

Sergt. R. Smith of our company goes with Capt. Gilmour. I wrote a letter to Will Pollock today. I have not heard from him for some time. I suppose you will see him in the city.

I hear that our Regt. is the only one in the Brigade that has received orders to march, and I suppose we are only going out

4. John Hodgson was eighteen years old when he enlisted as a private in the ranks of Company G, 48th Pennsylvania, in the summer of 1861. Advancing to the rank of corporal, Hodgson served with the regiment throughout the entirety of the war and was discharged in the summer of 1865. He died in 1888 at age 45.

on picket or something of that sort. John Clemens[5] wishes to be remembered to you. Nothing more to communicate. So I will close.

With much love to all
Your Affectionate Son
C.C. Pollock

P.S. Tell Margie that Pa must have been mistaken when he said that I did not inquire after her, for I inquired after every one particularly, and Lieut. Jackson, when I told him she was going to knit him a cap, clapped his hands and jumped about in a very excited manner and seemed very much pleased. He said I should tell her he was very much obliged to her for her kindness and was anxiously waiting for it.

Yours
C.C.P.

———◆•◆•◆———

Camp near Upperville Va
Nov. 4, 1862

*D*ear Ma

We have been traveling along slowly since I last wrote but have not seen anything of the rebs as yet. On Sunday morning when we left camp, the Col. ordered me to take command of Co. D which is now without any officer and I have had command ever since. On Sunday night Co. G went out on picket and Monday Morning Co. D and E were ordered to relieve them but we were not out more than a couple of hours before we were ordered back, on account of the regiment having marching orders. We marched until about 9 o'clock when we got up to where the Regt was encamped and then were sent out on picket again, but we were in a small stone house formerly used for drying tobacco; it had a fire place in it and it was not long before we were very comfortable. I made a tin cup full of coffee and with some pork and crackers made a very good supper. About 12 o'clock one of the pickets fired at some imaginary reb and alarmed the camp, and our whole Brigade

---

5. John Clemens was a private in the ranks of Company G. He enlisted with the company the previous summer and would be discharged on September 30, 1864, upon the expiration of his three year term of service.

was under arms. That I may do justice to the old Regt. it was none of them but one of the new ones belonging to our Brigade, the 7th R[hode] I[island]. I was asleep at the time, however and as none of our pickets saw anything we did not get up. This morning before we were relieved McClellan passed us but I did not get up. We arrived in the camp we now occupy about 11 o'clock this morning after a short march of two or three miles. We can hear artillery firing every day but we seem to get no nearer to it. I do not know whether we will leave to-morrow or not but if we do go it will not be until afternoon as they killed some fresh beef to night and it is not to be cooked until tomorrow. There is to be a mail leave here to-morrow; I write you these few lines.

No more at present.

Your Affectionate Son
C.C. Pollock

———————◆•◆•◆———————

Nov 14 1862
Camp at Sulphur Springs Va.

Dear Ma
I received your letter written in Phila. the other day, and as Louis Bright[6] is discharged and going home to day, I will send a few lines with him. We are now encamped quite near the place we were last August and everything looks as natural as it did then. The hotel is burned down and from the appearance of the house it must have been a very fine one. I was down to see it yesterday morning and drank some of the sulphur water. I do not dislike the taste of it at all. It must have been a very fine watering place in good time. They had billiard tables, ten pin allies and the bath house is very convenient with all the advantages you could wish for. Everything though is now knocked to pieces. There is nothing new going on and I do not know what to write about. I am very well with the exception of a cold. I hope you will send those things on with Capt. Gilmour as I am now pretty bad off for the want of clothes. I used to have an old woolen jacket when I worked at the lumber yard and I left it hanging up behind the office if you sent it on

---

6. Private Louis Bright, a twenty-eight-year-old telegraph operator from Pottsville was discharged on a surgeon's certificate on November 9, 1862.

by mail as I can wear it under my vest and it will be as good
as a couple of undershirts. I still wear the old felt hat that you
send to me before we left Hatteras and it is still very good
    No more at present.
                                        From Your Affectionate Son
                                                            C.C.P.

                              ✾ ✾ ✾

ALTHOUGH MAJOR GENERAL Ambrose Everett Burnside did
not actively seek nor necessarily desire army command (he had
twice turned down Lincoln's offers of army command earlier
that year and had only reluctantly accepted it in November),
he wasted little time in grabbing the reins and submitting his
plans for a new offensive. He understood perfectly well that
Lincoln—and an increasingly impatient North—wanted action,
even though winter was just a few weeks away. Indeed, from the
unseasonably cold temperatures and the snow that had already
fallen in Virginia, it seemed to many that winter had already
arrived. Burnside's plan was one based on deceit and swift
movement. He would concentrate his forces near Gordonsville,
giving Lee the impression that the Union army was continuing
to move in that direction, but then very quickly sidestep to the
southeast, secure Fredericksburg, then march on Richmond
from there. Lincoln was rather cool to the idea but, in the end,
gave Burnside his nod of approval. The president was quick to
point out, however, that Burnside's entire plan rested on speed,
telling the newly-minted army commander that if he moved
"very rapidly," he would succeed, "otherwise not."[7]
    Burnside certainly did move "very rapidly." On November
15, just one week after assuming army command and only a
few days after Lincoln consented to his plan, the distinguished,
heavily-whiskered general put his men in motion. And just two
days later, the advance of the army began arriving in Falmouth,
having covered more than thirty miles in just 48 hours. Directly
across the Rappahannock River from Falmouth was an almost
entirely undefended Fredericksburg. The nearest Confederate force was Longstreet's, which remained at Culpeper, some
thirty miles away from Fredericksburg to the west. Having sto-
len a march on Lee, many in the Union army expected, even
beseeched, Burnside to cross the Rappahannock immediately

---

7. Woodbury, 176-185.

Wartime view of Fredericksburg, Virginia, sketched by Edwin Forbes, looking across the Rappahannock River. (Courtesy of the Library of Congress)

and secure the undefended town. But Burnside would not; the waters of the Rappahannock were rising rapidly—especially after the recent rain and snow—and Burnside was afraid that if he crossed, he might trap a part of his army with the high waters of the river to their backs. He would not take that risk and instead decided to wait until the pontoon boats arrived. He was expecting that the pontoons would have been there upon the army's arrival since he had long since put in an order for them; unfortunately for him and especially for the soldiers in his army, delay, confusion, and incompetence all combined to delay the transport of the pontoons and they would not begin to arrive until November 24. By the time they arrived, so, too had Lee's army.

Marching through a cold and a drizzling rain, the soldiers of the 48th Pennsylvania reached the Lacy House on the high eastern banks of the Rappahannock, directly opposite Fredericksburg, on November 19, having broken up their camps at White Sulphur Springs. Next day, the Schuylkill County soldiers could plainly see Confederate troops taking up positions in town and on the heights beyond. Indeed, there was even some banter between them and their gray-coated foes, with jibes being shouted back-and-forth across the wide river. These Confederates belonged to Longstreet's command. Moving quickly in response to Burnside's arrival at Falmouth, Longstreet's men covered the thirty miles from Culpeper in a short time and were now taking up position on a piece of high ground immediately in rear, or to west, of Fredericksburg. At the same time, Stonewall Jackson's men were making their way from the Shenandoah Valley. When they arrived, Lee would connect them to Longstreet's right flank, extending the Confederate line south, parallel with the river, and guarding as many of the potential crossing points as possible. But with the arrival of Lee and the onset of winter, few

Arthur Lumley's depiction of Union soldiers sacking Fredericksburg on the night of December 12, 1862. As Pollock wrote, the 48th took part in this looting. (Courtesy of the Library of Congress)

of the soldiers in blue anticipated a crossing; instead, many of the men prepared themselves for winter quarters.

For the 48th Pennsylvania, those quarters were in a heavy pine woods roughly one mile east of the Rappahannock. As the men set up camp, some of the regiment's officers ventured over to the bluffs overlooking the river and watched as the people of Fredericksburg packed up their things and evacuated their homes, with "wagons heavily ladened with household things," and old men, women, and children "hurrying here and there with bundles and packages." If any of the 48th's soldiers felt any sorrow for these people being turned out of their homes during the cold season, they were far more concerned about keeping themselves as warm and as comfortable as possible while the temperatures continued to drop and as snow, rain, and sleet fell interchangeably during those frigid first days of December. It was not long before most of the pine trees in camp were cut down. As Oliver Bosbyshell wrote, the entire woods were "slaughtered." Soon log huts, complete with fireplaces and chimneys, sprung up. There was still the occasional drill and there was still some picket duty, but, for the most part, the men breathed a little easier in the belief—or, rather, the hope—that the winter would pass and the men would remain in their new log huts before another major engagement. But Ambrose Burnside would not—indeed, could not—let that winter pass in inactivity. Lincoln and the nation demanded action.[8]

And so, on a very foggy Thursday morning—December 11, 1862—the engineers of the Army of the Potomac at last built the pontoon bridges across the Rappahannock, which was certainly no easy task, especially for those attempting to construct them directly at Fredericksburg, for the town was filled with Confederate troops who shot down many of the bridge builders. To drive them out, Burnside ordered the town shelled. Buildings were knocked down and fires quickly spread. But those persistent Confederates remained. An amphibious operation was thus in order, with soldiers in blue being taken across the river in pontoons, under fire, to storm the town and drive those tenacious graycoats out by force. This accomplished, the engineers finished their work and the Union soldiers—having already been given three-days' rations and extra ammunition—began to cross. They would continue to cross the next day—December 12—and as Burnside continued to deliberate, vacillate, and decide upon his plan of attack, the city of Fredericksburg was looted, vandalized, and pillaged by the boys in blue.

As the Union troops tramped across those pontoons bridges and then helped to lay waste to Fredericksburg, many hundreds of yards beyond town Confederate soldiers watched and waited for the attack. Taking up a line of battle behind a stout four-foot-high stone wall that ran along the base of Marye's Heights, the Confederate position here was so strong, so fortified, with artillery well-placed on the heights, ready to sweep those open fields to their front, Lee believed Burnside would focus his efforts further to south, to get around his right flank, which was held by Stonewall Jackson's men. But this was exactly the reason why Burnside opted to launch a full-scale assault against Longstreet's line behind Fredericksburg. While the First and Sixth Corps were instructed to strike at Lee's right, the Second, Fifth, and Ninth Corps were directed to attack straight ahead, toward that formidable—indeed, as it

---

8. Gould, 95-97; Bosbyshell, 93-95.

turned out, impregnable—Confederate position. The result was wholesale slaughter.

The Battle of Fredericksburg ranks among the most lopsided battles of the war, with Union casualties nearing 13,000 men with little—nothing, rather—to show for so much carnage, so much sacrifice and so much bloodshed. Lee's casualties, on the other hand, were less than half the Union toll. All throughout the day, wave after wave of Union blue swept forward directly into the storm of lead and iron poured forth from those well-placed, well-protected Confederates along Marye's Heights. This butchery went on relentlessly for hours with one Union line after the next being mowed down. The attacks did not so much as dent the Confederate line behind Fredericksburg while blood flowed freely upon the frozen ground, dyeing it a crimson red.

While so much of the history of the Battle of Fredericksburg is dominated by the attacks made by the soldiers of the Second and Fifth Army Corps against Marye's Heights, it must also be remembered that the soldiers of the Ninth Corps also participated and their attacks were just as brave though just as futile. Included among the Ninth Corps troops who advanced to the front that sanguinary Saturday were those of the 48th Pennsylvania. Having crossed the Rappahannock on December 12, the men of the 48th bivouacked in the streets of town and did their part in pillaging, plundering, and vandalizing the historic town. Next day, the men were drawn up line of battle as Second Corps soldiers to their right were hurling themselves fruitlessly against that stone wall. Late in the afternoon, General James Nagle led his brigade forward and, said Captain Bosbyshell, "It was not long before the work of carnage began." A steady and deadly barrage of artillery and musketry fire welcomed the 48th to the fray. Making their way forward over the stiff and rigid bodies of those who had already been killed and the writhing forms of men suffering in the cold from non-fatal wounds, the regiment advanced to the top of a gentle rise of ground and from there, loaded and fired as best they could toward the gray kepis and black slouch hats rising above the stone wall. Expending all sixty rounds per man, the 48th was relieved just after nightfall. "All efforts to dislodge the enemy were unsuccessful," noted regimental historian Joseph Gould, rather matter-of-factly, "and the losses very heavy." Colonel Sigfried praised his men's efforts that day, writing that "Their line was steady and unbroken while advancing under the most murderous shelling of the enemy, and their fire deliberate, well-aimed, and effective." Still, when the regiment withdrew they had nothing to show for their actions, except for the sixty men who had been killed or wounded in the failed, forlorn assault. The survivors tramped back into the streets of town. "Fresh ammunition was distributed," wrote Bosbyshell, "and the men, literally worn out, soon fell asleep despite the angry tempest of lead still raining in front."[9]

Without question, the Battle of Fredericksburg was a disaster for Ambrose Burnside, the Army of the Potomac, and for the nation. Even so, it seems that Burnside—the man who never sought or ever wanted army command in the first place—was determined to attack again the next day, with his Ninth Corps and with himself leading the way. No doubt the men breathed much easier when they learned Burnside was talked out of it.

In temporary command of Company D, 48th Pennsylvania, for the duration of the campaign, Lieutenant Curtis Clay Pollock had survived yet another storm. Throughout it all, he stayed good to his word to write as often as he could and the letters he wrote home from the regiment's camps either "opposite" or "near" Fredericksburg both before and after the battle must rank among the most descriptive and the most insightful of all the letters he would send home throughout his time in uniform. The first was written soon after the regiment arrived on the eastern banks of the Rappahannock and directly across from Fredericksburg.

Camp opposite Fredericksburg Va
Nov. 22nd 1862

Dear Ma
We are encamped along the river just opposite the city and the Rebels occupy the other side. We have frequent communications with them and they ask us, how we like the election in N.Y.? and, what we think of Bull Run? Our fellows reply by asking how they liked South Mountain & Antietam and so they go on asking and answering but doing it all in

9. Bosbyshell, 94-98; Gould, 99-104.

good humor. There is nothing particular going on. The Rebels are running trains to Richmond but our batteries fire on them whenever they come in range. We sent a flag of truce over yesterday but I have not heard what it was about. I have a great deal of confidence in Burnside but I think he ought to move across the river, but he knows what he is about & it will all come in good time. I suppose Bob and Augusta have returned from their wedding tour. How do they appear to hit it [off]? I have not written to Mary yet but will do so before long. We have such poor accommodations for doing anything and everything is upside down. We rec'd a mail to day but no letters for me. I have not had a chance to wear my new uniform but will tomorrow on inspection if it is a clear day. We have had rain for the last few days except today and it is cloudy now and I think we will have a snow storm before long. Night before last it rained all night and the rain came through our tent making us all wet. I was just as wet in the morning as if I had been rolling in a gutter but I dried myself off before a fire which Walter[10] built in front of the tent. We are camped but a short distance from the place where we were when here before. The railroad is not in running order from here to Aquia Creek and I suppose that is one of the reasons why we do not cross the river, but they are now working at it and it will be done in a few days. We are supporting the battery belonging to our brigade and the balance of the brigade are camped back of us on the hill.

No more at present.

From Your Affectionate Son
C.C.P.

Camp opposite Fredericksburg
Nov 25th 1862

Dear Ma

I received your letter to day but as there is nothing going on I cannot promise to do much more than answer your questions. I did not say anything [about] our driving the Rebels in fine style because I did not know anything about it until I saw it in the paper but as it may be interesting I will give you an

---

10. Walter may have been a runaway slave who attached himself to the 48th and became something of a camp servant to the officers of the regiment.

account of it.[11] We received orders to march on Sunday Nov. 9 about noon; we were then lieing near Waterloo. We marched to Amissville and camped there. The next morning (Monday) we struck tents about 10 o'clock and started back on the same road we came. There had been artillery firing going on all morning at intervals but we being used to hear[ing] it, did not mind it much. We went back about one mile when we came up to Genl. Sturgis and he ordered us to go across a field to a ravine and then deploy the Regiment as Skirmishers and advance to the front. We were at this time to the left of one of the batteries that was firing and the wagons and some cavalry were rushing towards the rear as fast as they could, we thought it was a regular skedaddle; however, we marched up to a stone fence and laid behind that for an hour or so and then rec'd orders to move on slowly to the front. Well, we kept advancing and stopping until about 4 o'clock when one of the Genl's aids came up and told Col. Sigfried that the Rebs were trying to get around on our right flank so we immediately rallied the skirmishers on the reserve and then marched back to nearly the place we started from but more to the right. Here we rested until nearly dark when we were ordered to pitch tents. Thus ended the memorable day covering Nagle's Brigade with honor and never firing a shot. I was on picket during the night with Co. D. of which I am now commander, their officers all being away. The baggage train was shelled the day we left Sulphur Springs but we were far enough out of the way of them. Virginia is pretty well cleaned out of everything and I do not often meet any of the people as we are not allowed to go out of camp. Everybody is very well satisfied with the change of commanders, that I have heard say anything. Burnside just passed here a few minutes ago and was greeted with three cheers as he always is, whenever he comes around. If I wanted comfort I would rather be on Hatteras but if I liked all sorts of hardship I would like it better where I am so you can draw your own conclusions. You never told me whether you received those articles I sent in Lieut. Jackson's trunk. I wish you would send my gloves by mail if you have not already sent them.

From Your Affectionate Son
C.C.P.

---

11. Here, Pollock is referring to a skirmish at Amissville, Virginia, which took place in early November and in which the 48th played a minor supporting role. He is apparently responding to a question his mother had asked regarding the affair in one of her letters.

Camp near Fredericksburg Va
Dec. 1st 1862

Dear Ma
I received your letter to day and was very glad to hear from you as I had not heard for the last few mails. I am sorry I did not mention how pleased we were with caps. Lt. Jackson told me to say to Margie he was very much obliged and to thank her all sorts of ways. As for me I cannot say too much for her and I wear it on all occasions and it is very comfortable. I have it [on] now while I am writing. We have just had supper and as Walter is sick we have one of the men cooking for us. We had some scrapple for breakfast this morning which was presented to us and we are now having some made; it was very fine but I suppose you would not have thought much of it at home. We built a fire place in our tent when we first came but it did not operate very well, it smoked very much and did not give any heat so we covered it up to day and went to work and put up our tent differently and made another fire place out of logs with mud the fire is now burning and does [so] splendidly. The Colonel told us this morning that we were to have Sibley tents but how soon we will get them I do not know. They will be much more comfortable than these small shelter tents in which you have hardly room to move about. We had a Regimental drill this morning and a Brigade drill this afternoon. We had a great deal of sport on Brigade drill at the expense of these new Regiments; they are as green as the first day they came into field and their officers are as dumb as the men. They got into some jolly scrapes and had a great time getting out again. Do you know that you mentioned to me in your letter about Uncle Richard going home with Lulu & his taking a fancy to her the first time he saw [her]? I thought it might make a match but then, Harvey Boyle being engaged to her, I thought it could not be. However I am very glad to hear it & I hope he will have better luck than he had before. I am still in command of Co. D. though I mess with Capt. Bosbyshell and Lt. Jackson [of Company G]. I heard today that we were to move across the river on Wednesday. I have it from good authority, one of our men who is orderly to Gen. Sturgis told us. I intend writing to Mary this evening and a letter to Will. I wrote to Bob Hill

sometime ago; why does he not answer it? You can give that [illegible] to Aunt Annie if you think it will please her though I scarcely think it worth giving away. Flanagan and Humble are well and hearty and they both helped us to build our shanty. Humble did the plastering and as we have no such things as trowels in the army, he used his hands to plaster it up with and while he was up to his wrists in mud he remarked "that any fool could work with tools but it took a man to work without them." I was thinking of your dinner on Thanksgiving day but we did not make out so bad, we had roast beef and some other little fixings. I do not see how Harry Rogers got home on a furlough, it would be perfectly impossible for one of us to get home on one now, even if we could I do not think I would like to go on account of not knowing what moment we may move "onward to Richmond." I have tried to avert that scolding you threatened me in your letter of today how I have succeeded I leave you to determine. The band is out playing this evening but [it] cannot come up to our old band.

No more at present.

From Your Affectionate Son

C.C.P.

———————•◆•———————

Camp near Fredericksburg
Dec. 9 1862

ear Ma

Although I have not heard from you for some time, and we having a mail every day, I sometimes think I might say what you said to me in your last letter, about "being few and far between." We have not been doing much of anything since I last wrote, except lieing around in our tent reading. Last night we sat up until our wood was all burned reading "Pickwick," we having finished Chas. O'Malley a few nights before.[12] We received orders to get ready for an inspection at 3 o'clock today and just about the time we were dressed up ready to go out, the order was countermanded and instead we were to cook 3 days' rations, to be kept on hand, ready to move at a

---

12. Pollock may have been referring to the *Pickwick Papers* by Charles Dickens and *Charles O'Malley: The Irish Dragoon*, a novel by Charles Lever, published in 1841.

moment's warning. We have received several very conflicting orders within the last few days. Yesterday morning we had an order from Gen. Sturgis to set aside the drills for two days to enable the men to fix up comfortable quarters for themselves. That looked very much like winter quarters, but the General told me we would be likely to stay but a week or two longer. However the order to cook rations looks very much like a move, and you must not be much surprised to hear of the Army of the Potomac crossing the river. It is very cold lately, and if we have to do much more marching this winter we will freeze to death, because it is as much as we can do to keep warm now, and we have a very comfortable fire place. I only hope Burnside knows what is good for his army and not move this winter. I would like nothing better than to see Richmond fall but I do not think winter the time to do it. If we would have to march, and we only can carry one blanket, how do you suppose we would get along with 3 on a march and we have six here? It is almost impossible, let those persons at home say what they may. No doubt they sleep warm and comfortable enough in their feather beds while [the] poor soldier is nearly froze and has to get up two or three times a night to walk around and keep warm. You may think it strange what I say, but it makes me so angry to think about those persons at home who are always harping "Onward to Richmond" when they do not know what they are talking about. We had quite a heavy fall of snow the other day and the ground is now frozen very hard. I have often wondered why you never did anything about my gloves. I have asked about them several times and I need them very much now. If you have not sent them, send at once. I do not know whether I have ever told you that you can send quite large packages by mail, some of the men get even boots. That woolen jacket also would not be uncomfortable [in] such weather as this. We are sitting in our tent; Capt. is writing and Jackson is keeping the fire going, it is very comfortable inside but freezing out. I have not been writing for about a half an hour, having stopped that time to talk about love, poetry and the ladies. The subjects being brought on the floor by the Capt and so we had to set aside writing and discuss them. The band has been playing and a few minutes ago it struck up an old and favorite polka which made me think of the old dancing school and what I will miss this winter. By the way I believe Stouch is going to teach this winter. Do you intend letting Margie go? I would like to make her a Christmas present of a couple of quarters at dancing school. We have not been paid yet but expect to, all the other Regt. are being paid but ours, our paymaster has not yet arrived.

Your Affectionate Son

C.C.P.

I have a sore thumb and you must excuse bad penmanship.

C.C.P.

———•◆•———

Camp near Fredericksburg

Dec. 16 1862

*D*ear Ma

    I have received two letters from you within the last few days. I just write now to inform you of my safety; we were engaged on Saturday afternoon. I lost two men killed in Co. D and two wounded.[13] There was none of Co. G hurt, except one man who was detailed on the ambulance corps & he has a flesh wound in his arm. I will give you a detailed account as soon as we get fixed up again. We are in our old camp. We lost 62 killed, wounded & missing. I would have written before now but have had no opportunity.

Your Affectionate Son

C.C.P.

We arrived in camp last night about 12 o'clock. The firing was very severe all day Saturday. Our loss is estimated at from 7 to 10,000. I did not get the quantity. I have a very good pair of boots. I am in very good health. I rec'd a letter from Bob Hill last night before we crossed the river. With much love to all I remain

Your Affectionate Son

C.C.P.

I will write again to-morrow or next day.

---

13. Privates Henry Williamson and Thomas Kinney of Company D, 48th, were killed in action at Fredericksburg. One of the wounded, Corporal John H. Derr, died of his wounds on January 2, 1863.

Camp near Fredericksburg
December 18, 1862

_My_ dear Ma
    This is the first time, I believe, I ever attempted to
write a letter on a sheet of foolscap, but as I have a good deal
to communicate, I intend to try and fill it. I have received three
letters from you lately; one the night after the battle, another
last night, and one tonight from Charley Evans, who has just
returned. I also received a letter from Bob Hill last evening.
    Today a week ago (11th) we marched off about half a mile
from our present camp expecting to cross the river at once but
were halted there. All day we laid in mud about three inches
deep and listened to the artillery firing which was kept up in-
cessantly all day. Towards evening we were ordered back to
camp and hardly got there and our things off before we were
ordered to fall in again and off we started to cross the river but
we had not got farther than the place where we had lain all day
when the order was countermanded again and back we went
to camp. We slept very comfortably and were aroused before
daylight to get ready to cross. We had not more than eaten our
breakfast before the order came and on we started, this time
in earnest. When we arrived at the bridge we found it already
to cross. We crossed at the upper bridge, where they had two
down. I see by the papers that this is called the lower bridge,
but in fact it is the upper one being at the upper end of town.
Well, we got safely across, though the Rebs fired a few shells at
us while crossing and though they fell into the river it was too
far up to injure any of us.
    As soon as we crossed we were formed in line of battle along
the shore and afterwards we marched up into the street to let
other troops take our places. We laid in the street about half
an hour when we were again moved forward to the gardens
behind the house. Here we laid nearly all day and the men
wandered all over town bringing in tobacco, etc of which they
found in abundant supply in the town and as they were out of
money and no way to get it, it was very acceptable. They also
brought a number of books, some very handsomely bound and
works of the best authors. Co. G got a complete set of Waverly

novels[14], very finely bound in muslin. I have one of them. I did not run around much being afraid of the regiment moving. In one very handsomely furnished home a ball struck a piano and knocked it from the corner, in which it was standing to the center of the room and destroying it entirely.

Everything was apparently left in great haste and the men could be seen walking around with every imaginable article of household goods. One man brought into camp a large doll, quite as large I think, as the one Emily Potts has, others had lace, shawls, silk dresses and, in fact, everything. I was told that a man belonging to one of the batteries found a whole set of silver and carried it off.

About four o'clock we were marched down the street nearest the river to about the middle of the town and halted just in front of where a whole block of houses had been burned to the ground, nothing was left of them but the tall chimneys and the smouldering embers. Here we had orders to bivouac for the night and as we could not light any fires the men made their coffee and cooked their evening meal on the burning ruins. Soon after dark one of the chimneys fell down with a loud crash and as the men were lying all around under them at every little [illegible] there was we all supposed two or three must be badly injured, if not killed, but by good fortune all the men got out but one, who was not seriously injured, he being near the bottom.

Soon after this I changed my bed, having made it close to the fire, and not wanting any [chimneys] to fall on me, I moved to the other side of the road. It was quite cold, and I laid down to try and go to sleep. I do not know how long I slept, but I got awake feeling very cold, and, hearing a great deal of commotion around I got up and saw a crowd around one of the fires, and on asking what it meant, learned that another chimney had fallen down and hurt another man. I jumped up and went over. The doctor was there and I could tell by his face that he was seriously injured. He was carried off to the hospital but died before morning. [15] It was too cold to go to sleep again so I sat up on a narrow drawer and fell asleep with my head on

---

14. Exceedingly popular, the *Waverly Novels* were a set of best-selling novels written by Sir Walter Scott.

15. Private William Hill, a thirty-four-year-old coal miner from Pottsville who served in Company B, 48th, was killed by the fall of this chimney. Several other men were injured as well.

my hands, but I had hardly got to sleep before the drawer gave way and I fell into the fire and burned my wrist slightly. It did not take me long to get out of it, I tell you. Well, after that there was no more sleep for me that night.

Saturday morning rose as stated in the papers. About 10 o'clock we moved down the street to the lower end of town and laid there until about one o'clock. (The infantry firing commenced about 12), when we were moved out through town towards the firing. When we arrived at the outskirts of the town we were ordered to remain there in reserve, while the rest of the Brigade went out. We laid down behind a stable for some time, when one of the staff officers reported the rebels [were] going to charge, and then we were ordered to support the men already out. We started off on a double quick across the fields and as soon as the Rebs saw us they commenced pouring in their shells thick and fast, but we kept on and by our going at double quick we escaped a great many of their shells, which otherwise would have fallen directly in our ranks. Gen. Sturgis complimented us very highly on the manner in which we went up and said it was the best line he ever saw go into a fight. I have now got to the end of the sheet and as it is late I will go to bed and finish in the morning.

Friday Morning

After a run of about a quarter of a mile we reached the place where the infantry was firing. They were posted behind a small hill and were firing over the hill at the Rebs who were behind a stone wall at the bottom of the hill, on the top of which they had their breast works, and near the stone fence ran a small creek between them and us. We were lying down behind the hill for a few minutes waiting for a Regiment to fire all their ammunition before we relieved them. When they were through we went up to the brow and commenced well, we fired away, but could not tell whether we did any damage or not. We were relieved by other troops who had come up while we were firing, and we went back out of the road. There was a regiment coming up soon after we were through firing (163 N.Y.) and as soon as they saw some of us some [of] them fired right into us, taking us I suppose for Rebels, but after a great waving of flags on our part, they ceased firing and came up. They paid pretty dearly for their firing at us, for the Rebs seeing them stop dropped several shells right in their ranks and put them in great confusion. When they fired into us it killed two men, lying right at my feet, but never scratched me.

As soon as it was dark, we were marched back to town to get another supply of ammunition, and on the road we got mixed up with some other regiment and I lost my company. We went back to the place where we were the night before and, had hardly half the regiment but [Lt] Col. Pleasants soon came up with the remainder. I went in the house that Col. J.K. Sigfried was quartered in and slept very comfortably.

Sunday morning we got up with the expectation of fighting again, and in fact it was rumored that Gen. Burnside had ordered the 9th A.C. to take the fortifications by storm, but we were lying around all day, in suspense afraid to leave for fear the regiment might move.

I heard during the afternoon that the regiment that Heb. is in, was only a short distance off, and I started off to see him, but after hunting for him for some time and not finding him, I gave it up and went back. I found the regiment but no person knew where he was. I saw one of my old school fellows from Milton, H. Hinen. I slept in the same place that I did the night before, and the family who were living in the cellar came up occasionally and as there were two very pretty, and interesting young ladies who sang remarkably well, we managed to spend a very pleasant evening.

Monday morning came and we all were wondering what Burnside intended to do. We all thought it was folly to attempt to take the position which the Rebels held and we were getting anxious about lying around the town exposed to their artillery firing. The papers say so much about the men eager for the fray, but to tell the truth, you will not come across one man in the whole army who is not heartily tired of the whole thing and would like to see it settled any way at all. I thought I could see from the various movements about town that we were going to evacuate. The ambulance trains were running all day beside me carrying wounded men over the river on litters, old bed ticks, mattresses, chairs and in fact everything they could lay their hands on. This was kept up from morning until dark and I was told that the night before they were working quite as hard. Soon after dark we were marched off down the street the same way we went on Saturday and stopped at the same

place. Then the Colonel called the company commanders together and told us we were to go up to the outskirts of town and
occupy the houses. We were to make loop holes through them
large enough for one man to shoot through. From this I thought
we were to direct the attention of the Rebs to the front while
the remainder of the army went around and attacked them on
the flank but we had hardly got the work done when we were
ordered to fall in again and marched back to town and over the
same pontoon we crossed on before and marched up to our old
camp. Thus ended the five days fight before Fredericksburg.
There were some charges made on their fortifications but none
got any farther than the creek. I was very glad we did not have
to charge as we would have been almost entirely cut up. I believe that the position they hold is impregnable when attacked
on the front. General is said to have said it was worth 100.

We found our old shanty all knocked to pieces and for the
first night we slept in with some of the men. But now we have
one of our own again and much better and larger than the
first. For a small sketch of it I must recommend you to Mrs.
Bosbyshell and it is much better than I could do it. We have
fine large fire places in it and warms it up finely. Lieut. Jackson was detailed to take a party over the river to bury the dead,
and he tells us he has seen as much war as he wants to—He
saw General [Jeb] Stuart and several other Rebel celebrities.

I commanded Company D and lost two men killed and two
wounded. Co. G lost but one man wounded in the arm, not as
the rebels could see, when each brigade left town and could
have full sweep at them from that time until they got all the
way up and under the shelter of the hill. Some regiments coming up you could see the shells bursting directly in their ranks
and knocking men in all directions. Our regiment suffered less
than most of the others and the reason of it is, I think that we
went at it more systematically and did not get excited. Lieut.
Jackson had a very narrow escape, a shell bursting directly in
front of him and the powder burnt his neck and hands without
doing any further injury.

I wish you would send me another silk pocket handkerchief.

It was quite cold last night but we slept very comfortably in
our new house. The weather was very mild all the time we were
over the river, or the men would have suffered severely. We are
getting along very well and are in good spirits, and the only

thing we want to see is the war over. I think you will be pleased with this letter and about the only think that kept me at it so long was the thoughts of it pleasing you so much. I have had to stop and rest myself several times during the writing, but I have at last got it through and I am very glad of it.

With much love to all I remain your affectionate son,

C.C.P.

✳✳✳

TRAMPING QUIETLY ACROSS the pontoon bridge, the soldiers of the 48th Pennsylvania arrived back at their old camps, roughly one mile east of the Rappahannock River, during the very early hours of Tuesday, December 16. Although Pollock wrote that the men were still in "good spirits" Captain Bosbyshell remembered it differently, writing that the men were "worn out and disgusted" upon their arrival in their old camps, which likely better captured the sentiments of the men in the wake of the fiasco at Fredericksburg.[16] Pollock did record that the men increasingly yearned for the war's end and, as the weeks passed the young lieutenant would himself repeatedly express this sentiment, wishing to get back home with or without the Union preserved. The longing for home must have been especially pronounced around the Holidays, as the Schuylkill County soldiers spent another Christmas and New Year's Day hundreds of miles away from their homes and loved ones.

At last the soldiers went into winter quarters and kept themselves busy in fixing up camp and resuming all the usual routines of life in the army, and doing all they could to stave off the general despondency and low morale that so characterized the army throughout that winter of despair. Some of the officers sought leaves of absence, but General Edwin Sumner—commanding the army's Right Grand Division, which included the Ninth Corps—made it known that none would be granted. Undeterred, these officers reacted to Sumner's ruling by tendering their resignations. To teach the officers a lesson and to prevent this from becoming a widespread practice, Sumner approved their resignations, but did so by dishonorably discharging these men from service, writing that they had resigned disgracefully in the face of the enemy. A harsh measure, to be sure, but Sumner's tactic of making an example of these

16. Bosbyshell, 100.

Artist Alfred Waud's rendering of the infamous Mud March, which he labeled "Winter Campaigning." (Courtesy of the Library of Congress)

men worked. Unfortunately, a few of the 48th's officers were so discharged, including the hard-fighting Captain John Porter of Company I.[17]

1863 arrived on a Thursday and on that day, Colonel Joshua Sigfried wrote a lengthy summary of the regiment's past activities and included the hope that the New Year would bring the cessation of hostilities. "The old year is numbered with the past," wrote Sigfried: "To us as a nation it has been indeed an eventful one. Thousands of our brave sons and comrades in arms have yielded up their lives as willing sacrifices that the nation might be preserved. We enter today upon the new year, 1863. What shall be its history? May we hope ere its close to see peace restored to our now distracted country—a peace founded in justice, righteousness and universal liberty." The year would not, of course, bring an end to the war but it would witness a number of smashing military successes at such places as Gettysburg, Vicksburg, Chattanooga, and Knoxville. What was more, 1863 was the year the Emancipation Proclamation went into effect, making the destruction of slavery an avowed goal of the war, one on equal footing with the preservation of the Union. The Proclamation gave hopes to millions and was a critical step

17. Ibid., 100-102.

in the nation at last fulfilling its promises of "justice, righteousness, and universal liberty," as Sigfried had hoped.[18]

But the year began inauspiciously and discouragingly
enough for Union arms, at least in the east, with yet another
embarrassment for the luckless Ambrose Burnside. Near the
end of the January, after weeks of planning and strategizing,
Burnside commenced another offensive operation. His plan was
to keep Lee's army in place at Fredericksburg by crossing a
force there, directly at the town just as he had done in December. At the same time, however, he would lead the bulk of the
army in a northwesterly fashion, move it up the Rappahannock
and then cross it somewhere behind Lee's lines where he could
then come crushing down on the Confederate rear. The movement began on January 20 and, as it so often happened with
Burnside, that's when bad luck immediately struck. The skies
quickly grew grey and it soon began to rain. With the changing
temperatures, the rain would turn to sleet and freezing rain,
then back to rain and even some snow. The storm lasted for
days and turned the roadways into impassable rivers of mud.
The army slowed and got bogged down; in some places, cannons
and wagons were swallowed up by the mud. All the while, Confederate troops on the opposite river bank scorned and scoffed
at the drenched, mud-covered Yankees. "The artillery could not
budge a wheel," said Joseph Gould of the 48th, "the supply and
ammunition wagons were hub-deep in the roads. The troops
almost drowned, most of them being without a particle of shelter. It was cold weather, too," said Gould, "being the middle of
January." Burnside called the entire thing off and ordered the
men to return to their camps. Plagued by bad fortune and now
with even the elements conspiring against him, Burnside then
requested to be relieved of army command. Lincoln assented
and replaced him with the ambitious but hard-fighting Joseph
Hooker.[19]

As it had the previous year when the 48th was encamped
at Hatteras, the winter provided Curtis Pollock ample time and
opportunity to write letters home, keeping his family up to date
on all the regiment's activities and on all the camp rumors and
gossip, and providing him an outlet to express his growing disil-
lusionment and his earnest desires to come back home.

18. Sigfried letter reprinted in Gould, 103-107.
19. Gould, 109-110.

Camp near Fredericksburg Va.
Dec. 27th 1862

*D*ear Ma
I received two letters from you lately and would have answered them before now but I have felt so little like writing that could hardly get myself down to it. Besides I have a gathering on my thumb which rather incommodes my writing. The letter I received last night informed me of the mailing of my bundle, but as they are always rather longer coming I do not expect them until tonight. Gen Sturgis has been ordered to Washington and Gen. Nagle now commands our division. Col. [Thomas] Allard of the 2nd Md. has command of the Brigade and as he is not very well versed in Military tactics, we do not like our position very well, so as a 3rd Brigade is to be formed out of our division to be commanded by Col. Hartranft of the 51st P.V. He is without a doubt one of the bravest and best men in the army, & there is not a man in his Regt. but what would do anything he asked of them, so well they like him. He has asked Col. Sigfried about our joining his Brigade and said he would like very much to have us. There has been very little transpiring since the battle except a review by Gen. Sumner the other day but it did not amount to much. I was at Falmouth the other day and saw Lieut. Huff of the 53rd. The Capt. has just been reckoning up the amount that Uncle Sam owes us for the last six months and mine amounts to the small sum of $654.35. I have never had an answer from Mary and it has been sometime since I have written to her. If you have not sent that money, you need not as I have not much use for it now. I wanted it more on account of Christmas than anything else, but as it is now over I do not care about it. We had rather a dull Christmas but had a turkey for dinner for which we paid the small sum of two dollars; we also had potatoes and a few other etceteras. The Col. has been trying to get leaves of absence for the officers but so far has not succeeded. Gen. Sumner told him as soon as he could see two hours ahead of him he would give him some satisfaction. I am very much obliged to Pa for sending the jacket, though I will have no use for it at present, as it is not at all cold, also to Aunts Sarah &

Mary for their present, which will come very handy on many a cold day. We expect to go on picket again tomorrow but have not yet received the order. The young ladies in Pottsville must have left town, for you never mention them in your letters, at which I am very much surprised as you know how much I like to hear about them and how they are getting along. It has been cloudy all day and I think we will have a snow storm before long. I wish this war was wound up as we are all heartily tired of it and besides we are losing a great deal of valuable time which will never be regained.

With much love to all I remain
Your Affectionate Son
C.C.P.

Send me a couple pairs of stockings.

Camp near Fredericksburg
Dec 28th 1862

ear Ma

Although I wrote to you yesterday, I will write a few lines letting you know that I received your bundle and am very much pleased with everything it contained. The gloves fit me very well & I am very much obliged to my dear Aunts—The Regiment is on Picket today down at the river but having a boil on my neck which makes it rather stiff, I did not go. It is a very fine day and quite warm. There are a great many rumors in camp the last few days, one is that there are two corps coming down from Washington and that the 2nd and 9th are to go up and take their places. I do not know how true it is but hope it is so. Another is that our corps is to go to Suffolk. There is not much confidence to be placed in these rumors but they are always circulated and create a great deal of talk. I hope by this time you have received my letter giving you an account of the occupation and evacuation of Fredericksburg, it is about the longest letter I have ever written you and hope it will interest you. We are going to commence to-morrow to get ready for our New Years dinner and if we make out as well then as on Christmas I will be satisfied. Preparations appear to have been made to remain here for some time, though we have received no orders one way or another.

No more at present; From
Your Affectionate Son
C.C.P.

————•·◆·•————

Camp near Fredericksburg
Jan. 2nd 1863

*D*ear Ma

I sent word home with Louis Bright for some watch keys, and have never heard anything about them since. I gave him one that was broken so that you would know the size. I have no key now and am very much in need of one. Please send me three as soon as possible. I also would like to have some postage stamps. There is very little going on now about camp, and I have been off duty for some time, having boils on my face which makes it larger than there is any necessity for it being, but it is getting better every day and I hope soon to be about again. I had a letter from Mary night before last written in Phila. and I answered it last evening. I was in command of Co. D during the fight and lost two killed, more than any other Co. in the Regt. We were mustered for Pay on the 31st ultimo, and there is six months now due us. We have a visitor in the Company, he came last evening from Reading, and is a brother of one of our sergeants. Co. A, from Port Clinton, was the recipient of a splendid flag from the citizens of that [town], the other day, and it has all the battles we have been in painted on it. All the officers who have been promoted since we have been in service, had to go and get mustered out of the service on the old commissions and get mustered in on the new ones. Dinner is ready & I will finish afterwards.

Poor dinner, nothing but cold boiled ham and some—well, Walter calls it bread—it is made of dough without any raising in it and baked in a mess pan with a lid over it; you can judge for yourself. Also some tea. What do you think of the war by this time? I wish it was well over. There is no end of the "wishings I was home" in the army now. I would like to get off myself if I could but somehow or another I do not get sick at all & cannot get an excuse. I heard this morning that Gen. Sturgis who is in Washington, is trying to get his division on there, and that there was a probability that he would succeed. Today is quite warm and pleasant though we had a heavy frost last night. Do not forget the watch keys. I expect a letter from you this evening. If you ever get a chance to send any good things on, such as mince pies, sausages, or anything like that, I would be exceedingly well pleased. So with much love to you, Pa. Aunts Mary & Sarah and the youngsters.

I Remain Your Affectionate Son
C.C.P.

------◆◆◆------

Camp near Fredericksburg Va.
Jan. 5th 1863

ear Ma

I received your letter night before last, and would have answered it yesterday, but I heard that Capt. [George] Gowen [of Company C] had gone across the river with a flag of truce and had seen John Hughes. He is a Capt. in the Commissary Dept. and is well; he told Gowen his wife had a baby a short time ago. He wanted to know what we were doing here, and why we did not settle it, he said it could be settled in fifteen minutes by drawing a geographical line between the north and south. The Regt. was on Picket yesterday but owing to my sore face I did not go down. There are about thirty men in Co. D. for duty. Capt. Potts is now in Pottsville sick, Lieut. Kleckner has been promoted to Colonel of one of the drafted Regts. and the 2nd Lt. has resigned and gone home on account of a wound he received at Bull Run.

We were to have a Review of the 9th A.C. yesterday by Burnside, but it was postponed indefinitely. I think there is a move on the carpet and you must not be surprised to hear of the Army of the Potomac crossing the river again or else going back to Washington. I passed a very quiet day yesterday, doing nothing but read[ing] and sleep[ing]. Quite Stylish presents those of Uncle Richards, such a beau is worth having. We had an imitation of pot pie to day for dinner, but we all managed to eat our share. Capt. [John] Porter and Lieut. [John] Woods of our Regt. have resigned and this morning they started off. The Chaplain also left. The discharges they got was not exactly the thing, it read thus, "Capt Porter having tendered his resignation in the face of the enemy is hereby discharged the military service of the U.S." I would like very much to get home but I will not resign yet a while. What do you think of my coming home? I am getting dreadfully tired of this thing and the dear [Lord] only knows how long it will last. Please give me your opinion on the subject when next you write. John Sinn was here to see me the other day. He has sent in his resignation. Ed. Flanagan has not been well for some time and I think he will be sent to a Hospital before long. Humble is all right. If you get a chance send me something good to eat. Sausage, mince pies, &c &c. Tell Bob Hill I think he is treating me very badly, he scarcely ever writes.

Capt. Bosbyshell is trying to get to Washington. John Potts is quite dangerously ill from the affects of the wound he received here. I hope that Sturgis will get this division to Washington and then I could resign without any trouble. What do you think? Mary told me in her letter that she heard I was engaged and gave me a scolding for not informing of the fact as soon as it happened, bright idea is it not? Hoping to hear from you soon and that you are well.

I Remain Your affectionate Son
With much love to all
C.C.P.

Camp near Fredericksburg Va.
Jan. 7th 1863

Dear Ma

I received your letter of the 2nd last evening, and was very glad to hear from you. I have not much to write about but as you will like to hear from me, I will tell you all I can. I am glad to hear Margie has learned to skate; it is a very good and pleasant exercise. Jim I know would make a good skater as he learned very fast the first winter he tried. Jim & Frank must be getting quite tall, and little Annie you never say anything about her, how is she getting along? Does She never say anything about me anymore, or has she forgotten me entirely? And Margie she has become quite a young lady I suppose and has lots of beaus, does she belong to the choir? Has Bell Lee no other beau but Charley Bosbyshell? I understood that Dory Russell was at home now. I am sorry to hear of Sally Bright's illness; I hope she will soon be over it. The Dr. says my affliction is of the scrofulous order but it is getting better. There was but one place on my face that is very sore and I have been poulticing it and this morning it broke much to my relief. I would like to have had part of your Christmas dinner, though we did not do so bad under the circumstances. Has Fanny Hughes learned to skate yet? I remember I was trying to teach her the winter before I left. I understand that she and guy are very thick. How is it? It is a wonder you did not publish my letter. It seems to have gone the rounds pretty well. I never want any of my letters that I send home put in any of the papers as I see a good deal of that done. We had a grand review of the 9th A.C. yesterday by Gen. Burnside and it looked well. I rode up and saw it; it was a magnificent sight. Gen. Sturgis is in Washington and Nagle commands our division. Col. [Zenas] Bliss of the 7th R.I. commands the Brigade; he is a Regular Army officer. We are having a Brigade drill this afternoon. Capt. Bosbyshell is Brigade officer of the day, quite a big thing. Our chimney smokes so today that we had to put the fire out, but as it is not very cold it does not make much difference. There are still fresh rumors around camp that we are going to Alexandria, and I hope to gracious it is so, but the order seems so long in coming that I begin to think it is "no go." I understand that express will come through now, if so I would like to have a little something good. It is very easy to say keep your spirits up but to tell the truth there is hardly a man in the Army of the Potomac who is not downhearted, and I think we have reason to be. Another thing I do not believe is to be taken by way of Fredericksburg and about the only way I see is to go to Suffolk and advance on it from there. It is almost a perfectly level country and no rivers except the Blackwater. We heard the news of the defeat of Bragg at Murfreesborough. It was a hardly contested fight.[20]

    With much love to all, I Remain Your Affectionate Son

C.C.P.

I am very much obliged to Aunt Mary & Sarah for the trouble they are going through to knit my stockings.

---

20. Fought on December 31, 1862,-January 2, 1863, the Battle of Murfreesboro, or Stones River, in Tennessee, claimed nearly 25,000 casualties and resulted in a strategic victory for Union forces under General William Rosecrans, with the retreat of Confederate forces under command of General Braxton Bragg. This victory helped to restore some of the morale lost in the Union war effort that winter.

Camp near Fredericksburg Va.
Jan'y 9th 1863

ear Ma

I do not know what has become off all my correspondents. I have not had a letter from any except you for some time. I suppose you will wonder what has gotten over me writing so many letters, but the only reason I can give for it is because I feel like writing. My face is much better & is getting well I think, though I am not on duty yet. How does Aunt Mary & Sarah like Pottsville? I hope they are having a fine time. We are having a Division drill this afternoon. Gen. Nagle wants to show off his drilling capacities, as it is a thing we never had before in this dep't. Ed Patterson was here yesterday and today several other citizens from Pottsville who are visiting the 129th [Pennsylvania Infantry]. Bob Palmer was here a few minutes ago. He looks quite natural. Capt. [Bosbyshell] received a letter from his mother last evening and also one from Miss Stern, she is a very faithful correspondent and writes very often, she and Oliver Christian [Bosbyshell] seem very much attached to each other. Is the shop still running and do they have much work? Charley Dougherty was here this morning; he is a Capt. in the 96th. It is the first time I have seen him since I left home. We still hear of our going to Washington every day but I do not know anything officially about it, so we only hope it is true. I have been taking tincture of Iron for my affliction and I think it has done me a great deal of good. We are having very fine weather and not very cold.

I would like to have another shirt as I always cannot get a shirt washed every week particularly if we were on the march. I wish I knew what is to be done here but I think something will turn up before long. That cavalry raid of ours was a magnificent affair and is productive of almost as much good as gaining a battle. [General William T.] Sherman I think will fix the Rebs at Vicksburg before long, and Rosencrans has gained a signal victory Murfreesboro. I do not know what the troops at Suffolk are about to do but it is likely they will move before long. I have not heard any account of Averill; he is said to have left here with 15,000 Cavalry and is to make a dash through Richmond. I hope he will succeed. We heard that Will Bartholomew was killed at Murfreesboro and also that Baird Snyder was also killed at Dumfries in [Jeb] Stuart's late raid.

Isaac Lippman arrived here yesterday after a long absence and has quite a stock of goods down at Bell Plains. We had two officers from 129th here to dinner to day, Martin Coho & Capt. [William] Wren. Do you expect to send Julie to Pottstown to school again? She must be quite tall now. How I would like to see you all again. Is Pa ever troubled with rheumatism now a days? We are getting along as well as could be expected and hoping you are well, with much love to all.

I remain

Your affectionate Son

C.C.P.

———•◦•◦•———

Camp near Fredericksburg

January 14th 1863

ear Ma

I received your letter dated the 8th last evening and had been looking for one for some time. You spoke of paper being scarce and that I should always fill up the sheet, it must be getting more plenty as you only filled three sides. I was out to see Heb. yesterday and spent the day with him; he is much nearer to us than I thought he was. He has not changed at all, if any he has grown stouter. I had a very good dinner of turkey &c. One of the young fellows in the [illegible] was on to see him and brought a box. My face is entirely well again and I am very glad of it. Two commissions came on last evening for Company D. and I will be <u>relieved of my command</u>.[21] I hope they will order me to Washington City, or something of that sort. There is nothing new going on not even any new rumors, and the rumor about our going to Washington City, though it was kept up for a week or more, has I think died a natural death. It has been very cloudy for the last two days and I think we will have some rain before long. We had some very good corn Starch, made by the Capt. today for dinner. I have not received the stockings but will very likely get them this evening, & am very much obliged to Aunt Mary and Sarah for them. There are about 30

---

21. Pollock's temporary assignment as commander of Company D came to an end and he returned to Company G, resuming his duties as that company's First Lieutenant.

men in Co. D for duty. If Burnside intended remaining here this winter we will not get any more notice of it than we have now. The Army of the Potomac, last winter did not receive orders to go into Winter Quarters and I do not think we will. If Burnside sees any favorable opportunity of making a move, he will do it and if not I think he will remain all winter. The Capt. has been a little under the weather for the last few days but is coming around again all right. We expect to go on Picket to-morrow; we have not been on since last Sunday a week. The Balloon lies a short distance from our camp and we see it every time it goes up.[22] We have been fixing up our chimney today as it was nearly burnt out, so we plastered it all over again. Charley Loeser is First Lieutenant now, his Commission came last evening, the First Lieut. of that Co. was discharged on Surgeon's Certificate when we first came here. I have arrived at the end of the sheet so I will close with much love to all.

Your Affectionate Son
C.C.P.

———————•◦•◦•———————

Camp near Falmouth Va.
Jan. 19, 1863

ear Ma
       I received your letter last evening and as to the box you had better not send it as we are now under marching orders and are expecting to move at an hour's notice. None of the men have received any boxes yet and I hardly think it possible for one to come on and even if it would, it is not unlikely that we will not be here. The shirt I do not need very much at present and I think it likely the mail will reduce the price on packages in a short time. We were paid on the 17th and I want to send $200 home if I can, and one of the officers expects to get home on sick leave, and if he gets it he will take it. I am quite well again and all in very good spirits but still would like to get out of this war. Do you think it will ever end? I see by the paper that President Lincoln thinks the war will soon end but it is my opinion that this war is not going to end suddenly and in that

---

22. The army balloon corps, headed by Thaddeus Lowe, was a common sight during the campaign and would be used in reconnoitering and observing Confederate positions across the Rappahannock.

case the end is a long way off. You cannot wish me home more than I would like to be there. I am as you say a little better off than a private but still I have the privations to bear as well as them, and we have had our transportation cut down so often that we can scarcely carry anything now. It has been very cold for the last few days and I am very glad we have not moved, we rec'd orders to move on Saturday and have been waiting ever since, expecting orders every minute. It is not an easy thing to get into a Hospital and I would not go to one unless I was [so] sick that I could not walk. We have had butter since Isaac has been here and as for onions and dried apples we can buy them by the bushels, potatoes are not quite so plenty but still we have them very often. We had quite a laugh over the onions you were going to send in the box when they were so plenty here and we all like them very much. Our Contraband has given us notice this morning that he is going to leave and that he was to go to Pottsville. It was without doubt a magnificent sight the review of the 9th A.C. John Cather was here and I would have written by him but he was here so short a time that I hardly had time. He is a good fellow. I am afraid we will not get to Washington for some time to come unless the Rebs drive us back which I hope they will not. No more at present.

Your Affectionate Son
C.C.P.

Camp near Fredericksburg
Jan. 20th 1863

My Dear Ma
   I wrote you the other day but as we leave tomorrow I will write to let you know I sent $200 by express today which I hope you will receive. I sent to Aquia Creek where there is an Express Office. Gen. Burnside has sent an order, which will be read to night, saying that the army is to move to-morrow. No one appears to know where we are going to, but I suppose we will cross the river above Falmouth. I have been relieved of the command of Co. D. two commissions having come for two of the sergeants. I think we will have a snow storm before long. I have just heard that [General William] Franklin [commanding

the Sixth Corps] is moving toward the right, that is, up the river.

There is nothing doing since we received orders to march, and we have been kept in suspense ever since. Our darkie got off this morning and we are sorry to lose him as he was a very good one and honest. I suppose you will see him if he arrives. You can pay the debts that I owe at home and do what you please with the balance. I owe Helms in Schuylkill Haven $12.75 which I would like you to pay. I bought a jacket from him but as I did not like it I sold it again.

We have a new servant which Walter got for us before he left and I think he will make a good one. Col. [Simon] Griffin of the 6th N.H. has returned and as he is Senior Colonel in the Brigade, has taken command. He is a good officer and knows his business. Sturgis I hardly think will return and I suppose in that case Nagle will have command of the division permanently. I will send this letter by Isaac if he will take it for very likely the mail will be stopped. I have nothing more to write about, so I will close with much love to all.

I Remain Your affectionate Son
C.C.P.

Camp near Fredericksburg
Jan. 26th 1863

My Dear Ma
I received your letter the other day but have not had a chance to answer it before as we were on Picket yesterday. We have our Headquarters at the Lacy House and were very comfortably fixed for Pickets. I heard a Rebel band playing last night in Fredericksburg, the first one I have ever heard. They played several times and played splendidly. Col. Pleasants, Capt. Gowen, and myself occupied one of the rooms and just before dark, we had two visitors who came down to see what the army looked like. One was some judge from Vermont and the other an old union citizen of Alabama. He says he is acquainted with the Sterrets but could not give me any information about them as he has not been home for some months and does not know where his wife and family are. I have never come across a Southerner who is so bitter against the south. He calls

them all sorts of names. They remained with us all night and started off for Washington again this morning though I do not think they got a very extended view of the army. Burnside has just issued an order turning over command of the Army of the Potomac to Gen. Hooker. I do not know what to think about it but if they only keep on the way they are doing now, I think the Confederacy will soon be recognized and I guess the sooner it comes the better. The express is open to Aquia Creek and if you send the box directed to there in care of Gen. Nagle I think I would get it., as we send down every week after it. You need not send the shirt yet as the trunk is now so full that it takes all skill in packing which the Capt. has to get all in and I do not know that I particularly need it just now. I do not owe Bob Hill a letter and if he does not write soon I will get offended at him for I wrote to him about a month ago and have not rec'd an answer yet. Mary also neglected to answer my letter. Send plenty of good things to eat for I feel very much like piling into about a bushel of anything that is good. You know that I like mince pies & turkey. Could you not send me some stewed cranberries? I think it likely some of us will get home shortly, the Capt. says he expects to go before the army moves again. I do not know if I am turning Democrat, but I know if they do not do something that is going to strike hard at the heart of this Rebellion I will be a Peace Republican or Democrat either [way].

It makes me feel bad to think I am missing all the skating this winter when every person at home are enjoying themselves so much. The Paymaster is here again to pay us for Nov. & Dec. and I believe will pay us to-morrow or next day. I hope you rec'd the $200 I sent the other day. Hoping you are all well; I remain with much love to all.

Your Affectionate Son
C.C.P.

Camp near Fredericksburg
Feb. 1st 1863

Dear Ma,
I received your letter on the 29th ult and would have answered it before now but have been on duty for the last two

days. We receive express here now and if you can get a box off, you had better send it. We never left our camp on that grand expedition that got stuck in the mud, and I am very glad we did not get off, for the mud was awful. I went up to see Heb the day after Franklin's Division returned to their camp, and they had not returned, so I waited a couple of hours and at last they came mud up to their knees and they had been detained longer than the rest, building corduroy roads to enable the artillery and wagons to get back. I suppose you have seen John Clemens by this time and he can tell you all that is going on and a little more too if he likes. There is some talk of getting furloughs in a day or two but I suppose it will be three or four weeks before I can get off as there are some who have not been home but I intend to come as soon as I possibly can. I am very anxious to get home and see you all again for a short time. I do not dislike the service but it is being away from home so long that makes us get down in the mouth, now and then. If I could get home every few months I believe I would rather be in the army and I would rather be in the field than in garrison. There is something so picturesque in an army encamped or marching in the field and if I was to make a business of soldiering I would choose to be in the field. You need not be afraid of my trying for that kind of [dishonorable] discharge [as Porter and Woods]. I would rather remain always than accept such a one. The mud around here is so deep you can hardly get through it. The other day I went down the country to subpoena a witness for the Capt. who is Judge Advocate of a Court Martial, and I used to think that the horse would stick fast every few minutes and I had to walk every step of the way. If I was to start to-morrow for home I could be in Philadelphia just in time to witness the wedding. I do not think Heb will be able to get off but he is very anxious to go. I sent $200 home by express and I hope you have received by this time. I was on Picket last Sunday down at the Lacy House and in the evening I heard a Rebel Band playing, the first I ever heard and they played very well indeed. The Regt. was on Picket yesterday but [Lieutenant] Jackson was down with the Company.

Your Affectionate Son
C.C.P.

Camp near Fredericksburg
Feb. 5th 1863

*D*ear Ma

I received your letter with the handkerchief the other day. We are getting along here as well as could be expected. The weather has been rather stormy lately and the ground has become frozen very hard but today it commenced snowing and I think it will turn to rain. I have been wanting to ask you to send me a pocket photographic album with photographs of the family. I have seen a great many and they are very nice to have out here. Get one large enough so that I can put a couple in that I have here. Tell Bob Hill that I would like to have one of his and his wife's. Also Aunt Mary's and Sarah's. I wrote to Bob Hill before we left Pleasant Valley and he has never answered my letter. They have commenced giving furloughs and Gen. Nagle went home yesterday. None of our Regt. has gone yet but are expecting to leave every day. I expect I will get off if they keep it up long enough but I heard last night that orders had been received that no more furloughs were to be given to the 9th A.C. from which I suppose that Burnside is to be given a new Dep't. and is going to take his old Corps with him. I will be very well satisfied with that arrangement and I do not think there would be any discontent among any other Regt's to do the same. I have been making myself comfortable since this cold spell set in by loafing in the Hospital Tent, which is large and has a good stove in, our own being very uncomfortable and smoky. The Capt. has been rather unwell for the last few days and today he has been over here all day. I am writing this here now and am nearly roasting though I am off at one end of the tent. In our own house you have to hug the stove to keep any way from freezing. We keep very good hours lately, over here until about 11 o'clock P.M. and then get up at 9 A.M. or a little later. We have a great many standard books here now and I am reading them. We have Shakespeare and I am going to commence it in a day or two. Wood is very scarce here. The teams going three and four miles for it. Today Lule was married and I have been thinking about it several times today. I have not seen Heb for the last few days but I do not think he got off. We commenced having officer school today and got along very well. The conversation now going on is on the beauty and merits of the Young Ladies of Chester County. Capt. Bosbyshell upholds the ladies and Pink Loeser says the country sticks in them and he prefers city ladies. No more at present.

Your Affectionate Son
C.C.P.

P.S. 7 o'clock P.M.

I have opened this letter to let you know that orders have just been received that we are to start for Fortress Monroe to-morrow or next day.

C.C.P.

CHAPTER SEVEN

Springtime in Kentucky, a Summer in New England, and a Winter in East Tennessee

February 1863–January 1864

A MBROSE BURNSIDE'S BRIEF and disastrous tenure as commander of the Army of the Potomac lasted just eighty days before coming to an end on January 25, 1863, shortly after the ignominious Mud March. A day after being relieved of his command, the rather luckless Burnside penned a heartfelt farewell to the troops with "an especial farewell" to his "long tried associates of the Ninth Corps."[1] Burnside's position at the helm of what was by then a downhearted Army of the Potomac was taken up by Joseph Hooker who immediately set about making some sweeping structural changes. Among other moves, he abolished Burnside's Grand Divisions, consolidated the cavalry into a single corps, and, in early February, sent the Ninth Corps away from the army, ordering it to report for duty at Fortress Monroe.

Ever since its attachment to the army at the outset of the Maryland Campaign the previous September, the Ninth Corps had been seen by many in the Army of the Potomac as something of an outsider and its long service under and strong attachment to the departed Burnside only served to fuel the dislike many felt for this itinerant corps. Hooker explained that sending away the Ninth Corps would "conduce to the good feeling and efficiency of this army, and perhaps to that of the 9th Corps."[2] Conversely, the soldiers of the Ninth Corps had felt no special fondness or strong connection to the Army of

---

1. Woodbury, 249.
2. Joseph Hooker to Asst. Adjt. Gen. J.C. Kelton, February 6, 1865, printed in *Report of the Joint Committee on the Conduct of the War at the Second Session of the Thirty-Eighth Congress* (Washington, D.C.: Government Printing Office, 1865), pg. 189.

the Potomac. Indeed, many within the Ninth Corps, including Lt. Curtis Pollock, welcomed the new assignment and felt relieved to be departing their winter camps with the Army of the Potomac near Falmouth. Joseph Gould, historian of the 48th, reflected the sentiment of the regiment when he recorded that the orders separating the Ninth Corps from the Army of the Potomac and to proceed to Fortress Monroe "was received joyfully by the command."[3]

Setting off first by rail to Aquia Landing and thence by steamer down the Potomac, the 48th Pennsylvania arrived at Fortress Monroe late on the evening of February 10, "and under its protective walls," noted Oliver Bosbyshell, "the steamer dropped anchor for the night." The next morning, the vessel steamed upriver several more miles to Newport News where the regiment finally disembarked. The soldiers of the 48th would remain there for the next forty-five days, waiting out the cold winter days and awaiting word on their next assignment. Few, if any, in the ranks could have then predicted that their next assignment would ultimately carry them all the way to Lexington, Kentucky—some 600 miles to the west—and from there another 220 miles south to Knoxville and to the mountains of east Tennessee, where they would find themselves encamped by year's end. For the moment, they were simply content with where they were, enjoying their new billet at the familiar tramping grounds at Newport News, where, over the next six weeks, "Many amusements were indulged in;" amusements, said Oliver Bosbyshell, such as "horse racing, cricket matches, base-ball and the like."[4] The uneventful stay at Newport News also allowed Lieutenant Pollock plenty of time to write home, though his surviving letters from February and March 1863 are relatively few.

Newport News, Va
Feb. 15th 1863

*D*ear Ma

I received the other day a letter from you and Mary and Mary gave me a long description of the wedding. I am glad to hear that the money arrived safely. I received something

---

3. Gould, 112.
4. Bosbyshell, 102-103.

like $400 but I had to pay a good many debts that had been standing for some time. I suppose you are aware of our change of base, we are all very well satisfied with it and are very glad to leave the Army of the Potomac. We had a very pleasant ride down here on board the *North America*, a very fine boat.[5] Capt. [Bosbyshell] & I had a stateroom together, and it was furnished in tip-top order. I think Mary's photograph is a very good one and I hope you will soon send me on that photographic album and the photographs of the rest of the family. We lost our tents in moving and I have been sleeping with the Doctor in a large Hospital tent but we expect to get new ones in a few days. I started the day after we arrived here to go to Ft. Monroe to see if I could See [illegible] but the boat had left & I could not get off the next day on account of going on picket. I had command of one of the Picket stations and got along very well. It was very cold and I caught a severe cold but am much better today. I expect to go down tomorrow if I can get off. Col. [Sigfried] & [John] Clemens came back yesterday and of course we got all the news. His coming back and giving such a good account of home, makes me want to come home more than ever but I guess it will be some time before I can get off. We have a very fine camp about ¼ of a mile above our old one. I expect to go to Ft. Monroe tomorrow, but I will try and get someone to go in my place. It has been raining almost all day. I have been sleeping in the Hospital tent since I have been here. I have no more to say at present so I will close with much love to all.

I Remain Your Affectionate Son
C.C.P.

I would have had written sooner but had no opportunity.
C.C.P.

———————

Newport News Va.
Feb. 21st 1863

Dear Ma,
I received your small letter this evening and being unoccupied I will answer it immediately. There is very little going

5. Apparently, Pollock was alone in his thoughts about this particular ride aboard steamer *North America*. Joseph Gould and Oliver Bosbyshell both noted how overcrowded the steamer was with the soldiers of four regiments and how "decidedly uncomfortable" the journey was.

on now except fixing up our camp. We have all received new tents and are fixed up very comfortably. I met the Major of Heb's Regt. on Sunday before we left and he told me he had gone. We did not get off until Monday morning. You need not be much afraid of my not trying to get a furlough if there was any to be gotten. We had rain here for two days but it has cleared off and for the last two days we have had very fine weather. Dory Patterson was over here last evening; he looks very well and is very stout. I have just received a detail to go on guard tomorrow. Col. Sigfried went to Norfolk this morning and will not be back until tomorrow. Do not forget the send me that photographic album. I am waiting for it. Also that box; I am looking for it every day. We expect to move to Fort Monroe before a great while and I think we will have a fine time there if we can only get to go. I went down to Fort Monroe the other day but it was so wet I could not get around much. I would like very much to have a short leave of absence to get home for a few days but I guess it cannot be. I heard today from Thad Boyle. Col. Kleckner[6] is in camp this evening and he told me Thad has sent in his resignation and expects to have it approved and will go home shortly. I will try to see him before he goes. I receive very few letters now-a-day's I do not know what has become of all my correspondents. I have not received that letter from Bob Hill yet.

I was glad to hear that Heb got home, he was very anxious to get off. Did you see him? John Clemens[7] is very loud in his praises of all the young ladies in town. He says Kate is very sick not expected to live. How is she getting along now? I was very sorry to hear she was sick as she was always a particular friend of mine.

With much love to all
I Remain Your Affectionate Son
C.C.P.

---

6. Charles Kleckner, a thirty-year-old merchant from Ashland, Pennsylvania, entered service as 2nd Lieutenant in Company D, 48th PA. Promoted to 1st Lieutenant, he resigned his commission in the 48th to accept the colonelcy of the 172nd Pennsylvania Infantry.
7. John Clemens, a private in Company G entered the war in 1861 at age 18. He was discharged upon the expiration of his term of service in September 1864.

Newport News Va.
Feb 25th 1863

*D*ear Ma

As Major Wren is going home to-morrow I will write a few lines with him. We had a review this morning of the 9th A.C. and a magnificent affair it was. The [corps] looks much larger than I supposed it was, and the troops looked remarkably well. We were reviewed by Gen. Dix[8], he is quite an old man but is very straight and fine looking. We have our camp fixed up in tip top style and it is very clean and neat. I wish Pa could come on and see me it is not such a great distance and Fort Monroe is worth seeing. He could come very handy with Maj. Wren when he comes back and I do not think I will hardly be able to get home for some time. We expect to be paid again the beginning of March, for four months. Have you sent the box yet? I have been expecting it for some time. We are having very fine weather the last few days and I hope it will continue. We have made a ball and bats and wickets and tonight we expect to get up a game of town ball. The mail has just come in and no letter for me.

Much love to all.

Your Affectionate Son
C.C.P.

Newport News Va.
March 5th 1863

*D*ear Ma,

The Captain is going home to day and I will write a few lines by him. It is now some time since I have heard from home and I feel rather anxious. I received a letter from Mary yesterday giving an account of the school. I do not know what to write about. I will try and get home as soon as possible but I

8. Major General John Adams Dix, born in New Hampshire in 1798, was just fifteen years old when he entered the army during the War of 1812. Resigning from the army in 1828, he later became a U.S. Senator from the state of New York and, at the outbreak of civil war, was appointed a major general of volunteers. Dix held command of Fortress Monroe from May 1862 to July 1863. Dix died in 1879 at age 81; Fort Dix in New Jersey is named in his honor.

do not know of any excuse by which I can get off. Capt. Bosbyshell will tell you how hard it is to get off. Patterson was here
last evening and says he is going home on the 15th. Hardell[9]
is going home with the Capt. It has been very cold here for the
last few days. I would like to have a pair of fine boots but I do
not know how to get the right fit. Ed. Flanagan is much better
but not quite right rid of his cold yet. You can send that Photograph album with the Capt. when he returns. Capt. Porter
gave me that letter you sent by him. We live very well. Fresh
Beef, Mutton Chops, Eggs, Fresh Bread, Butter &c &c Capt.
[Bosbyshell] will call on you and tell you all the news.

From Your Affectionate Son
C.C.P.

✹ ✹ ✹

ON MARCH 25, 1863, orders arrived rather unexpectedly for
the soldiers of the 48th Pennsylvania to pack up their gear and
"leave at once"; suddenly, their six-week stay at Newport News
had reached its end and now the regiment would be heading
west. Having already campaigned in North Carolina, Maryland,
and Virginia, the regiment was now on its way to the war's Western Theater of operations. For the next year, it would serve in
Kentucky and in the mountains of East Tennessee still with the
Ninth Corps, which now formed part of the Army of the Ohio.

Even after the twin disasters of Fredericksburg and the Mud
March, Abraham Lincoln was not yet willing to part ways entirely with Ambrose Burnside and in March, he named Burnside as
the new commander of the Department of the Ohio, which, at
that time, encompassed Ohio, Indiana, Illinois, Michigan, and
eastern Kentucky. Among other duties, Burnside's new assignment would call upon him to suppress Confederate raids and
incursions and maintain a strong presence in Kentucky to restore and preserve peace in that divided Border State. Burnside
would also take steps to quell the festering anti-Union and anti-
Lincoln sentiment that was increasingly on the rise, particularly
in southern Indiana and Illinois, but also in Kentucky and even
in Ohio. Finally, and perhaps most importantly, Burnside was
to plan for an invasion and occupation of eastern Tennessee, an

9. William H. Hardell was a First Defender along with Pollock in the Washington Artillery and
a member of Company G, 48th Pennsylvania. A 22 year old merchant, Hardell was mustered
into the regiment on September 6, 1861, and by war's end would be promoted to the rank of
1st Lieutenant.

Pre-War Image of Downtown Lexington, Kentucky. (Courtesy of the University of Kentucky Special Collections)

area with strong ties and loyalty to the Union and an important region militarily because of the rail lines that ran through the state, which connected southwestern Virginia with Chattanooga and northern Georgia. To help fulfill these missions, Burnside sought more troops and he specifically requested that his "long tried associates" of the Ninth Corps travel west with him. Thus, it was that in late March those orders arrived for the soldiers of General Willcox's and Sturgis's divisions—the 48th Pennsylvania included—to leave their camps at Newport News and report to Burnside in Kentucky.[10]

Boarding the steamer *John A. Warner*, Lieutenant Pollock and the soldiers of the 48th sailed up the Chesapeake to Baltimore, embarking upon a new campaign and entering upon the next chapter in the regiment's history. From Baltimore, the regiment traveled by train north to York, Pennsylvania, and thence to Harrisburg, before moving westward to Altoona and Pittsburgh. Train cars then carried the soldiers of the 48th fully across Ohio and to Cincinnati, where they arrived on Sunday, March 29. The veterans would not soon forget this whirlwind journey west. Oliver Bosbyshell described the trip as

10. Woodbury, 261-262.

an "exceedingly delightful one. It was much in the nature of an ovation, as crowds greeted the 'boys' at every station, and a plentiful supply of good things was constantly distributed by friends. At the town of York, Mifflin, Altoona, and Pittsburgh, in Pennsylvania, Caddy's Junction, Newark, Columbus and Cincinnati, Ohio, bread and coffee were also provided." When the regiment got off the train cars at Pittsburgh, they were escorted to City Hall where a great meal was prepared "and greatly enjoyed." Then, upon arriving in Cincinnati, the regiment was gathered in the Market House and given "a most appetizing feast." The journey across Ohio was especially enjoyable—and especially memorable. As Bosbyshell noted, "The enthusiastic crowds of girls, boys, women and men that greeted the regiment at every stop, was an experience so charming to the men who had been so long campaigning in a country hostile to them, that it made the trip satisfactory in the extreme." Yet, as pleasant as the journey may have been, the soldiers of the 48th Pennsylvania would soon find their first assignment in the war's Western Theater was to be exceedingly more so, for soon after their arrival they discovered that they would be detailed to serve as provost guards for the city of Lexington, Kentucky. This meant that while other units of the Ninth Corps were either sent out to chase after marauding bands of Confederate cavalry or sent further south to augment U.S. Grant's forces closing in on Vicksburg, the 48th Pennsylvania was given something of a break—a reprieve—from active field duty and, instead, would spend the next five months patrolling and policing the streets of Lexington.[11]

Joseph Gould recorded that the regiment's main duties as provost guards "consisted of furnishing guards for the railroad stations, ordnance depots and jails, also in patrolling the city day and night to preserve order." Gould also remembered Lexington as "a very pretty city" and he described their time there as "very pleasant." "How we loved to be doing duty in this city," wrote Gould, "plenty to eat and to wear, little or nothing to do in the way of duty, amusements of all kinds and everything that could be of service to make a soldier happy." Oliver Bosbyshell was more effusive when he wrote of the regiment's stay in Lexington as "one long happy holiday." Indeed, it was not long before Lieutenant Pollock and other battle-hardened soldiers of

11. Bosbyshell, 104-105; Gould, 113.

the 48th fell in love with the city. And, conversely, it did not take long for the Union-leaning people of Lexington to love the 48th. In late May, young Andrew Snyder—the drummer of Company H—wrote in a letter home that the "people like us very much, and say that this is the best-behaved regiment that has ever been here." Evidence of the people's fondness for the 48th was made clear in late April when orders arrived for the regiment to depart the city and report back to duty with its brigade while the 1st Tennessee regiment was to relieve them and take over provost duties. When they got word of this, the people of Lexington took up a petition and presented it directly to General Burnside at his headquarters in Cincinnati, requesting that the 48th stay. Burnside agreed and countermanded the orders.[12]

The 48th thus remained in Lexington until early September, all the while continuing to win the affection of the city and returning that affection as well. "Every man had his clothing, arms and accoutrements in first-class shape," said Gould, "Our drills were perfect, and round after round of applause greeted our manual of arms from the crowds of visitors who came to camp to view the evolutions of the troops and listen to the music of our very excellent band. . . ."[13] As could have been expected, many of the young and single soldiers in the regiment very quickly fell in love with some of the young ladies from Lexington and its surrounding towns.

The 48th Pennsylvania first arrived in Lexington early on the morning of Tuesday, March 31, after having crossed the Ohio River in a ferry boat from Cincinnati to Covington and, from there, having taken train cars to their new home. The regiment at first took up quarters on the city fair grounds, then in the city itself—in vacant homes and in hotel rooms. On April 11, however, the 48th was ordered out of the city proper and directed to a new campground on the edge of town. This new camp was enclosed by a large wooden fence and included a large hemp warehouse, which, said Bosbyshell, "made comfortable barracks for the companies—amply spacious for all needs."[14] The officers established their headquarters in large tents erected outside the warehouse. Curtis Pollock, along with his friends Captain Bosbyshell and Lieutenant Henry Jackson, as the

---

12. Gould, 113-116; Bosbyshell, 106-108.
13. Gould, 114.
14. Bosbyshell, 106.

commissioned officers of Company G, would have occupied one such tent. Soon after the regiment's arrival in Lexington, young lieutenant Pollock resumed his letters home.

—————————•◆•—————————

April 5th 1863
Lexington Ky.

*M*y Dear Ma
        I guess you will think it very strange that I have not written for so long a time, but the reason (and I know it is a poor one) that we have been in so unsettled a state that I had no opportunity. And I do not feel a bit like writing now but I know that you will be anxious about me so I will write a few lines to let you know that I am in good health and spirits. Col. Sigfried is Provost Marshal of the City and the Regt. is doing Provost Duty in it. I am on guard to day and have been kept pretty busy all day. I will write a long letter in a few days giving you an account of our journey here. We had a very pleasant trip. If we can only stay here it will be also the most comfortable quarters we ever had. The Regt. is quartered in two houses and we have a room with the officers of Co. B. We were paid the day before we left camp to come into town and I received $426.[15] I will not send any [money] home as I am going to try and get there myself as soon as possible. No more at present.
                                Your Affectionate Son
                                        C.C.P.
Direct to Washington, D.C.

—————————•◆•—————————

Lexington Ky.
April 13th 1863

*D*ear Ma
        I received the letters sent by Flanagan and Evans, but have not received any by mail, except one from Mary. We are getting along very well and like our new duties. I am on guard

---

15. This was equivalent to four months' pay. Joseph Gould wrote that the paymaster arrived soon after the regiment reached Lexington and, afterward, the city "received a coat of red paint. . . .[while]Some of the members [of the regiment] received several days in No. 3 jail, which they fully deserved."

to night and it is 1 o'clock A.M. I am sitting in the Provost Marshal's office writing. We had a splendid trip from Newport News here and we all enjoyed it very much. We saw plenty of pretty girls along the road and we would get out at the stations where the train would stop and talk to them and when we came across any while [the] train was going, we had notes prepared and would throw them out the window, kiss our hands to them and wave our handkerchiefs. Indeed we had quite a jolly time. The scenery along the Juniata [River] is beautiful, and going across the plains from Altoona to Pittsburg the scenery is said to be perfectly beautiful but as it was very foggy we did not get to see much. We had four engines attached to our train crossing the Alleghenies and they had tough work to get us up. I was very much taken with Ohio. Every town we passed through the depots were thronged with pretty girls and there were so many of them. It was on Sunday when we passed through and everybody was dressed up in their Sunday go-to-meeting clothes and looked well. There was one particular young lady who was down at the cars and with whom I fell desperately in love, her name I found out to be Sue Sterling and she kissed her hand to me. We passed through Columbus about 12 o'clock at night and we did not get to see much of it. I was nearly left behind here. Capt. [Bosbyshell] & I got out to get our coffee pot full of coffee and before we got to the place where they were dishing it out, the train started and Capt. [Bosbyshell] got right aboard but I was not going to lose the coffee so I took the pot and ran to the place but it was almost all gone so that I could only get a few tin cups full, and when I started for the train it was about a hundred yards ahead of me and going very fast. Well, I did some tall running about that time with the old coffee pot in one hand. I just managed to get up to the last car and get aboard. They all thought I had been left. I met a gentleman in Pittsburg by the name of Whitney and he took me around and treated me first rate and I had quite a jolly time. We arrived in Cincinnati about 11 o'clock Monday morning and were marched to the Market House where a table was set for the men. One of the Hotel keepers then invited the officers down to take dinner at his hotel and it was there I ate the first buckwheat cakes I had tasted [since] the last winter; they were very good and we had some of the best sausage I ever ate. After dinner we crossed over to Covington got on the train and after waiting until nearly dark, we started for Lexington. We rode all night and when I got awake the next morning I found myself here, and a very fine city it is though they are a great many Secesh. about. I have become acquainted with some Union ladies and spent a very pleasant evening with them and last night I escorted one home from church. I saw on the street to day a daughter of the Rebel General Preston[16] she is rather a fine looking girl but not pretty. I expect to get acquainted with quite a number of ladies this week and I now have the photographs of two very pretty young ladies here. One of them is a namesake of Sallie Bright's, her name is Bell Bright. The town clock has just struck two and I am very sleepy so I hope you will excuse this hastily written letter. We have been quartered in town for some time, but today we moved out to the outskirts, and send our details in every day. Col. Sigfried commands this post and Gen. Wilcox has relieved Gen. [Quincy] Gilmour who has been here and commanded the central district of Kentucky. I do not know whether I shall be able to get home or not but as soon as I think there is any show, I will try it.

Your Affectionate Son
C.C.P.

———————◆———————

Lexington Ky.
April 21st 1863

*D*ear Ma

I received a letter from you some days ago and I am not sure I answered it so I will write a few lines today. I am getting along very well and am much taken with this city. I have become acquainted with quite a number of young ladies and spend nearly every evening in their society. The young ladies here are, as a general thing, the most agreeable and interesting I have every met with. I spent last evening with three very agreeable young ladies and I invited one to go to a concert next Friday evening. I have had my teeth fixed. I had eleven plugs put in and it cost me $30. I have had a great many things to buy since I have been here and I also lent a good deal of

----

16. This is most likely General William Preston (1816-1887), a Kentucky native who offered his services to the Confederacy and rose to the rank of brigadier general.

money to some of the officers who were at home and spent their money there so I do not think I can send any home this time. You must remember that we are in the city and a person must have a great many things that we do not need when on the march. Such as kid gloves &c &c. I am on guard today and am writing this on the desk of the Broadway House. The officers all get their meals here when we are on guard. I do not know whether I have told you that we have moved out of town and come down every morning on guard. We have a beautiful camp about a mile from the main street. The men are quartered in a large empty barn and we have tents and are fixed very comfortably. We have had some very warm weather since we have been here and it has been very dusty but it rained the other day and it is now quite pleasant. I had my photograph taken the other day and I think it is a splendid picture. I would send one with this letter but they are all out at camp. I have just been offered a horse so I will ride out and get one. The men have been behaving themselves very well since we have been here and the people of the town have a very good opinion of us. The Brigade has moved on to Richmond [Kentucky] and I think very likely will go to Cumberland Gap before they hold up. Lieut. Jackson is acting asst. Provost Marshal on Gen. Wilcox's staff so the Capt. & I are alone with the Company. I have become acquainted with some very fine young men here in town & I manage to pass my time very agreeably. No more at present.

> Your Affectionate Son
> *C.C.P.*

——————◆•●•◆——————

Lexington Ky.
April 25th 1863

*D*ear Ma

I am on guard and I have just had my supper. I get my meals at the Broadway House when I am in town. I just had your letter handed to me and will answer it at once. Also find enclosed one of my photographs. Gen. Nagle came to town this morning on a brief visit; the Brigade is now at Winchester, Ky. I took a Miss Julia Shaw out carriage riding yesterday afternoon and had a very pleasant ride. We went all around town and I had all the objects of any personal interest pointed out to me.

I saw the house in which Gen. Preston's family resides. He is a Gen. in the Rebel army. After we got back I took another young lady to the old folks Concert and had a very pleasant time. The way I managed to get introduced was through the Capt. He was down town as officer of the day soon after we came here and met Mr. Shaw who is considered the strongest Union man in the place and he invited Capt. & Col. Sigfried to take tea with him. They went and then one evening when the Capt. was going up to make his party call I proposed going with him, and we went. Since then they have introduced me to several other families. I think you are mistaken about these ladies. I don't think they are as lazy as those further south.

The Commissioned Officers of Company G, 48th Pennsylvania, pose for a photograph while at Lexington, Kentucky. Captain Oliver Bosbyshell is seated; standing left is 1st Lieutenant Curtis Clay Pollock, and right is 2nd Lieutenant Henry Clay Jackson. (From the John D. Hoptak Collection)

I bought some white pocket handkerchiefs at an Auction the other day and Miss Annie Shaw is going to hem them for me. There are two families of the Shaw's here, two daughters in one and three in the other and after mature deliberation, I really think they are the finest lot of girls I ever met, and they are smart too. They have one of the finest Cemeteries here that I have ever seen. I was all through it yesterday afternoon. I had to stop writing to go to the Theatre, the officer of the Guard has to go every night to examine passes. They played the *Hidden Hand.* I did not see all the play as I could not stay until it was out. I have not been to Episcopal Church yet but intend to go tomorrow. The first Sunday we were out in camp and I could not get into town the next Sunday I went to Methodist Church with the Miss Shaw's and last Sunday I was on duty. It is now 1 o'clock A.M. and I would write more but have nothing to say so with Much love to all.

I remain
Your Affectionate Son
C.C.P.

Lexington Ky.
May 13 1863

*D*ear Ma

I received your letter the other day and was much pleased to hear from you. You seem to think that I will go right off and get married, well I think I could get a very good wife here if that was my intention but as I might have some trouble supporting her after the war is over I do not think I will try it. The ladies here are different from ladies further south, and if you only knew them I think you would like them. Some of our officers have gone home on furlough but only for ten days and I think it is hardly worthwhile to come home for so short a time. If you and Pa could come on and see me and bring Mary or Margie along, you would not only see the most beautiful country you ever passed through but also a great part which you would be interested in seeing. I was at a hop given to Gen. Wilcox and staff at the Phoenix Hotel and was introduced to two daughters of Cassius M. Clay, and two very fine young ladies they are too.[17] I enjoyed myself very much and made several acquaintances. I danced nearly every set and made myself generally agreeable. There were quite a number of pretty girls there but not so many as would have been if the weather had been better. We have been talking about having a fishing party for some time; a party of about eighteen and it has been put off several times on account of the weather but yesterday it came off and a splendid time we had of it. The stage[coach] came to camp for Col. Pleasants, Capt. Bosbyshell, Lieut. Jackson, Hardell and myself and then started for the ladies. We got them all aboard, but one, Miss Julia Shaw and she was sick and could not go. We were all very sorry as she was one who took most interest in getting it up. However we got off by 6 ½ o'clock AM and started for a creek about eleven miles in the country. We had a great deal of fun going Capt. Bosbyshell threw himself away entirely, cutting up and making a great deal of fun generally. We got out about 10 o'clock got our fishing poles ready and two of the young ladies said they were going to take charge of me

17. Cassius Marcellus Clay was a prominent Kentucky politician and abolitionist who, in 1863, was serving as the United States' Ambassador to Russia.

and I must do as they said. So we three started up the creek by ourselves and after walking about a half a mile we sat down under a tree and had quite a sociable chat and fired at a mark with my pistol. We did not do much fishing though I caught four during the day. This afternoon a darkie brought me a very magnificent bouquet; a present from some lady down town. I have it now before me and it is <u>so</u> sweet.

Your Affectionate Son
C.C.P.

Write soon.

Lexington Ky.
May 24, 1863

*D*ear Ma

I received your letter by the hands of Alex. Govan, and was very glad to hear from you. We are getting along old fashioned and are all well. Will Gillingham[18] is going home tomorrow and Maj. Wren has resigned and is also going.[19] Gen. Nagle I suppose will be at home ere this reaches you.[20] He was out at camp the other day and made a short speech to the Regt. Maj. Wren I understand is going to address the Regt. this evening on dress parade. I am going to send a lot of photographs with Will Gillingham of officers in the Regiment. You can either keep them at home or send them to Mary just as you please. We have had very good news from Grant last evening and I only hope it will be confirmed. There was a large ball given at Gen. Wilcox Head Quarters on Thursday evening but I was not

---

18. William P. Gillingham was a 22 year old carpenter from Pottsville who enlisted into the ranks of Company G, 48th Pennsylvania, in September 1861. He was discharged on a surgeon's certificate in September 1863.

19. Major James Wren, who originally commanded the Washington Artillery during the early days of the war then went on to command Company B of the 48th before being promoted to major, resigned on May 18.

20. In early May, 1863, Brigadier General James Nagle resigned on account of poor health. Nagle had raised and originally commanded the 48th Pennsylvania before his elevation to brigade command in the early spring of 1862. The soldiers were sorry to see their first commander bid farewell. Private William Atkinson of Company G wrote that Nagle was "beloved by his whole command" and that he was "the embodiment of a true soldier, a strict disciplinarian; he was humane and kind as a father, or dear friend. . .he was brave, prudent honest and good, and his form, countenance, and bearing inspired the beholder with the belief that he was born to command. In the closing of his military career our country loses one of her bravest, most honest, patriotic and faithful officers" Nagle's military service was not quite ended, however, for later that year he helped to raise the 39th Pennsylvanian Emergency Militia and, the following year, commanded the 194th Pennsylvania Infantry. Nagle died of heart disease in August 1866 at the age of 44. (Gould, 119)

invited. Capt. Bosbyshell got an invitation through Col Sigfried. It was a splendid affair, one of the most grand balls ever given in this part of the country. I was not down at church this morning as Capt. went and there has always to be one officer with the company. We had a large fire here on Friday. The building occupied as a hospital caught on fire from one of the flues and before we could get the engines to work it had got too far to be stopped. I was on Guard at the time and the engine house was opposite the guard house so I got my men to get the engine out and pulled it up. But it had not been used for so long a time that it was some time before we could get it to work. It was the first engine on the ground. The patients were all gotten out and nearly all the Hospital stores. It was quite a large building and was formerly a Medical College. I spent last evening up at Shaw's and had a very pleasant time. I went down on horseback in the afternoon and took one of the young ladies out riding but we met with an accident on our way home. By some unaccountable means the lady fell off the horse but did not hurt herself at all. As good luck would have it I had a very quiet horse and when she fell, he never moved an inch. She was not minding what she was about and lost her balance and fell right over. The weather is now very warm and any quantity of dust. I will try and get home as soon as possible but you know I must wait my turn. Hoping you are all well I close.

Your Affectionate Son

C.C.P.

— · ◆ · —

Lexington June 8, 1863

*D*ear Ma

I received a letter from you yesterday and as the Capt. is going home to day I will send this by him. We were paid the other day but I cannot send any home as it now takes all my pay to keep me, for I have a great many more expenses here than I have ever had before. [The] Capt. will tell you the reason he got home again so soon and I will now have to wait until he gets back before I can get off but as soon as he returns I will come home.[21] There is very little going on here now.

---

21. Captain Oliver Bosbyshell returned back home to get married. He returned to Lexington, with his young bride, on July 8.

The 9th Corps has passed through here on its way, I think to Vicksburg, but no person knows for certain. Their orders are to go to Cairo [Illinois] and I do not see any other place where they could go except to Vicksburg after going there. I came off Guard yesterday morning and was so tired to go to church but went down in the evening. You ask in your letter if I never visit any other ladies except the Miss Shaw's. I do visit several other families but am more intimate at Shaws than at any others, and like them better. I rec'd a letter from Mary and Sallie Bright yesterday and they both tell me not to come home until July; well, that will suit me very well and I think I will act on their advice. Tell [illegible] I will answer her letter sometime this week. I do not feel a bit like writing this morning and I hardly know what to write about. I will send home most of the pictures of Capt. [Bosbyshell], [Lt.] Jackson & myself and I want you to give them around to all my relations; you need not give any out to the family. The other night on guard two drunken soldiers got into a fight and one drew his pistol and shot the other in the leg. I arrested them and the wounded fellow was sent to the hospital and the other proved that he did it in self defense so he got clear.

I have nothing more to say So I will close.

With much love to all

I remain

Your Affectionate Son

CC Pollock

———◆———

Lexington June 18, 1863

*D*ear Ma

I received your letter to day, after getting back from an excursion into the country. I went to Shelbyville with some young ladies to attend a commencement at one of the schools there. I had a very pleasant time and would liked to stay a little longer. I started on Tuesday and came back to day. I met with quite a number of very pretty and interesting young ladies. When we started to come back this morning it commenced to rain quite hard but did not last long. Shelbyville is about 50 miles from here on the Louisville and Frankfort R.R. The Band tents are just behind ours and they are singing away at a great rate that I can hardly write. They are now singing "Three Blind Mice" and making great noise over it. [The] Capt. told me that he would explain to you as soon as he would see you how it was that he managed to get so long a leave. As soon as he comes back I intend to make an application for a leave and I guess I can get it. I want to be at home when Mary is there. You speak of my spending too much money. I do spend more than I ought to but I do not gamble nor drink but little but still it goes I hardly know where. Things are much more expensive here than at home and I have been getting some new clothes, and these two trips I have taken I did not go free. We have had a little excitement here lately on account of Raids the Rebels have been making in the southern part of the state. Last Saturday evening when I was on guard I had orders to keep everything in readiness as a raid was expected here, but they did not get this far. I see from the papers that they are getting up into Penna. but I guess you have enough men at home to keep them all out.[22] I will be on guard tomorrow and it is very likely it will rain; it looks much like it to night. The news from Vicksburg and the Army of the Potomac is not very good and I am afraid will be worse in a day or two. I sometimes think that this war will never be over that it will last until they can get no more men from the North or the South'rn Confed. has all her men killed off and that will be some time. It is hard to tell how long we will remain here, we may be ordered off at almost any moment or we may stay for six months to come. I have had a splendid time since we have been here. In fact I am down town almost every evening having social chats with some of my quite numerous lady friends. You asked me once if I would not like to have a photograph of Fanny Hughes and I told you I would but you have never sent it yet. Did she ever say anything about a paper I sent her? No more at present.

Your Affectionate Son
C.C.P.

I sent you a copy of the *Kentucky Loyalist* did you ever receive it?[23]

22. Here, Pollock is referring to Confederate General Robert E. Lee's second invasion of Union soil, which culminated at Gettysburg in early July 1863.
23. While the 48th was stationed at Lexington, Private William P. Atkinson of Company G, a printer by profession, commenced the publication of a weekly newspaper from a confiscated printing office in the city. He titled it the *Loyalist* and, according to Oliver Bosbyshell, it was a "bright, newsy paper, filled with good local matter."

Lexington Ky.
July 5th 1863

Dear Ma

I received your's and Mary's letter day before yesterday and had been looking for it for some time. We are getting along old fashioned and had quite a time yesterday. On Friday evening I went to a ball at the Broadway Hotel and had a very pleasant time. It was very warm dancing but I managed to get through with quite a number of dances. It broke up about 4 o'clock A.M. and then I got in with a party of Gents and we went down town and got a lot of firecrackers and started in the 4th of July in the city of Lexington. I had to be out at camp at 6 o'clock as we were to have a parade and I left the party down town, tieing packs of crackers to darkies' coat tails and seeing them run as if the old scratch were after them. We started down town about 7 o'clock with about two hundred men and marched all over town and when we got to the Court House Square we went through the Manual of Arms and the firings and did it very well. We did not get back to camp until about 11 I took a good wash to cool myself off. Such warm weather I do not think I ever experienced before, the perspiration just rolled off me in small creeks.[24]

I laid down after dinner and slept all afternoon and as we were going to have some quite extensive fireworks in the evening I went down town to bring a young lady up. I did not get up when it first commenced but what I did see was very beautiful. It rained a little in the afternoon but cleared up before dark. I have been asked several times by the Miss Shaw's that when I go home I must bring Margie out with me and they have invited her to stay with them. So as soon as the order is revoked and I can get leave I am coming home and if you will let her I will bring her back with me. I am sure she would have a pleasant time and be well treated. I was at another fishing party that went down to the Kentucky River about a week ago. We started from Judge Kincade's [home] about half way between here and the river. Mrs. Kincade is a very fine lady is very well

---

24. Joseph Gould wrote about celebrating the Fourth of July "with a very pretty street parade through the city during the day and fireworks at night. Our camp was crowded with the elite of the city, and everybody went away happy."

acquainted with Mrs. Hunt. She has one daughter. The two Miss Brand's were along and a Miss Ernst from Covington. She says her father formerly lived in Pottsville and I think very likely Pa has known him. She is a very fine young lady, not so wild as the rest of the party were but steady and quiet. We had a pleasant time considering the warm weather. I would like very much to get home now as Mary is home from school we could have a jolly good time. The news is very favorable here from Penna and I think we are doing very well all round.[25] No more at present.

From [Your] Affectionate Son
C.C.P.

Lexington Ky.
Sunday July 12th 1863

*D*ear Ma

I received your letter from Capt. Bosbyshell who has ar-rived here safe and sound. I have been introduced to his wife and like her very much. I asked Col. Pleasants about my going home and he said he would see the Gen'l. about [it], as a week or two ago he issued an order not granting furloughs, but as soon as that order is revoked I intend to put in my application. We have had considerable excitement here within the last week on account of [Confederate General] John Morgan's raid, but it has all subsided now. Our Reg't. was ordered out and we had all our things packed up and removed to the fort and we went out and barricaded the roads and dug some entrenchments, and were fully prepared for his coming., but after lieing out for two days we were ordered back to our old camp and are now fixed up just the same as before we left it.[26] On Thursday evening, Co's. G, I, & K received orders to be ready to march at 7 ½ P.M. with two days' cooked rations. We went out to the

---

25. Union forces under Meade and Grant had, indeed, secured two important victories at Get-tysburg, Pennsylvania, and Vicksburg, Mississippi, respectively, on July 3 and 4, 1863.

26. It appears that not long after Pollock penned his July 5 letter home, reports circulated through camp that famed Confederate cavalier John Hunt Morgan—who was also a resident of Lexington—was galloping into town with his band of horsemen. Gould wrote that "the long roll was sounded and we sprang out of our blankets, and, hastily dressing ourselves, were soon in line." Each man carrying 60 rounds of ammunition, the regiment marched out to Fort Clay and "loafed around all day." Morgan never showed.

fort and there were five wagons and they gave us horses to ride and we started out on a grand scout. It seems there had been reported at Hd.Qrs. that 150 Rebels had crossed the Kentucky River at a place called Mundy's Landing and we were ordered to go out and capture them. The distance is about thirty miles from here and we rode all night and by morning I was pretty tired and sleepy and we stopped about an hour to rest. I laid down on one side of the road and went to sleep at once and never waked until we were ready to start again. We arrived at the place about 5 or 6 o'clock A.M. and found that the Rebs had recrossed the night before and some of our Cavalry [went] after them but as our orders were only to go that far we got ready to go back. We got a very good country breakfast at a farm house and then we got some corn for the horses and started back again. It was very warm though the day was cloudy and we had no rain. We stopped at a small town and got our dinner and about 5 o'clock P.M. [We] arrived at Lexington very tired and sleepy. It was the first scout I have ever been on and I like it very well. Only we were disappointed at not meeting the Rebs. I am on guard today and will not be able to get to church. It has been quite cloudy for the last few days and I think we will have rain before long. The news from all around is very cheering and John Morgan is I think cut off entirely and will never get back to Tenn. with one half the men he took out.

Much love to all
I remain Your Affectionate Son

Tell Pa to write to me. What is grandpa's direction in Phila.?

C.C.P.

❊ ❊ ❊

POLLOCK'S LETTER OF July 12 would be the last he would write from his comfortable quarters at Lexington, Kentucky. Next day, new orders arrived, which were addressed specifically to him. General Orders No. 32, Department of the Ohio, dated July 13, 1863, stated in part that 1st Lieutenant Curtis Pollock of the 48th Pennsylvania was to proceed all the way to Brattleboro, Vermont, to help take charge of a camp of drafted men who were being organized there. These orders appear to have been quite unexpected; if he had made application or volunteered for such an assignment, he made no mention of it in

The Bodley-Bullock House in Lexington, Kentucky, served as headquarters of the Union Provost Marshal. Several of Pollock's letters home were written from inside this home. (Hoptak Photograph)

any of his letters home. The records as to how exactly this came about are simply not clear. Either way—whether he volunteered or not—Curtis Pollock soon bade a temporary farewell to his comrades in the 48th and to his friends in Lexington and set off on the nearly 900-mile journey. Having already served in North Carolina, Virginia, Maryland, and Kentucky, Pollock was now on his way to a new and different kind of service in Vermont.

The summer of 1863 witnessed the nation-wide implementation of the controversial Enrollment Act. The patriotic fervor that had swept the nation during the war's early days had almost entirely vanished and with volunteers no longer as forthcoming as they were in 1861, the government now implemented conscription. Consequently, even as the United States cheered and celebrated the news of the twin victories at Vicksburg and Gettysburg, conscription agents throughout the North began calling names and drafting men into service. The Act and especially its implementation were met with widespread criticism and much opposition, and even triggered some of the worst urban rioting in American history in the streets of New York City from July 13-16. In the coal regions of Pollock's own Schuylkill County, Pennsylvania, resistance to the draft was also especially prevalent. The previous October, when the state government was doing all it could to turn out volunteers and conscripts, protests—some quite violent—broke out in Potts-ville, Minersville, and in the coal mining villages and farming communities in between. Miners went on strike and to help restore order—and to get those coal mines back in operation—Secretary of War Edwin Stanton authorized Governor Curtin to send military forces into Schuylkill County while President Lincoln wrote that in such "extreme" cases, he would be con-tent with simply the *appearance* of executing the law.[27] Thus for any Union official—military or political—helping to implement the draft was an unenviable and sometimes dangerous task. But from his few letters written during this time, Pollock would seemingly make the best of his new duties—and of his time in New England.

Pollock did not describe his journey to Brattleboro, Ver-mont, at least not in any of the surviving letters. Nor do we know exactly when he arrived. Indeed, the next letter in the col-lection—dated August 10—was written some 200 miles further east of Brattleboro, from Long Island, in Boston Harbor, where Pollock had escorted a contingent of drafted men. As it turned out, Pollock would remain in Boston longer than he had antici-pated before returning to Brattleboro. But just as he had while stationed in Washington and in Lexington, Pollock was sure to take some time to explore his new surroundings.

Long Island Boston Harbor[28]

Aug. 10, 1863

Dear Ma,

 I have now been here one week and would have writ-ten to you before now but expected to get back to Brattleboro every day since we have been here. I came down here with some drafted men and have to stay and take charge of them

---

27. Alexander K. McClure, *Old Time Notes of Pennsylvania*, Vol. I, (Philadelphia: The John C. Winston Company, 1905), pgs. 540-547; for more on the unrest in Schuylkill County see Grace Palladino, *Another Civil War: Labor, Capital, and the State in the Anthracite Coal Regions of Penn-sylvania, 1840-1868* (New York: Fordham University Press, 2006).

28. Long Island, located near the center of Boston Harbor, is approximately 2 miles in length and encompasses some 225 acres. Camp Wightman, a training and rendezvous camp, was established on Long Island. As Pollock would note, a number of drafted men would attempt to desert from Long Island by swimming to the mainland and some would drown in the attempt.

but hope I will be relieved before long. Long Island is about 6 or 8 miles below Boston, it is a very pleasant situation but I am very tired of it and want to get back to Brattleboro as I left some interesting lady friends there. I have been up to the city twice since I have been here and have seen a good deal of it. Yesterday I went down to Fort Warren[29] and the Boston Light House in a sail boat and had quite a pleasant time. There were about 1,200 drafted men went away from here yesterday and day before; 800 went to the Army of the Potomac and 400 went to Newberne. We have about 160 in our camp and they are a very good set of men. Some of those that went away the other day were some of the hardest cases I ever came across. They were mostly New Yorkers who came to Boston and came down here as substitutes.[30] There is not much of any interest going on here except the running away of these conscripts, but it is a hard matter for them to get off the Island. There is a large hotel but miserably kept; none of the rooms are furnished and they give us very poor meals. I did not bring anything along with me when I came on, as I expected to go back the next day, so I am in rather a bad way for clothes. However I think we will get back to-day or tomorrow. Direct as before to Brattleboro now. I suppose Pa has gotten home by this time

　　　　With much love to all, I remain your affectionate Son
　　　　　　　　　　　　　　　　　　　　　　　　　　C.C.P.

————————◆•◆◆————————

　　　　　　　　　　　　　　　　　Long Island Boston Harbor
　　　　　　　　　　　　　　　　　　　Aug. 18th 1863

*D*ear Ma
　　　I received your letter yesterday and you think it has been very strange that I have not written but the reason was that I was ordered down here and expected to go back every day and I was going to give you my impression of Boston as soon as I got back, but day after day passed and I was not relieved and

---

29. Completed in 1861, Fort Warren was a 28-acre fortress built to defend Boston Harbor. During the Civil War, it was used mainly to hold high ranking Confederate prisoners.
30. One controversial aspect of the Enrollment Act was that it permitted conscripted men to hire a substitute to serve in his stead. Many of these substitutes had no intention to ever serve but would desert at the first chance. Often, these men would offer themselves up again as substitutes, only to collect the money and then desert once more.

day after day I put off answering your letter, until I was here one week when I received orders to remain here on whatever duty the Genl. com'd'g might direct, so here I am and likely to remain for some time to come. I wrote to Mary a few days ago and I suppose she will think from my letter that I am on the point of committing suicide or something more desperate still, but you can inform her that I am still in the land of the living and in the best of spirits. Most of the young ladies I met at the Wesselhoeft were from Boston and they will be coming home soon and I intend to try and find them out and enjoy myself as much as possible while I remain here. We have had quite a cool spell of weather here for the last few days and as usual I have caught a severe cold in the head. There was another detachment of 1,000 men went off this evening for the Army of the Potomac and 200 from our Vermont camp, we still have about 150 here who will go off in the next load. I should like very much to get home for a week or two now, but I am afraid there is a very small chance. However I shall try it in a week or two when the conscripts will not come in as fast as they do now. We get from thirty to fifty almost every day. Pink Loeser was down here the other day with a squad but went back immediately; he says they are having a fine time in Brattleboro. Lieut. Matthews 2nd Maryland is here with me; he is Adjutant and I am Quartermaster of our detachment. We are fixed very comfortably here in our tents except a floor which we hope to have before long. We have cots with a straw mattress and enough blankets to keep us warm. To day after the troops had left their camps I went around and picked up two chairs and two axes. I am very sorry to hear Grandpa is unwell and hope he will soon recover. I have had but one short note from Capt. Bosbyshell. I think it very strange he has not written to me. I think there must be a letter down there for me. I think I will have to write to Sallie Bright and ask her if she has forgotten me already or likely she believed in the following

When absent from lips that we love
We make love to the lips that are near

Much love to all
From Your Affectionate Son
(C.C.P.)

———◆◆◆———

U.S. Barracks
Brattleboro Vt.
Sept. 9th 1863

*D*ear Ma
    I received your last letter a few days ago and had just written one. There is nothing going on here and I have little to do except go on guard when my time comes. I am now living out at camp on the outskirts of the town but I go into town whenever I please.[31] We have a man who furnishes us with as much to eat as we want. I have become acquainted with most of the village girls and like them very well. I ate a [illegible] with one and caught her and last evening she presented me with a very nice pocket handkerchief with my initials worked on in German Text. It is very handsomely worked and I think a good deal of it. I have not been on any picnics this week but have been down town every night calling on some of the ladies. The water [illegible] are beginning to thin out but I still visit the Wesselhoeft quite frequently. I was down there this morning rolling ten pins with some young ladies. We have a couple of foot balls out here and we exercise ourselves every evening kicking them about. Do you still get the Kentucky Loyalist? They never send it to me. The draft is nearly over here and all the conscripts will be here by the end of the week, and then if we are not put on recruiting service, we will likely be ordered back to Kentucky, though Major [William] Austine told Capt. Brannan that we would be the last detail to leave. It is now decided that we will not go to New Orleans as a detail from the Regiments has come on here. They arrived but a short time ago and came by the way of the Mississippi River. There is nothing more to tell so I will close.
    With much love to all.

Your Affectionate Son
C.C. Pollock

---

31. Located in the far southeastern corner of the state, along the Connecticut River, and bordering New Hampshire, the picturesque Brattleboro is one of the oldest communities to have been established in Vermont.

Brattleboro Vt. Sept. 1863

Dear Ma
    I have been intending to write you every day for the last week but have been putting it off from day to day, on account of my having had so gay a time. I have been on two picnics during the week and two hops and then going to see the girls in the mean time. I have just become acquainted with the village girls and I have had a splendid time. I have nothing to do of any consequence and can come and go when I please. There are a very gay set of young ladies here and it is a person's own fault if he cannot enjoy himself. I am on guard to day and I think will have some rain. We went on the first picnic to Chesterfield Lake and a beautiful place it is. There was only a small party of ten went and we enjoyed ourselves so much that we concluded to try it again, so on Friday we had another and went to a place called South Vernon and had quite as gay a time as before. I called on a lady last evening from New Hampshire who is a very intimate friend of Norman Farquhar's wife; she is a very pleasant and agreeable. She lives in Portsmouth. I had a very pleasant time, and have not enjoyed myself so much in one evening for a long time. Her name is Miss Ladd. I understand you are having a gay time in Pottsville now. I wrote to Mary some time ago but have not received an answer. You need not be afraid of my drinking as I scarcely ever drink anything now. I have given it up almost altogether. The draft is nearly over in this state but I do not think we will be ordered back to our regiment for some time as Major Austine says we will be put on Recruiting Service and if that is the case it will be just as probable that we will stay six months of more.
    With much love to all.

I Remain Your Affectionate Son
C.C.P.

———•◆•◆•◆———

U.S. Barracks,
Brattleboro, Oct. 3, 63

*D*ear Ma,

I received your letter a few days ago, just before I started for Boston, and put off answering it until I returned. I left here for Boston on Tuesday morning and arrived there at 2 ½ PM. I had eleven conscripts to take down to Long Island. I got them down that afternoon, and went up to the city again that evening. I went to see J. Willy Booth play *Richard III* and was very much pleased with him[32]. It is the first time I have seen a tragedy played. I went down to the Island next day as I had some business to transact and stayed all day, and that evening I went and saw 'Cuba' in her celebrated act of *The French Spy*.[33] She is a very fine actress and this play is particularly well adapted to her style of playing. I returned on Tuesday and in the evening went to a country dance about five miles below here where I had a very gay time. Nearly all the officers who are here went along. It kept up all night and I did not get home until 5 o'clock A.M. Those Yankee country dances are great things and a person can have a good time. I have learned several new dances since I have been here. We were paid two months pay, a week ago yesterday which did not come any out of the way. I sent Mary $5 before I left for Boston. The weather has been milder for the last few days than it has been and to day we are having quite a shower. I have not seen Miss Ladd for some time, but I believe she is still here. I have heard nothing lately about leaving here and it is impossible for me to tell when I will leave. I am very glad to hear that some of those gents about home are drafted and hope they will have to go out. Hoping you are all well & with much love to all.

I Remain Your Affectionate Son
C.C.P.

I am very sorry to hear that Grandpa is so unwell and sincerely hope he will soon recover. [34]

---

32. John Wilkes Booth, of the famed Booth acting family, was a well-known stage actor, known for his portrayal of Shakespearian characters, including Richard III. Just eighteen months after this performance, in April 1865, Booth shot and murdered President Abraham Lincoln at Ford's Theater in Washington, D.C.
33. Pollock certainly enjoyed going to the theater and "Cuba" must have been the name of a well-known actress.
34. Curtis's grandfather—Reverend Jehu Curtis Clay—passed away on October 20, 1863, at age 71.

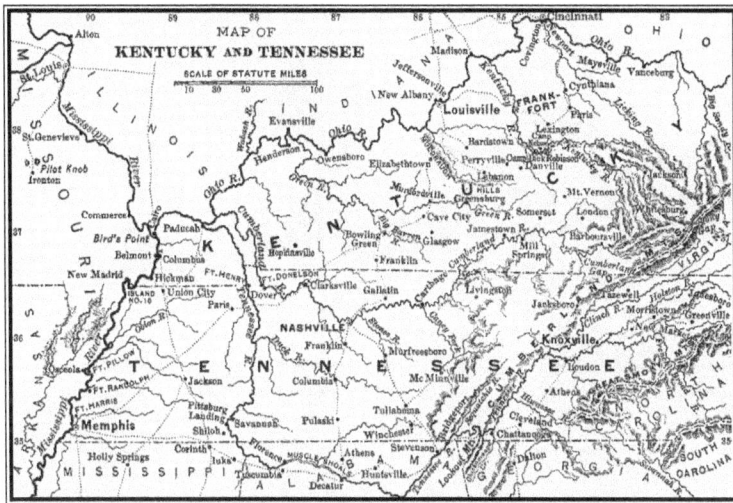

From April 1863 until January 1864, the 48th Pennsylvania campaigned in Kentucky and in eastern Tennessee, serving first as provost marshals in Lexington and then participating the campaign against Confederate General James Longstreet's force at and around Knoxville. The regiment went into winter quarters in the cold and snow-covered mountains northeast of Knoxville. (From Battles and Leaders of the Civil War, *Vol. III)*

✳ ✳ ✳

IN EARLY SEPTEMBER, 1863, while Lt. Pollock was stationed in faraway Brattleboro, Vermont, his comrades in the 48th Pennsylvania packed up their gear and departed Lexington. At last, the regiment's idyllic five-month-long stint as provost guard for the city had come to an end. Their orders were to report first to Nicholasville, Kentucky, and from there to make their way to Knoxville, in eastern Tennessee, where they would rejoin the Ninth Corps and the other forces Burnside had gathered for his command.

The liberation of east Tennessee was one of Burnside's principal objectives as commander of the Department of the Ohio, for not only was this region important militarily and strategically but its population was composed predominantly of loyal Unionists, who, for the first two years of the war, had suffered from plunder and persecution while under Confederate occupation. Burnside began planning for this campaign soon after assuming his new command but much of that spring and summer of 1863 would be consumed with other matters. Soldiers of his Twenty-Third Corps, for example, spent much of this time chasing after Confederate General John Hunt Morgan and his band

Wartime view of Knoxville, Tennessee. (From Battles and Leaders of the Civil War, *Vol. III)*

of horsemen while most of Burnside's Ninth Corps had been taken from him and sent to Mississippi where it played a supporting role in General Ulysses Grant's campaign against Vicksburg. In mid-August and with a motley assortment of soldiers from various organizations, however, Burnside, at last, got underway, setting out from Kentucky and marching south, across the rugged mountains and into Tennessee. By this time most of the Confederate forces that had been stationed in east Tennessee had been ordered south to Chattanooga and Burnside thus found little in the way of opposition. All along the route, the people of east Tennessee received Burnside's columns triumphantly and greeted these blue clad soldiers as their deliverers. Knoxville was reached in early September and it was there where Burnside, who had entered the city to a hero's ovation on September 3, set up his headquarters. Among his first orders of business upon arrival was getting his "tried and bronzed veterans" of his Ninth Corps back. The orders thus went out and from various points, the well-traveled, well-seasoned soldiers of the "wandering" Ninth Corps began to make their way to Knoxville and back to their beloved commander Burnside.[35]

After so long and so pleasant a stay at Lexington, the soldiers of the 48th naturally expressed much sadness and regret at having to leave. They had grown fond of the city and its people; many of the men had fallen in love. But orders were orders and on September 10, the 7th Rhode Island Infantry arrived to take their place and assume their duties and the 48th Pennsylvania

---

35. Woodbury, 302-326.

departed, amid the waving of handkerchiefs and the shedding of tears. It was, declared several of the soldiers, as tough and as tearful as when they first left their own homes and families in Schuylkill County. As the train cars pulled away, the soldiers doffed their caps and "cheered vociferously" until they were out of sight. The 48th Pennsylvania was heading back to the front and back to more active operations. But little could the men have known that this next campaign, while not the bloodiest, would nevertheless prove to be their most grueling, most tiresome, and most demanding of the entire war, particularly following immediately in the wake of their five-month-long sojourn in Lexington.

The 48th Pennsylvania's campaign in east Tennessee began with a seventeen-day, 221-mile march from Nicholasville, Kentucky, over rough, rugged, mountainous terrain, oftentimes on "rough, stony and generally troublesome" roads to Knoxville, where they arrived late on the afternoon of September 28. After so long and so wearying a march, the soldiers of the 48th spent the next few days resting and in exploring the city. They were generally impressed by Knoxville; "the whole place," wrote Oliver Bosbyshell, "indicated plenty and prosperity," while the surrounding countryside was "very beautiful." Especially heartening were the expressions and manifestations of support and loyalty from the people of east Tennessee. In early October, the regiment set out by rail and on foot on what proved to be a short, whirlwind campaign in the mountains of northeastern Tennessee and near to the Virginia state line, during which they participated in some supporting action at the Battle of Blue Springs. By nightfall on October 15, they were back at the campsites near Knoxville having covered a total of 97 miles by rail and 72 miles on foot in the past eleven days. Back in Knoxville, the men cheered the news of the reelection of Andrew Curtin as governor of Pennsylvania but events further south were not nearly as encouraging.[36]

On September 19-20, just three weeks after Burnside's triumphant entry into Knoxville, Confederate forces under Braxton Bragg routed General William Rosecrans's Army of the Cumberland at Chickamauga, some 120 miles southeast of Knoxville. Afterwards, Bragg's men pursued the retreating Federals and had them cornered at Chattanooga. Instead of striking again, however, Bragg settled in for a siege. Hounded by the authorities

36. Bosbyshell, 117-123.

in Washington to help the beleaguered Rosecrans, Burnside, in late October, began to shift his command south. His men only made it as far as Loudon and nearby Lenoir's Station, some twenty-five miles south of Knoxville, before new orders arrived instructing Burnside to remain where he was. The soldiers of the 48th thus settled in and proceeded to make themselves "as comfortable as possible." They remained at Lenoir's Station for the next three weeks.

It would be there, on the afternoon of November 10, where Lieutenant Curtis Pollock rejoined his command and resumed his duties with the 48th, his four-month stint helping to oversee the implementation of the draft in Vermont and Massachusetts having ended.

Pollock found the regiment comfortably quartered and pleasantly situated. The prevailing thought at that moment was that the men would spend the winter there but this was not to be, for Braxton Bragg had other ideas. In early November, with his men continuing to confront the trapped Union soldiers at Chattanooga and even as Federal reinforcements under Grant and Sherman were moving in, Bragg decided to detach a part of his army, under General James Longstreet, and send them north into east Tennessee. Bragg's hope was that Longstreet could quickly destroy Burnside's forces and then return to Chattanooga before Grant's reinforcing column arrived. Having played a critical role in the victory at Chickamauga, Longstreet objected strongly to these orders believing it would expose both his command and Bragg's to failure. But Bragg insisted and on November 4, Longstreet set out. He took with him two divisions of infantry, totaling some 12,000 men, and a 5,000-man division of cavalry. News of Longstreet's movement triggered panic in Washington, with the country's civil and military authorities now fearful of Burnside's safety. Burnside, however, sensed a great opportunity. Instead of falling back immediately to Knoxville, Burnside proposed he move forward, make contact with Longstreet's forces, then fall back slowly, doggedly, to Knoxville, drawing Longstreet after him and thus allowing Grant to strike at Bragg's reduced force at Chattanooga. It would be, said Oliver

The northwestern bastion of Fort Sanders, Knoxville, Tennessee. (From Battles and Leaders of the Civil War, *Vol. III)*

Bosbyshell of the 48th, "a mighty game of chess." Grant loved the idea and on November 14, Burnside set it in motion.[37]

The plan worked beautifully for the Union, with Longstreet taking the bait and embarking upon a chase that led him toward the strong Union positions at Knoxville and ever further away from Bragg at Chattanooga. The two sides came to blows first at Lenoir's Station then, more substantially, at Campbell's Station. Longstreet continually tried to get in between Burnside and Knoxville, but Burnside, correctly anticipating Longstreet's every move, never allowed this to happen. The weather was wicked—rain, sleet, and ice in near-freezing temperatures—and the roads back to Knoxville were veritable quagmires. Marching through the night on November 15 and 16, Burnside's men got little in the way of rest. They arrived safely back in Knoxville during the early morning hours of November 17 covered with mud and wholly exhausted. There, they took up positions in the impressive network of earthworks and fortifications that had been built under the direction of Burnside's chief engineer, Colonel Orlando Poe, and there, they awaited Longstreet's next move.

Longstreet led his men to Knoxville and, like Bragg had done at Chattanooga, he decided to settle in for a siege. But his men were never able to completely encircle the city and though much reduced, rations and supplies were still able to make their way to Burnside's men. Longstreet ultimately decided to attack but not before additional reinforcements arrived from Bragg. Days

---

37. Woodbury, 327-351; See also Earl Hess, *The Knoxville Campaign: Burnside and Longstreet in East Tennessee* (Knoxville: The University of Tennessee Press, 2013), and Alexander Mendoza, *Confederate Struggle for Command: General James Longstreet and the First Corps in the West* (College Station: Texas A&M University Press, 2008).; Bosbyshell, 127-140.

would pass before, finally, early on the morning of November 29, Longstreet struck. The result was disastrous for the Confederates. Concentrating their assault on the Union bastion known as Fort Sanders, Longstreet's men charged forward and were simply mowed down. In all, the attack lasted just over thirty minutes and, in the end, resulted in over 800 Confederate casualties. Burnside's losses that morning amounted to just 13 men killed and wounded. What was worse for Longstreet and his men, it was in the wake of this disastrous assault that word arrived confirming the rumors that Bragg's army had already been soundly beaten by Grant at Chattanooga (November 23-25). Rather than return to Bragg's forces in northern Georgia, Longstreet decided to remain in east Tennessee. In the meantime, Grant dispatched a force under General William T. Sherman, sending it to Burnside's relief in Knoxville. With news of Sherman's columns approaching, Longstreet retired to the northeast where he would ultimately settle in to winter quarters, being shadowed though not vigorously chased by elements of the Ninth Corps.

For the Federal forces in east Tennessee, the campaign against Longstreet was highly successful and for their commander, Burnside, an especially redemptive one. At the same time, it was grueling and thoroughly exhausting. Lieutenant Pollock and the veteran soldiers of the 48th endured the sleepless nights and the difficult marches along those slushy, almost impassible, roads. They were engaged at Campbell's Station and again during the siege of Knoxville. Upon returning to Knoxville, "hard work fell upon the men," as they plied picks and shovels to further strengthen the defensive lines surrounding the city. At the same time but in faraway Gettysburg, Pennsylvania, President Abraham Lincoln had delivered his immortal address, reminding the nation what, exactly, this war was all about and seeking to rally that nation to unite in order to carry out the unfinished work yet remaining. A week later, on November 26, the people of the North observed its day of Thanksgiving but for the men of the 48th in the trenches of Knoxville, there was no turkey, just quarter rations. Fortunately for the regiment, however, casualties were low. Throughout the entirety of the campaign, the regiment lost five men killed or fatally injured, eight wounded, and five more either captured or listed among the missing.

Following Longstreet's failed assault on Fort Sanders and his subsequent withdrawal toward Virginia, the soldiers of the 48th were among those who departed Knoxville and headed toward the mountains to the northeast, to keep a more careful eye on their gray-coated foes. There was some maneuvering, some elaborate games of chicken, but there would be no more substantial fighting—at least not against any Confederate forces. Instead, as the men finally set in to winter quarters near Blaine's Crossroads, Tennessee, they battled hunger, frigid temperatures, increasingly poor weather, and general war weariness. It was most assuredly a far cry from their idyllic spring and summer days in Lexington, the soldiers of the 48th now spent most of their days simply trying to keep themselves warm, huddling close to campfires and struggling to build adequate shelter. There they would spend yet another Christmas and another New Year's Day hundreds of miles away from their homes and families in Schuylkill County. The snow fell heavily that winter in the mountains of eastern Tennessee; the temperatures barely rising above freezing. It would be a season regimental historian Joseph Gould described as their "Valley Forge Winter." Sergeant William Wells of Company F declared that the condition of the men "was deplorable in the extreme." Still, the men did their best to keep their spirits up. As Wells later recalled, "Never did men bear greater hardships in camp life than did the troops in East Tennessee in the winter of '63-'64. Hungry, half-clad, shelterless and footsore, they bore all uncomplainingly for the land they loved so well and the flag they followed."[38]

Most of the talk in camp during that "Valley Forge Winter" revolved around the issue of reenlistment. For the soldiers of the 48th who had marched off to war in September 1861, their three-year terms of service were set to expire in September 1864. Not wishing to lose so many of its good and veteran soldiers, the government set out several inducements for those who would agree to serve another three-year term, including a bounty and a thirty-day furlough. It seems that at first, there was just a lukewarm reception to this within the ranks of the 48th but as it turned out, by early January 1864 more than three-quarters of its soldiers, including Lt. Pollock, chose to reenlist. For these men, this meant a much-needed and long-overdue visit home.

---

38. Gould, 147-153.

On January 13, Pollock and the men who decided to serve another "three years or the course of the war" term, departed their
chilly winter quarters and began the long journey home. This
journey first took them back to that Kentucky city they loved
so much and where so many pleasant memories were made:
Lexington. It was a joyful return— "like a homecoming," wrote
Oliver Bosbyshell. It would last just two "very happy and enjoyable" days, however, before the reenlisted veterans of the 48th
once more set out; this time, though, they would be heading
back to their real homes in Schuylkill County.[39]

Lieutenant Curtis Pollock's letters from east Tennessee are
sparse and in them, he barely mentioned the campaign and the
battles against Longstreet's forces. Having returned to the regiment on November 10, his next letter home—at least the next
one that survives in the collection—was penned on December
19. He would write but twice more before his return to Pottsville.
In his letters, Pollock talks about life in camp and about the "all
absorbing topic" of reenlistment. He also described how he spent
his Christmas, which, sadly as it turned out, would be his last.

———•◦•———

Camp in the Field about 20 miles
above (miles above) Knoxville Tenn
Dec 19, 1863

*D*ear Ma

We have just camped in the woods. On last Tuesday
night we were about 20 miles farther up the valley but just after dusk commenced our retreat, the Rebs after us. On Thursday we made a stand about a mile below where we are now but
they declined coming up. Our Brigade is in the advance and we
are doing Picket duty on the outside line. I do not know where
they are, but guess they are not a great distance off. We have a
large force in East Tennessee and if they give us battle I think
they will be whipped badly. The only thing that troubles us is
that our rations are short, we are now living on half rations. I
have been keeping a diary and as soon as we get settled down I
will copy it and send it on. I commenced it when we left Camp
Nelson up to the present time, with the exception of a few days

---

39. Bosbyshell, 141.

when nothing of interest happened. We have had a harder time and suffered more hardships than we have ever before since we have been in service, but still we hold up under it very well and if we only had enough to eat would get along very well. As for myself I have managed to get along very well between foraging and the commissary I have always had plenty to eat but the men do not get along so well. But in a few days we expect to be better supplied. It has been quite cold the last few days but I have managed to keep pretty warm. I have rec'd two letters from you since the siege has been raised the last one dated [December] 2nd which I rec'd yesterday. I think it will be safe to send that letter which came from Brattleboro. I think it must be from Miss Lawrence and likely has her photograph in it; put it in another envelope and send it on. [Edward] Flanagan and [John] Humble are standing here beside me and wished me to say they are well and have good appetites but not much to satisfy it. I expected, until within a few days, to spend my Christmas in Lexington but I am now beginning to think that I will enjoy it in the field. I have not seen my valise since I have left Camp Nelson and thought it was lost, but a few days ago I heard of its safe arrival in Knoxville and I expect it will be here in a day or two. Did you receive the letter I sent through before the siege was raised? It was sent by a Courier to Cumberland Gap and then mailed.

Lieut. Jackson is still in Knoxville but I expect he will be here before long. The night we made a stand, below here, it rained all night & we had no tents or blankets. I stood up by a fire all night and tried to make myself as comfortable as possible. Gen. Burnside has gone to Washington and Gen. Foster has assumed command.[40] We have two corps from Thomas and a division of cavalry.[41] Longstreet wants to attack us; I think he will have a warm reception. It is understood here that [Confederate General Richard] Ewell has reinforced Longstreet but I do not know how true it is.[42] We have a great deal of Cavalry in this department but they do not amount to much. They do not know how to fight. If they get into a skirmish and have one

---

40. Following the Battle of Fort Sanders, Ambrose Burnside, who had been battling illness, asked to be relieved of command of the Department of the Ohio. His request was granted and his place was taken by Major General John Foster.
41. General George Thomas replaced Rosecrans as commander of the Army of the Cumberland and two of his divisions were sent north to east Tennessee following the Battle of Chattanooga.
42. This proved to be a false rumor.

or two men wounded they call it a great battle. I believe I have told you all I know so I will close.

With much love to all, I remain
Your affectionate Son
C.C.P.

P.S. I ordered some photographs in Lexington and want some sent to Aunt Sarah in Milton & one sent to Anna Pollock in Williamsport and one sent to Mag. in Phila. I do not remember now whether I promised any more but do not give any out of the family. I would like to have one sent to Aunt Annie if she has none. Mary can exchange some of them with some of the girls, whose pictures I have not got. The two Wheelers for instance. As I believe I half promised to exchange with them. I have written this last by the light of the camp fire in front of my tent. We were paid the other day but there is no opportunity of sending it home. I drew $214.95 I will have plenty of work to do as soon as we get settled down. I have a lot of papers to make out and it is drawing near the end of the month and the muster rolls will have to be made out.

Hoping to hear from you soon
I remain
&c.
C.C.P.

Camp near Blane's Cross
Roads Tenn.
Dec. 26, 1863

Dear Ma

I am kept very busy at present making out Muster Rolls and a great many other papers that a Company Commander has to bother himself with. Christmas has passed, and a very dull one it was for me. The day before Christmas we were out and made a reconnaissance but the Rebs. had just left. I have never felt so tired as I did that night when we got back to camp. There has been a great deal of talk of the 9th Corps leaving Tennessee, since Burnside has left us, but now that has given way to the all absorbing topic, "reinlistment." They are trying to get our Regt. to reinlist, but with the exception of a few of the Companies they do not succeed very well. There are only two

men in G. who are willing to reinlist. I heard this evening that
there were one hundred and sixty-four in the whole Regt. The
Government offers all those who reinlist thirty days furlough
and the bounty. If three fourths of the Regt. enlist they will allow them to go home in a body, and those who refuse are to be
put in other Regt's and companies to do duty until their term
of service expires. I have no idea what we will do here now. The
Rebels have evidently left this immediate vicinity but whether
we are to follow them up or remain here I do not know. As soon
as I get through all the writing I have now on hand I will copy
my diary and send it to you. It has been raining nearly all day
and as we have nothing but the shelter tents to do everything
in, I have not gotten through much work. I received my valise
as a Christmas present and it is the only one I have rec'd. It
has been all this time on the way from Camp Nelson here. I
picked up a young contraband the other day. He run away
from the Rebs. when they evacuated before Knoxville. He says
his "Massa" is a private and had him with him to carry his
knapsack and other drudgery. He calls himself "Dick." He tells
some wonderful stories about what the Rebs do, but I think he
has a rather strong imagination.

I am quite anxious to get that letter that came to Pottsville
for me for I imagine there is a photograph in it. Did you ever get
any of those pictures of Reilly and myself. I should very much
like to have one. I suppose by this time Mary has arrived again
at home and I need not ask if she has enjoyed herself. How is
Marge and Charley getting along? I heard something about a
young man being seen with a young lady and after that she
could not be found. How is it?

> With much love to all I remain
> Your affectionate Son
> *C.C.P.*

Camp near Blaines Cross Roads Tenn
Jan. 1. 1864

*D*ear Ma
It is now nearly two weeks since we have received a mail
and I do not hear anything about our getting one. The regiment has nearly all reinlisted and it is expected we will start

for home in about two weeks. Co. G. has not done as well as other Companies only six having reinlisted.[43] Some of the other Companies have gone in a body. It is very cold to day and now as I am writing the ink freezes to the pen since I have to stop every few minutes to warm my hands. We have very changeable weather here, one day it is warm and pleasant and the next very cold. I have been on a Court Martial for the last few days the first one I have ever been on. Our rations are still very short but we manage to get enough around the country to make up the deficiency.

There is very little going on here in the way of news. We never hear anything, and I have not seen a paper for a long time. As to the Rebs, no one about here appears to know where they are and seem to care less. We are still doing Picket duty. One Regt from our Brigade are about to start for home in a day or two. (the 21st Mass.) They have all reinlisted. It is too cold to write so wishing you a Merry Christmas & Happy New Year I will close with much love to all.

I Remain Your Affectionate Son
C.C.P.

---

43. Pollock either received a false report or undercounted the number of Company G men who did reenlist, for far more than six did so.

CHAPTER EIGHT

"Wasn't That a Splendid Charge?"
February-August 1864

———•◆•———

O N WEDNESDAY, FEBRUARY 3, 1864, the people of Pottsville braved cold winter temperatures and turned out by the
thousands to welcome home the war-weary, veteran soldiers of
the 48th Pennsylvania Infantry. Many of these returning soldiers were their sons, husbands, fathers, and brothers whom
they had not seen since they first marched off to war more than
two-and-a-half years earlier. Having learned early that morning that the regiment would be arriving sometime during the
afternoon, the people of town made every preparation to give
the veteran soldiers a hearty welcome home. Streamers of red,
white, and blue ornamented the city, hanging from homes and
businesses alike, while American flags, both large and small,
were displayed everywhere throughout Pottsville. Banners bearing the names of all the great battles in which the regiment
saw action were draped along Centre Street while three large
medallions bearing the names "Nagle," "Burnside," and "Sigfried" were suspended from wires strung across Mahantango
Street. Finally, at 3:30 that afternoon, after much anticipation
and amidst a tremendous cheer and hearty applause, the train
cars carrying the returning heroes arrived, drawing to a halt at
the Mt. Carbon station on the southern end of town.[1]

For Curtis Pollock and the soldiers of the 48th Pennsylvania, now officially on their thirty-day furlough, the long journey
home had begun more than a week earlier and more than five
hundred miles away. On January 25, the soldiers bade farewell
to their friends and acquaintances in Lexington before setting
out on the Kentucky Central Railroad for Covington. There they
remained until the evening of January 31 when, said Captain

---

1. Bosbyshell, 142.

Bosbyshell, "the start for home began in earnest." The regiment made its way to Cincinnati where the men received their pay and where they boarded yet another train, which carried them through Columbus, Ohio, and then on to Pittsburgh, where they were treated to a "fine supper" provided by "the good people" of the city. Altoona, Pennsylvania, was reached early on the morning of February 2 and later that evening, the regiment arrived at the state capital of Harrisburg, where the men stretched their legs and bedded down for the night. Next morning, a special train was procured and the soldiers were eagerly on their way home. All along the route from Harrisburg to Pottsville, people turned out to wave and cheer on the men; it was, said Gould, "one continuous ovation." Finally, Pottsville was reached and amidst the cheering throng that had gathered, the regiment detrained, formed up into line in front of the elegant Mansion House and listened as Congressman James Campbell stood to deliver some welcoming remarks and to present to the regiment a new stand of colors that had been prepared by the ladies of Pottsville.[2]

"Officers and Soldiers of the 48th Regiment," exhorted Campbell, "I have been honored by the ladies of Pottsville, your sisters, wives, and mothers, with the pleasing duty of presenting this flag, guidons and markers, as their testimonial to and appreciation of your patriotism, bravery and devotion to the cause of the Union." Campbell asked that the regiment carry these new flags alongside the "tattered" ones they brought home with them, those that had been "rent in conflict, but of stainless honor." Over the past two years, continued Campbell, the people of Pottsville and of all Schuylkill County had been keeping the soldiers in their prayers and had "watched with sympathetic bosoms" the soldiers' "trials, bravery and suffering—the deadly struggle, the sufferings in hospitals, on the weary march and by the dreamless bivouac, all heroically borne" by the soldiers of the 48th. And while "they have shed tears for the gallant dead," they had turned out that day "with words of welcome and smiles of gratitude to greet their returning brothers and husbands." After a few more remarks, the regiment broke into three vigorous cheers. Colonel Sigfried thanked the people for their gift, promising that the new flags would either be returned from the field of battle in honor or not returned at all.[3]

2. Gould, 155-158; Bosbyshell, 141-144.
3. Gould, 158-159.

After this stirring ceremony the soldiers of the 48th paraded through the city to the cheers of the people who had gathered along the streets or from those who watched from windows or balconies above. At the head of this procession rode General James Nagle, the man who had originally raised and recruited the regiment and who had first led it into battle before a deteriorating heart condition forced his resignation from the army the previous May. Behind Nagle paraded the Pottsville Band, followed by soldiers who had been wounded in battle and earlier sent home on discharge, now led by Major James Wren, formerly of the 48th. Behind these wounded warriors marched the returning soldiers of the 48th, glad to be home, no doubt, and much heartened by the reception. "A more animated spectacle is rarely witnessed here," summarized the *Miners' Journal*. More than forty years later, regimental historian Joseph Gould still remembered the great ovation the regiment received upon its return, musing that "If monuments and pensions had been in order at this time every member of the 48th could have had a monument twelve feet high, with an eagle on top of it, promised to him when he would die and a pension of $20 or more per month for the balance of his natural life."[4]

The parade route took the men up Centre Street and to the Union Hotel where another welcoming speech was made, this one by Mr. John Bannan. And as he did in response to Campbell's address, Colonel Sigfried once more made a thankful reply, this time, however, he "spoke of the spirit that had animated his men in re-enlisting," and expressed his hope that the regiment could, by new volunteers, be recruited back up to its full strength when the furlough expired and when it returned to the war. With that, the soldiers then broke ranks and entered the hotel where they enjoyed a fine and welcoming dinner prepared by the women of Pottsville. Afterwards, noted Oliver Bosbyshell, "[t]he boys were dismissed, and each found home in the shortest space of time."[5]

For Lieutenant Curtis Pollock, home was but a short distance away. He had marched proudly at the head of his company as the men turned their heads left-and-right, hoping to catch a glimpse of their families and old friends who may have come out for the occasion. Most of the men from Company G were from Pottsville or from nearby St. Clair, so they arrived back

---

4. Ibid., 159-160.
5. Bosbyshell, 144.

to their homes much sooner than their comrades who hailed from such places as Minersville, Tamaqua, Schuylkill Haven, or Port Clinton. Yet no matter where they resided, all were glad to be back home, if only for thirty days, and all were no doubt happy as they bedded down in warm beds instead of on the cold ground and as they enjoyed hearty meals instead of their usual accustomed ration of hardtack and salt-pork.

The soldiers who returned home likely shared their stories from the battlefield and from the various campaigns that had thus far marked the regiment's history while at the same time they caught up with those whom they had been for far too long separated. For the past three years, young Curtis Pollock had been writing home regularly from the front but now he had the chance to tell of his experiences first-hand, either at the dinner table or in front of a warm fireplace. He may have told of the long marches, of the many miles the regiment traveled on foot, on water, and on rail, campaigning in North Carolina, Virginia, Maryland, Kentucky, and, most recently, in mountains of east Tennessee. Perhaps he spoke of the bloodshed, of the horrors of his combat experiences at 2nd Bull Run, Antietam, Fredericksburg, and Knoxville. And he may have told of the people he had met along the way, especially the pretty young ladies who had captured his heart and his attention while in Lexington. Young Curt also listened as his mother and father talked about what had gone on in Pottsville during his absence—of marriages and childbirths and even of the funerals of those he had known but who had since passed. He learned also of the opposition to the draft and the growing labor unrest that had broken out throughout the county over the past two years—in places such as Heckscherville and in other coal patches and farming communities between Pottsville and Minersville and Tremont—and about how volunteer soldiers from New York and New Jersey had been brought in to help restore order and, in some places, to impose martial law—and to keep those coal mines at peak operation. More importantly, though, Curtis Pollock listened as his younger brothers and sisters talked about all the growing up they did while he was away at war.

Although this was a furlough, there was some regimental business the officers had to attend to. As Colonel Sigfried stated from in front of the Union Hotel, it was his hope that the 48th could be recruited back up to full regimental strength. This cry would soon be taken up in the pages of the *Miners' Journal*: "The regiment had 340 men on its return, and we hope to see this gallant Schuylkill County regiment not only re-enlisted here, but to see it return under its able officers recruited up to its original strength. The 48th is unquestionably one of the finest infantry regiments in the service," boasted the *Journal*, "No better material ever left a community to fight for freedom and for the rights of men." Regimental headquarters was established in Pottsville. And there, throughout the month of February and into early March, a steady stream of new volunteers began to arrive, signing their names—some eagerly, others no doubt with a little trepidation—to the regimental rolls. Some came from Pottsville itself; others from Schuylkill County's near and distant towns, townships, and hamlets. Many were young; eighteen-year-olds or almost-eighteen-year-olds who were much too young to have enlisted when the first calls went out three years earlier in 1861 but who were now of fighting age. Some of these "new" volunteers had seen prior service, having previously served and having been honorably discharged from some of Schuylkill County's nine-month regiments, such as the 129th Pennsylvania. But no matter their motivations for doing so, enough of them had volunteered during that winter of 1864 for the 48th Pennsylvania to soon be recruited back up to nearly full strength.[6]

"While at home," reflected regimental historian Joseph Gould, "'the boys' enjoyed the relaxation from their nearly three years of hard and dangerous service, hugely." Yet, in what must have seemed like the proverbial blink-of-an-eye for many of the "boys," their thirty-days' furlough inevitably came to an end. Officially, their furlough expired on March 4 and on the following day, the soldiers—veteran and rookie alike—assembled in Pottsville. Once there, however, they received the welcome news that their leave was to be extended for two more days. Then, on March 7, after the soldiers assembled once again, they learned that their leave had been extended, this time for another week. So again, it was back to their homes or back to a local hotel or boarding house for these men, most of whom were no doubt pleased that they could now spend some additional time with their families. But that time would finally come to an end on

---

6. *Miners' Journal* article reprinted in Gould, 160.

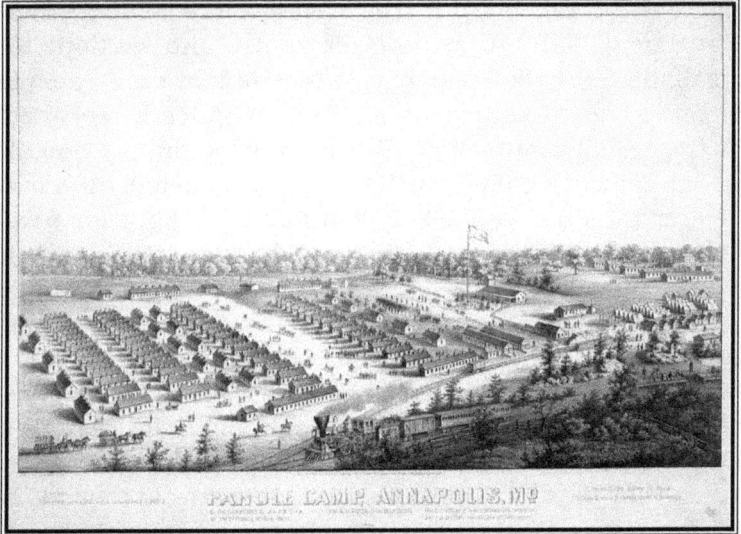

Camp Parole, Annapolis, Maryland. Once more returning to the "seat of war" following their furlough, the soldiers of the 48th Pennsylvania rendezvoused and spend several weeks in camp at Annapolis before embarking upon the bloody Overland Campaign. (Courtesy of the Library of Congress)

March 14. That day, the regiment assembled in Pottsville and paraded down Centre Street to the Mt. Carbon station. As they had when the regiment returned home six short weeks earlier, the people of Pottsville once more lined the streets, cheering on the men and waving flags. But this time it was a more somber, more tearful occasion, the people fully realizing that they may be saying goodbye to their sons, husbands, brothers, and fathers for the last time.[7]

It was on that March 14 that Curtis Pollock embraced his family and kissed his siblings goodbye for the final time, and if, on that Monday afternoon, his mother and father, and brothers and sisters had journeyed down to the train station to watch the young lieutenant climb aboard the train car, it would have been the last time they ever saw him alive.

The thought that this might be the case surely crossed William and Emily Pollock's minds, as it did for many of the people now waving their loved ones goodbye and bidding them farewell. Conversely, as the train began pulling away from Pottsville that late winter day, many on board surely felt that they may never see home again. The veteran troops were certainly more aware of

7. Gould, 160-161.

the dangers that lay ahead, once the ground thawed and warmer temperatures arrived, when active campaigning would once again commence. But not even the most seasoned, veteran soldiers on board those train cars could have ever imagined just how deadly and just how savage the fighting would be that spring, in the tangled Virginia Wilderness and on the crimson, blood-soaked fields of Spotsylvania, Cold Harbor, and Petersburg.

Yet all that bloodshed was still several weeks away. For the moment, the first stop for the 48th after they departed Pottsville was the state capital at Harrisburg, where they arrived late on March 14 as a heavy snow began to fall. Two days after the regiment's arrival there, Curtis resumed writing letters home.

Harrisburg
March 16th 1864

*D*ear Ma

We arrived here safely on Monday evening about 11 and were quartered in the Vol. Refreshment Saloon. I went to a hotel and we slept in a bed. The next morning we marched out to Camp Curtin and Camped just outside the camp. We at once commenced to pitch tents in the midst of a very heavy snow storm, which made it very uncomfortable. The storm however did not last very long and we soon got our tents all up.

We went down town again last evening and slept at the Hotel; however now we have a floor in our tent and a stove and there will be no necessity for us going down again.

Thad Boyle is here; I have seen him several times. It is reported in camp that probably Gen. Burnside will visit us today but he has not come yet. We will be very nicely fixed up in a day or two. Four officers and a number of men are going home recruiting today, but none of "G"'s officers. We have commenced drilling & this morning I had the company out for the first time for a long while. I will try and get this of[f] by this afternoon mail if I can.

It is quite cold now & if we did not have a fire we could scarcely stand it.

Write soon
Your Affectionate Son
C.C.P.

※※※

THE REGIMENT'S STAY in Harrisburg would prove a short one, as the men soon received orders to proceed to Annapolis, Maryland, where the various regiments and batteries of the Ninth Army Corps were directed to rendezvous. Departing Harrisburg on March 18, the soldiers set off first by rail to Baltimore and from there via steamer to Annapolis where they arrived the following day. The 48th would spend the next six weeks at Annapolis, wondering what their orders would be and speculating where the next campaign would find them. Lieutenant Pollock wrote frequent letters home during the regiment's stay at Annapolis, for it seems it helped him deal with the growing boredom at the regiment's inactivity. The weather during those six weeks was generally poor, mostly rainy, while drilling and guard duty was tedious and wearying. Worse, sickness began to spread, especially in the form of small-pox, which killed a number of 48th soldiers even before the shooting recommenced. By the middle of April, a feeling of homesickness took over Curtis and he began longing for home. He even began stating his disappointment that he had not resigned while home on furlough. He also began to grumble again about Col. Sigfried and especially about Lt. Col. Pleasants and, as he did two years earlier, he asked about the possibility of his father working to get him another assignment, specifically that of a staff officer as a general's aide-de-camp. But, yet, for all the "disagreeable weather," and despite the drilling and the complaints about "very little going on," there was some changes being made—some major, some minor—and many of them affected Pollock directly.[8]

While at Annapolis—at a place they dubbed Camp Hartranft, in honor of General John Hartranft who was placed in command of the rendezvous camp there—the soldiers of the 48th watched as other Ninth Corps regiments arrived—some were familiar, veteran ones; others, though, were brand new, having just been recently raised and organized. Among the latter were eight regiments of African-American soldiers, organized into an entire division of United States Colored Troops (U.S.C.T.) and officially organized as the Fourth Division, Ninth Army Corps. Burnside had requested the ranks of his corps be augmented with these black units and he welcomed them with pride. Watching these new soldiers drill caught the attention of the Schuylkill County

Born in Buenos Aires, Argentina, Lt. Col. Henry Pleasants assumed command of the 48th Pennsylvania in the spring of 1864. He and Pollock seemed to have had a sometimes strained relationship. Pleasants famously engineered the tunneling of the Petersburg Mine in the summer of 1864. He died in 1881 at age 47 and was buried in the Charles Baber Cemetery in Pottsville, very near to the Pollock family plot. (Courtesy of Mr. Ronn Palm and the Museum of Civil War Images)

men and many were skeptical about their ability to withstand combat. As Oliver Bosbyshell recalled, "many doubted whether the colored boys would prove faithful under fire," but this doubt was soon set to rest, noted Bosbyshell, "by their excellent work in the subsequent campaign."[9]

The all-black Fourth Division of the Ninth Corps, commanded by Brigadier General Edward Ferrero, was broken down into two brigades, each with four regiments. It was up to Burnside to decide who should lead these brigades and in early May, at the outset of the Overland Campaign, he called upon Colonel Joshua Sigfried of the 48th Pennsylvania, wanting him to take command of Ferrero's First Brigade. "I wanted you with the 4th Division," Burnside later told Sigfried, "because you were one of my best officers, and commanded my entire confidence and

---

9. Ibid., 147.

esteem." But Sigfried hesitated. He was honored by the invitation but taking command of an entire brigade of black soldiers was not an easy decision as there was a special risk involved for a white officer to do so, since the Confederate government had already made it known that any white officer captured in battle while leading black troops would be put to death on the grounds of inciting insurrection. Weighing more heavily on Sigfried's mind, however, was the thought of parting ways with the 48th, especially at the outset of a new campaign. Ultimately though Sigfried yielded and in early May he bade farewell to the soldiers of the 48th Pennsylvania, whom he had led for the past two years, and entered upon his new command. When Sigfried departed, Lt. Col. Henry Pleasants took command of the regiment.[10]

In Pleasants, Curtis Pollock and the soldiers of the 48th had a new commander. But Sigfried's elevation and transfer to brigade command would also have a more direct impact on the lieutenant. When Sigfried accepted Burnside's offer of command, he did so with the condition that he could select his staff officers. Burnside agreed and Sigfried tabbed Captain Oliver Bosbyshell to be his assistant-adjutant general. This left a vacancy at the head of Company G, a vacancy that would temporarily be filled by Lt. Curtis Pollock, since he was the company's next highest-ranking officer. He never received a formal promotion to captain, however; rather he would retain his rank of 1st Lieutenant but now have the added responsibility of commanding the entire company. He remained in such capacity through all the battles of the Overland Campaign, from the Wilderness to Cold Harbor and during the mid-June attacks at Petersburg.

There were other changes as well. In addition to a new commander, the soldiers of the 48th would also receive new rifles while at Annapolis, trading in their Enfields for the much better Springfield rifled-muskets. And it was there, at Annapolis, where the soldiers of the 48th got their first look at the newly-minted Lieutenant General and General-in-Chief of all United States armies, Ulysses S. Grant, when he toured the Ninth Corps's camps in mid-April alongside Ambrose Burnside.

Grant had come east after having orchestrated a number of impressive victories in the war's Western Theater. It was Grant

---

10. Samuel T. Wiley, *Biographical and Portrait Cyclopedia of Schuylkill County, Pennsylvania,* (Philadelphia: Rush, West and Company Publishers, 1893): pgs. 495-496.

*Lieutenant General Ulysses S. Grant, one of the principal archi-
tects of the Union victory in the Civil War. (Courtesy of the Library
of Congress)*

who had engineered the victories at Forts Henry and Donelson
and at Shiloh in 1862 and who, in 1863, captured Vicksburg
and smashed Bragg's Confederate army at Chattanooga. Now,
in early 1864 and just before the spring thaw and the return to
active campaigning, the forty-two-year-old general traveled to
Washington to accept his new rank and his new command and
to develop a new strategy, one that would, hopefully, end the
war once and for all. Fully aware of the importance of armies
working together, Grant planned to launch simultaneous offensive actions across the war's various theaters. General Nathaniel Banks, with an army of 25,000 men and assisted by a
naval fleet under Admiral David Farragut, was to move against
Mobile, Alabama, while General Franz Sigel, with 10,000 men,
was to move south, up the Shenandoah Valley, destroying Confederate resources, including the Virginia & Tennessee Railroad

while at the same time keeping a small Confederate army in check. Further south and east in Virginia, General Benjamin Butler would advance from Fortress Monroe and along the James River and head toward either Petersburg or, especially, Richmond, which Grant believed would be thinly defended. Tearing up rail lines and damaging resources, Butler's force was to threaten the Confederate capital and, if possible, take it. These three campaigns—under Banks, Sigel, and Butler— were intended to be secondary to the major thrusts launched by General William Tecumseh Sherman in Georgia and General George Gordon Meade in Virginia. Sherman was directed to dive deep into Georgia and set after Joseph Johnston's Army of Tennessee and the city of Atlanta. Like the other generals, Sherman was also directed to inflict as much damage on Confederate war resources as possible. Finally, in Virginia, Meade, the victor of Gettysburg and still the commander of the Army of the Potomac, would target General Robert E. Lee and his once seemingly unconquerable Army of Northern Virginia while driving toward Richmond from the north. "Wherever Lee goes," Grant told Meade, "there you will go also."[11]

Grant's plan was a good one, or, as Sherman said, an "enlightened one." By maintaining a relentless pressure across the board, Grant hoped to prevent the Confederates from taking advantage of their interior lines and inhibit their ability to shift and shuffle men to various fronts to meet individual threats, as had been the case throughout much of the war's first three years. And by doing as much damage as possible to its resources, Grant's hope was to cripple the Confederate effort at continuing to wage and support this already costly and destructive war. For his own part, Grant opted to travel along with Meade's army in Virginia rather than confine himself behind a desk in Washington. Meade had offered to resign but Grant would not allow it. Still, once the campaign commenced, it would be Grant, and not Meade, who increasingly called the shots. Grant's grand offensive was scheduled to begin on May 4, 1864, and the hope was that the war would be over within the next eight months, by November, and especially before the presidential election. 1864 was, after all, an election year and both Lincoln and Grant were hoping to wrap things up before the voters cast their ballots,

---

11. Donald Stoker, *The Grand Design: Strategy and the U.S. Civil War*, (New York: Oxford University Press, 2010), pgs. 351-353.

to help Lincoln's chances at re-election, of course, but also to ensure the nation would be preserved and slavery abolished before a new administration could take over in the event Lincoln was defeated.[12]

In his letters written during the regiment's six-week stay at Annapolis in early 1864, Curtis Pollock wrote of seeing Grant and recorded his impressions of the man who would ultimately engineer the Union's victory. Pollock also noted the return of those members of the regiment who did not re-enlist and who thus spent the entire of winter of '63-'64 in the cold, snowy mountains of east Tennessee instead of at home on furlough. He also wrote of the arrival of new recruits and he spoke of the new weapons, the black soldiers, the lousy weather, his homesickness and boredom, of the problems he had encountered with a few of his superiors, and of all the things he did to help pass the time, which ran the gamut from singing songs to reading Shakespeare, from attending a circus and, of course, to writing letters to his "Dear Ma":

                                        Camp Hartranft Annapolis Md
                                              March 29th 1864
*D*ear Ma
        Your letter of the 25th was duly rec'd and I was very glad to hear from you as I had been expecting to hear from you for some time. I am very sorry to hear Mary is so sick, write immediately and let me know how she is. There is very little going on here now except drilling. We have four drills a day and I attend nearly all of them. I do not know whether I have told you that Capt. Bosbyshell has left us again & I am again in command of the company. It is very stormy to night and the wind shakes the tent so that I can hardly write. Mrs. Bosbyshell came on last evening and is down town with Capt. I have not seen her yet. I wrote a long letter to Lizzie Lawrence the other day also one to Maggie Shaw. I also wrote to Margie. I was down town to Church on Sunday for the first time I have been out of Camp since we arrived here. There are some very pretty young ladies here I understand, but I have not seen any of them yet.

12. Ibid.

We now have quite a large company and new recruits coming in nearly every day. We received three today. The weather has been very bad since we have been here. One very heavy snow storm and two or three heavy rains. & I think before morning it will rain again. Our new recruits are learning very fast but as yet we have no muskets for them. All the men that we left back in Tennessee are to be sent to us again but I do not know how soon they will arrive. We have not heard anything about going away yet. There was another Negro Regiment come in to day, all armed and equipped. I will not be able to send any money home now as I will require all I have to keep us in provisions until the paymaster arrives, Lt Jackson being entirely broke. I think the paymaster will be along in a week or so, in that case I will send the money immediately. Dan McGinnes goes home tomorrow. Maj. Gilmour arrived today but brought no letter for me. It is now blowing & raining quite hard, but if our tent will only stay up it will make very little difference to me. We have very comfortable quarters with, stove floor and bunk and I can devote my time to-morrow to writing if it keeps on raining.

With much love to all
I Remain Your Affectionate Son
C.C.P.

Write soon.

——————•◦•——————

Camp near Annapolis Md
April 1st 1864

*D*ear Ma

As John Reagan[13] goes home tomorrow on a five day furlough I will send a few lines by him. We are getting along very nicely here in camp & I have only been down town once since we arrived. Capt. Bosbyshell's wife is here but I have not seen her yet. I would like you to send back with Reagan "East Lynne" and Orpheus C Kerr's papers[14] as we have very little reading matter here. I intended to bring them with me but forgot it. It is raining again today but not very hard. Col. Pleasants has gone to Lexington on a seven days leave. Some say he is to be

---

13. Jno. J. Regan: Private, Company G, 48th Pennsylvania. Enlisted 2/26/1864, age 21; Mustered Out 7/17/1865.

14. *East Lynne* was a best-selling English novel authored by Ellen Wood and published in 1861. Robert Newell, an American author and humorist, authored *The Orpheus Kerr Papers*, which was a collection of fictional letters and articles written by Newell under the pseudonym "Orpheus C. Kerr," and which were largely satirical and comical in nature.

married, he did not say a word to me about his going before he started. I think he might have at least told me he was going.[15]

I have not had any letters except from you since I left home. Which I think is very strange. I wrote to Henrietta Wheeler last night thanking her for her photograph. If it is not for writing now-a-days I do not know what I [would] do with myself and I have written more letters since I left home than I have done before for a long time. I have not gotten over the effects of being home yet and I often wish I could get back again—but there is no chance of my coming home now even for a few days as I could not have sufficient reason on which to ground an application for a leave. I suppose all the girls are getting along old fashioned. Does Sallie Loeser come up on the hill as usual? Give her my regards. I have just had supper and we did not have any Dress Parade on account of the rain.

I do not know of anything else to tell you so I will close.

With much love to all
I remain
Your Affectionate Son
C.C.P.

Write soon.

⎯⎯⎯•◆•⎯⎯⎯

Camp Hartranft
Annapolis, Md
April 5th 1864

*M*y Dear Ma

I received your letter in due time and was much pleased to hear Mary is so much better and hope she will soon be entirely well again. I received a letter from Lexington the other day. I have not heard from Miss Lawrence yet. I do not see why she is so long answering my letter.

There is very little going on here. I was down town Tuesday evening and spent it with Mrs. Bosbyshell.

We have had very disagreeable weather for some time now. It has been raining ever since yesterday afternoon and looks as if it would keep up all night. I have been on guard today but

---

15. In 1860, and after just a few months of marriage, Pleasants lost his first wife, Sallie Bannon, when she died of an unknown ailment at the age of 31. This thrust Pleasants into a deep depression and, according to family lore, he had entered the army in 1861 in the hopes of being killed on the battlefield. But in 1863, while stationed in Lexington, Kentucky, Pleasants met and fell in love with Annie Shaw. Presumably, the two were married in the early spring of 1864.

have not seen much of my guard. It has been so wet that we only had a few men on post so I let them get along themselves the best they could. Margie has been having decidedly a gay time. Did she tell you everything Underhill told her? I suppose he was stuffing her up with some of his nonsense. I would like Mary to try and get Emily Baber to give me her photograph in exchange for one of mine. I should like to have it very much. There are no signs of our getting paid yet but I do not think it will be long before we will. Lt. Jackson has applied for a leave of Absence for 15 days and I guess he will get it. It has to go to New York to be approved by Gen. Burnside.

We have had a good deal of small pox in the Regt. since we arrived here but the cases are taken immediately away to the small pox hospital which is situated on an Island in the river.[16]

We have had no drills today on account of rain. I expect Col. Pleasants will be back in a day or two, his time now having nearly expired. I have been lounging around camp all day, hardly knowing what to do. The stove in my tent has been smoking nearly all day. Making it very unpleasant in the tent so I loafed around to other tents whose fires did not smoke. It is now after taps and I expect to go to bed in a few minutes. We have been in the habit of singing a great deal to pass away the long evenings but have not done any to night

Hoping to hear from you soon
I remain
Your Affectionate Son
C.C.P.

———•◦•◦•———

Camp 48th Pa. Vet. Vols.
Annapolis Apr 13. 1864

*M*y Dear Ma

I received your two letters since writing. I have been intending to write since last Sunday but have been putting it off from day to day.

There has been very little going on since I last wrote. I did not get down town last Sunday. Last evening I went down to the circus which is now here. We have a new doctor his name is

---

16. As it was in all Civil War camps, disease was, indeed, prevalent in the camps of the 48th PA at Annapolis. As Pollock noted, many fell ill and at least eight soldiers of the regiment died of disease during their six-week stay there.

Smyser from Norristown. He is a very fine fellow. He graduated with Charley Dougal in Phil. a short time ago.[17] Gen. Grant & Burnside went through camp today. We were all drawn up to receive them. Gen. Grant is a small, common looking man; [he] had quite a shabby coat on and Major Gen. shoulder straps. The same ones I suppose he had before he was appointed Lt. Gen. Burnside looks just the same as ever and we get to like him more & more every day. It seems strange how it affects everybody when ever he makes his appearances. as for me my blood seems to course faster through my veins whenever I see him.

We gave them three cheers but persons standing outside said when we gave the three for Burnside, they were the loudest.

Sergt. Jones has his wife here now and I have given them up my hut. It is rather disagreeable for me but I do not object to it. Lieut. Jackson has gone home on a 15 day leave & promised me he would call. Very likely he has been there by this time. Nearly all the men we left in Tennessee are now here but have not yet been sent back to the Regt. but I suppose they soon will be. A new Chaplain has been appointed for our Regt. and he arrived a few days ago. He is a Methodist I think, and a pretty smart man.[18]

Col. Sigfried and the officers who were with him at home returned to night. I have not seen them yet. Dan McGinnes,[19] I suppose you know, has resigned and is now at home.

You have been mentioning to me in every letter since I left home about that money I owe Will. You know well enough if I had it I would send it at once. Please do not mention it again as I am almost sick of hearing it. Col. Sigfried has arrived now & I think we will soon be paid.

Hoping to hear from you soon
I remain Your Affectionate Son
C.C.P.

---

17. Dr. Eugene M. Smyser (1842-1916) graduated from the University of Pennsylvania in 1864. On April 8, 1864, Smyser entered service as Assistant Surgeon in the 48th Pennsylvania Infantry and remained with the regiment until war's end.

18. Levi B. Beckley (1823-1895), a Methodist minister from Schuylkill Haven, PA, arrived in Annapolis and was mustered into service as the regimental chaplain of the 48th Pennsylvania at the rank of captain on April 11, 1864. He remained in this position with the regiment until the end of the war. Joseph Gould remembered Beckley fondly in *The Story of the Forty-Eighth*, writing that he "proved to be an able person, a fluent, emphatic expounder of the Gospel, and an intensely loyal, patriotic man."

19. Daniel D. McGinnes was serving as the regimental adjutant when he tendered his resignation on March 18, 1864.

If Mary thinks I do not want to hear from her tell her not to write. I rec'd Margie's letter to day & will answer it tomorrow. I am glad to hear of Mary's recovery. With much love to all; write soon.

Your Affectionate Son
C.C.P.

———————•◦•———————

Apr. 21st 1864

*M*y Dear Ma
        I have just rec'd your letter and am grieved to learn you are in such bad spirits. We are just on the eve of our departure for some unknown land & I am very busy. Capt. Bosbyshell is on Gen. Potter's staff and I understand it is to be a permanent appointment.[20] Could you not get enough influence to bear to get me a Staff appointment from the President? I am sick & tired of this Regt. for we are all used like dogs. I would like an appointment as Aide de Camp. I think I could get it with a little trouble. Pleasants is hard enough to get along with but you know what Sigfried is. The 21st Mass have orders to start on Saturday morning at 4 O'clock. Margie is not very confidential. Though she told me a good deal about Underhill.

I was never more surprised in my life than when I heard of Frank Campbell's death. When I last saw him he seemed perfectly well again. I have some photographs taken here and enclosed find one for Emily Baber. I think they are pretty good. We received new arms. The Springfield Musket is a very superior arm. There are now 78 men in the company and are learning to drill very fast. I would like very much to see you on here but you would scarcely have time to come now as we will all leave here in a day or two. I am very much obliged to you for correcting my mistakes and hope you will always mention any mistakes I make. You do not wish me home any more than I would like to be there.

I sometimes wish I had resigned while I was home on furlough. I mentioned my liking to leave to service in one of my letters to Liz and rec'd a very patriotic letter in return. She said she hoped never to hear of my carrying it into action., that the Union was as worth fighting for now as [it was] in

———

20. General Robert B. Potter commanded the Second Division, Ninth Corps; Bosbyshell's appointment as an officer on Potter's staff officer was only a temporary one.

the beginning. I have had one letter from Miss L. but not from Maggie Shaw. I have been rather down hearted these last few days but I guess I will get over it in the excitement of an active campaign.

With much love to all.

I Remain Your Affectionate Son
C.C.P.

✳ ✳ ✳

CURTIS'S MOTHER, EMILY, responded immediately to this last letter her son wrote from Annapolis in which he told her how "down hearted" he had become and how he sometimes wished he had resigned from the army. She did her best to offer some comfort, asking him to "try and keep a good heart" and reminding him that his country needed him and that he was at his "post of duty" and that they must bear the sacrifices while the nation was at war.

———————

Pottsville
April 25 1864

My dear Curt,

Your letter was received on Saturday and as Col. Sigfried and Jack Humble leave this morning, I have risen earlier than usual to have this ready to send by them. Mary wrote to you several days ago—expecting to send it with Humble—but as he did not go as soon as he expected, it will be sent this morning with mine. This is a rainy unpleasant morning and I hope you are not having such weather as this. I regret to hear you are not satisfied with your position in the Regiment. We would like very much to get you the appointment you desire, if possible. But we don't know how to go about it. Mr. Campbell is in so much trouble now I don't like to mention it to him, and as he exerted himself in your behalf before—don't like to trouble him again. I wish Oliver [Bosbyshell] could have remained in command of the company. I think it is a responsible position for you but I hope you will endeavor to do your duty and give satisfaction. Whatever business you are obliged to attend to, always be in time, don't procrastinate. You have the name of being lazy but I hope you will lose it by your good conduct here after. Pa says if you wish us to use any influence in your behalf you must send some money home; that nothing can be done without money now-a-days. He has just come downstairs and told me to tell you this.

You will be surprised to learn that your Pa has left the Lumber Yard, and is attending to the Coal business. He has charge of a Colliery beyond Mill Creek about four miles from here and is to have a salary of eighteen hundred dollars which is certainly better than a thousand. I hope he will get along well with it and give satisfaction.

We have a cow and a Calf and I suppose will have plenty of milk when the calf is sold.

There was a large Confirmation at our church the other night, about thirty persons were confirmed. Mr. Baker & Emily, Mr. Heylinger, Kate & Ida Brooks, Mr. Bright & Sally and Col Dewees who is present sojourning in this region, and attending to the gardens & asparagus beds.

There is to be a reading and Charades to-morrow night at Andrew Russell's for the benefit of the Sanitary Fair. Price of admission twenty-five cents. Col. Dewees has invited Mary and I purchased two tickets for Jule and Jim. Sally Bright, Loeser Brooks, Lucy Whiting are the parties who perform.

I feel in much better spirits than when I wrote you before, and hope you are feeling better too. Try and keep a good heart, I think Miss Julie is right. You are at the post of duty and your country needs your services although it is rather hard for us at home. But we must be willing to make some sacrifices and if you have your health and pass safely thru the perils of this war, I shall be truly thankful. We must be more patriotic Curt, you and I both. I hope you will not go where we shall not hear from you frequently. Try and write often.

Margie wrote Mary and I quite a letter about Underhill. She declares she don't care anything about him and will burn his letters if she receives any more.

Mary and all the family send much love.

Your affectionate Mother
E.C.P.

❄ ❄ ❄

IT WOULD BE a few days before this letter and those encouraging words reached Curt, for, as he had indicated, the regiment was on the eve of the new campaign, the one that had been engineered and developed by Grant. The soldiers of the 48th were not quite sure where they would next be assigned, having already seen service with various armies in North Carolina, Virginia, Maryland, Kentucky, and Tennessee. Their questions were finally answered and all the speculation settled when, in late April, Burnside's Ninth Corps received orders to join up with the Army of the Potomac in northern Virginia. After six weeks, the 48th Pennsylvania at last broke camp at Annapolis and on April 23 set out for Washington, arriving there on the morning of April 25. Later that day the Ninth Corps proudly paraded through the heart of the capital, being cheered on by hundreds of the city's residents lining the streets. At noon, Pollock and the soldiers of the 48th Pennsylvania once more caught sight of President Lincoln who was standing upon the balcony of Willard's Hotel, along with Ambrose Burnside and "other distinguished men." Oliver Bosbyshell remembered that, "All day long tramped the men of the Ninth Corps—their splendid bearing calling forth enthusiastic cheers from the thousands of people gathered to witness the pageant."[21]

In all, the regiment marched eleven miles that "very hot day," passing through Washington and finally arriving at Alexandria, Virginia, where they went into camp. It was a busy time for the regiment, and on April 27, Lt. Pollock had only the time to scribble out these few lines to his mother:

------◆◆◆------

Camp near Alexandria Va
April 27, 1864

My dear Ma
    We are just on the eve of marching & I think we are going to the Army of the Potomac. I am well & all right. The mail is to be stopped for 60 days I have time to write no more.
Your Affectionate Son
C.C.P.

❄ ❄ ❄

THAT EVENING AND well into the night Pollock and the men of the 48th marched twelve miles from Alexandria to Fairfax Court House, to the very same camping grounds the regiment had used following the retreat from 2nd Bull Run two summers

---

21. Bosbyshell, 146-147; Gould, 174.

earlier. Heavier marching was required of the men the following day, April 28, and it was becoming increasingly more difficult for the officers to keep the ranks closed up as the temperatures continued to rise and especially since there were now so many rookie soldiers in the ranks, soldiers who were unaccustomed to the long and wearying marches. A march of fourteen miles brought the 48th through Manassas and all the way to Bristoe Station. The road behind them, said regimental historian Joseph Gould, was "strewn with blankets, overcoats and other clothing" the men had tossed aside during the day, to lighten their load. The soldiers got a welcome respite at Bristoe Station, where they remained for the next few days mainly performing railroad guard duty.[22] On April 30, Curtis Pollock found the time to pen a lengthier letter home. He told of the regiment's jubilant parade through Washington, of the difficulties of the march, and of an unfortunate encounter he had with Lt. Col. Henry Pleasants.

Camp at Bristoe Station Va.
April 30th 1864

My Dear Ma
        Yours and Mary's letters came duly to hand the day we laid near Alexandria and I was much pleased at receiving so long a letter. I wrote you a few lines on our leaving Alexandria but did not have time to write any more. We have been marching steadily since our departure from Annapolis but I have been getting along remarkably well. We have relieved the Penna. Reserves who have been doing duty along the Rail Road and our Corps is now scattered along in its stead. I suppose we are to keep up communications and act as a reserve at the same time to the Army of the Potomac. We are very comfortably situated; our camp is on the top of a hill commanding the country for several miles around. Our passage through Washington was quite a triumphant one. We were cheered considerably and all the windows of the houses were filled with ladies who waved their pocket handkerchiefs very assiduously, and I received sweet smiles from several of them and a special wave.
        I have at last received the crowning stroke from Col. Pleasants. The evening of the first day's march when we arrived in Camp, he publicly insulted me grossly.

---

22. Gould, 174-175.

We were marched very hard for the first day and though I had nothing to carry, it was as much as I could do to keep up, and what could I do to the men who had their heavy knapsacks on? A great many of them gave out, and I was commanding the Company, Capt. Bosbyshell being Officer of the day. I came into Camp with Comparatively few men, he [Pleasants] rode up to me and swore I was not fit to command a Company and several other insulting remarks loud enough to be heard nearly all through the Regt. I told him that I could not help it if they marched the men so hard as to make them so tired they had to fall out. I have not had any thing to say to him since, except what I could not possibly nor do I intend to have as long as I am with the Regt., which I hope will not be long. Col. Sigfried is commanding the Brigade, Gen. Potter being sick. Capt. B. is on Picket tonight & Lieut. Jackson, who has just gotten back, is on Camp Guard so I have the Tent all to myself to night. I was on Picket night before last but had a very quiet time. The country about here is so much infested with guerillas that it is unsafe to go a mile from Camp alone. However there is no incentive to leave, for the country about here is entirely exhausted. I will answer Mary's letter in a day or two. So with much love to all.

I Remain Your Affectionate Son
Curtis

※ ※ ※

THE 48TH PENNSYLVANIA remained at Bristoe Station until May 4; that "fateful Fourth of May," as regimental historian Bosbyshell wrote, for that was the day designated by Grant as the jumping-off date for his great, grand offensive. On that Wednesday, hundreds of thousands of Union soldiers would be on the move, all throughout the South. Spring, at last, had arrived and with it would commence what proved to be the bloodiest and most destructive of all the four years of America's fratricidal conflict. The casualties—particularly those that would be sustained in Virginia over the course of the next five weeks—were simply appalling and unlike anything the nation had ever before experienced. From the start of the campaign through the second week in June, in Virginia alone, nearly 100,000 soldiers in blue and grey fell. Yet Grant knew and understood the frightful arithmetic; the Union could much more easily replace its casualties while the Confederacy simply could not. Soon this war would become

Panoramic view of the Battle of Spotsylvania as it appeared in Frank Leslie's Illustrated newspaper. (Courtesy of the Library of Congress)

one of horrific attrition. Despite the losses and despite the evergrowing criticisms from newspapers and from those on the home front, Grant would not be deterred. Despite some tactical setbacks, he did not back away. Rather, he continually led his army south and continually went after Lee, confident that this new strategy, bloody though it may have been, would ultimately end the war and bring peace at last to the shattered nation.[23]

When the soldiers of the Army of the Potomac first began crossing the Rapidan River on May 4, it inaugurated what historians have long since dubbed the Overland Campaign, a grueling, tremendously bloody forty-five-day campaign that ended outside of Petersburg, Virginia. All along the ninety-mile route from the Rapidan to Petersburg the fields were stained red with blood while thousands of freshly-dug graves dotted the landscapes. And wherever the soldiers of both armies traveled, they dug deep into the Virginia soil. They also felled trees for use in constructing earthworks and building defensive fortifications that proved nearly impregnable to frontal attacks. From the outset of the campaign the combat was constant, relentless. In years past, the two armies would slug it out, then back away from one another and the major battles occurred once every few weeks or even every few months. Those days were now gone and a new kind of war emerged. Now, it was *every* day that the men were on the front lines, subjected to artillery and to sharpshooters' fire, while the major pitched battles now became a frequent occurrence. It began on May 5-6 at the Wilderness, then continued from May 8-21 at Spotsylvania, on May 23-26 along the banks of the North Anna River, then further south to Totopotomoy Creek and Cold Harbor, where the two sides confronted one another

23. Stoker, 368.

A school teacher from St. Clair, Pennsylvania, Lt. Henry Clay Jackson was a respected member of Company G, 48th Pennsylvania. Captured at 2nd Bull Run, wounded at Fredericksburg and again at Knoxville, Jackson was killed in action at the Battle of Spotsylvania on May 12, 1864. His remains were interred at the Fredericksburg National Cemetery. (Courtesy of Mr. Ronn Palm and the Museum of Civil War Images)

from May 30-June 12, after which Grant shifted his thinking and his strategy, focusing even further south and deciding to strike at Petersburg, one of the last major transportation and supply hubs for the Confederacy. The fighting there began on June 15, 1864, and would continue for the next three days with Grant's men launching a series of frontal assaults against well-entrenched Confederate soldiers, who were taking advantage of a well-designed maze of earthworks, trenches, and fortifications. The lines could not all be carried and, seeing the slaughter, Grant, on the night of June 18, settled his army into the trenches. And there they would remain for the next ten months, until April 2, 1865, when, at last, Lee's ever-thinning, ever-lengthening lines collapsed under the weight of a massive assault.

The 48th Pennsylvania Infantry—forming part of the Second Division, Ninth Army Corps—would be heavily engaged throughout the entirety of the Overland Campaign and would sustain heavy casualties. Losses suffered by the regiment at the

Wilderness, Spotsylvania, Totopotomoy Creek, the North Anna, and at Cold Harbor, totaled nearly 300 men, killed or wounded, including some of the regiment's best soldiers and officers and a good number of Lieutenant Pollock's friends. Those who survived the slaughter did their best to try and make sense of the army's movements and of Grant's intentions. They also did their best to make sense of this new kind of war with all its attendant carnage. They quickly grew weary and exhausted, both physically and mentally, their bodies and their minds taxed and tested as never before. Yet through it all, Lieutenant Pollock tried to find the time to write to his "Dear Ma." With the constant maneuvering and near constant fighting, however, Pollock's letters became less frequent. Indeed, only six letters written by Pollock during the Overland Campaign survive. The first of these was penned on May 16, nearly two weeks after the regiment first crossed the Rapidan and just four days after the horrific slaughter that was Spotsylvania. On May 12, in its attacks there against Heth's Salient, the 48th Pennsylvania lost 129 men. It would prove, in terms of numbers lost, to be the regiment's second worst battle of the war, behind only 2nd Bull Run, where they lost over 150 men, mostly captured or missing.[24] Among the slain at Spotsylvania was Pollock's friend and fellow officer Lt. Henry Clay Jackson of Company G. Pollock's letters home during this campaign came to resemble a roster of the killed and wounded as he reported on those lost, gunned down on the fields of Spotsylvania or Cold Harbor or along the Totopotomoy Creek.

In the Rifle Pits near
Spottsylvania CH
May 16th 1864

My Dear Ma
        We have just been told that a mail would leave today, and though I have written but yesterday I will write you a few lines to day, for fear that the letter should not reach you.[25] Lt. Jackson was killed on the 12th; he was lieing quite near me when he was shot and was hit in the neck just above the collar bone. He did not live more than 15 minutes after being hit. I

---

24. Gould, 174-186; Bosbyshell, 148-150.
25. Pollock's letter of May 15, 1864, has not been found within the collections of the Historical Society of Schuylkill County. Perhaps, as he had feared, the letter never did reach home

had him carried out immediately and he was afterwards buried by Wm. Atkinson who took all his things.[26] We are lieing here holding our position. I would like to know what Grant is going to do. It has been raining for the last five days and the roads are in a very bad condition, perhaps that has something to do with our being here so quietly. On the 12th the 2nd Corps captured 8000 prisoners and 40 pieces of Artillery and 39 stands of Colors. They surprised the Rebels before they were awake and walked right over them. I saw Capt. Mintzer from Pottstown on Saturday he came around to see me but had no news.[27] Everything that is going on is kept very quiet. We have heard the rumor of the capture of Richmond but do not know whether to believe it. We have also heard of Sherman's success in Georgia. We have been lieing in the same position for the last five days although the positions of some of the other troops have been changed. I will write you every opportunity.

With much love I remain
Your Affectionate Son
C.C.P.

Co. G lost 2 killed and 9 wounded in the fight of the 12th and on the 6th we had 2 wounded, and on the 11th one was

---

26. The death of Henry Jackson would be deeply felt in the regiment. "Lieut. Jackson was a noble fellow, and idolized by his men," wrote Joseph Gould. Robert Reid of Company G echoed Gould's sentiment when he wrote of the death of Henry Clay Jackson. "Among the many killed" at Spotsylvania, said Reid, "none was more deeply regretted than Lieut. Henry Jackson." In his own regimental history, Oliver Bosbyshell, who had served alongside Jackson from the very start, wrote that the lieutenant was an "able and fearless officer, much liked in the regiment." Jackson was a school-teacher from St. Clair. He was 24-years old when the war began and stood 5'7½" in height. He rose steadily in rank and, along the way, happened to find himself among the casualties at most of the regiment's battles. He was captured (and later exchanged) at 2nd Bull Run, wounded at Fredericksburg, and wounded again at Knoxville. On May 12, 1864, at Spotsylvania, Lieutenant Jackson was advancing next to Sgt. William Auman of Company G. "He was struck in the neck by a rifle ball," related Auman. "I helped to carry him out. He died while we were carrying him to the hospital. When he was struck he fell against me. I asked him where he was hit; he whispered, 'I don't know,' and then his head fell to one side, and I saw that he was dying. He never spoke again." In the 1865 publication *Memorial to the Patriotism of Schuylkill County*, the editors included biographical sketches of many of the county's prominent Civil War soldiers. Among those highlighted was Lt. Jackson and in speaking of his death, it was written: "Thus fell Lieutenant Jackson, faithful to every duty, and though sensible of danger and perils, yet braving them with heroic disregard of self. He had determined if life were spared to remain in the army till the last organized force of the rebellion was overthrown. Gifted with a vigorous physical organization, considerable energy, a clear and active mind, ready utterance, strict integrity, and withal modest and affectionate, his friends had high hopes of his success in a civil profession, but he was reserved by Providence to be one of the numerous martyrs in behalf of the preservation of the Union, and the honor and free institutions of our country." Lt. Jackson's final resting place remains in the Fredericksburg National Cemetery. (Gould, 179-181; Wallace, 529).

27. Pollock may be referring to Captain William Mintzer of the 53rd Pennsylvania Infantry, Second Corps.

wounded by a chance shot.[28] Capt. Bosbyshell is with Col. Sigfried in the Negro Brigade. Col.[Sigfried] is commanding the Brigade and Capt. [Bosbyshell] is Asst. Adjt. Gen. Wm. Williams was the other man killed. None of the men you know are hurt. John Hodgson is all right and I do not know of any in the Regt. being hurt that you know. Dick Jones was grazed with a ball but not of much account. He has gone to Washington. We are very strongly entrenched here and so are the Rebs. and when a break is made some one will have to suffer. Our rations have been rather short to day on account of the roads. The wagons not being able to get up.

I believe there is nothing more to tell you.

Your Affectionate Son
C.C.P.

There were 136 killed and 1 wounded in the Regt. since fight began.[29]

***

CURTIS'S MOTHER EMILY, wrote in response to her son's letter of May 16, in which she lamented the death of Jackson and implored young Curtis to be careful and to look to God for solace and protection.

Pottsville
May 21 1864

My Dear Son,

We were very much pleased yesterday to receive a letter from you giving an account of your later movements and losses. We all regretted to hear [of] Jackson's death but are very thankful that you sustained no injury. After every battle always try and let us know who are killed and wounded. It is a great satisfaction to the friends here. Capt. Bosbyshell always did it, and Mrs. Hutten came up to us and wanted to know if we had heard particulars from you. I am sorry you have lost

28. Company G's casualties at Spotsylvania on May 12 totaled four men killed or mortally wounded and nine men wounded.
29. These include the casualties sustained at the Wilderness and on the road south to Spotsylvania.

Capt Bosbyshell and if I was him I would not fancy being in the Negro Brigade. I expect you will have some severe fighting yet—but somewhere there is an over-ruling Providence who can protect you as well on the Battlefield as at home. Trust in Him always and may you be ever enabled to do your duty as a soldier and a Christian. Do not be rash, however. I trust you may never fall into their hands a prisoner. It seems to me, the vengeance of Heaven will surely overtake and fall heavily upon those wretches for their treatment of our poor prisoners. No savages could be more brutal than they have been, for what can be worse than a slow death by starvation.

I have been to the city lately to see Margie, and invest the money left me by Uncle George, Margie has not been well. I shall be glad when the time is up for her to come home. I do not like the school at all. It is too strict for her.

Mr. Sidenham, your Grandpa's [successor] is to be married next month to Julia St. Clair, and Mary is invited to be brides-maid. I suppose she will accept. Miss St. Clair lives in Norris-town, but I think Mary will go to the city, also, and be there at the time of the Sanitary Fair. Your Uncle James has moved up to Twentieth & Race and Logan Square is being fitted up with Fair Buildings. The young girls here are having readings and Charades, the proceeds to go to the Fair. Mary, Sally Loeser, & Bright Bosbyshell, Tom Foster etc all take part. Mary is down town all night with Sally Loeser. I have not time to write more. Hoping to hear soon of your health and safety.

I remain your Affectionate Mother
E.C.P.

✳ ✳ ✳

ON MAY 21, 1864, Lt. Pollock and the soldiers of the 48th left Spotsylvania behind, though the memories of the sanguine fields there would never drift far from their minds and neither would the memories of those friends and comrades whom they had lost and who now laid buried there, shallow in the Virginia soil. Grant, although stymied and his men very much bloodied at both the Wilderness and at Spotsylvania, was determined to keep moving on. He ordered the army south once more, toward the North Anna River, ever hopeful of placing his Army between Lee's and Richmond, thereby forcing Lee out in the open where the Army of Northern Virginia could be destroyed. But again,

Union artillery supports an infantry attack at the Battle of Cold Harbor, as sketched by Alfred Waud. (Courtesy of the Library of Congress)

Lee could counter Grant's movements and his men were able to establish a strong line of defenses on the south banks of the North Anna before the arrival of Grant's blue-clad soldiers. The result was yet another bloody battle in what was already a very bloody campaign. The 48th Pennsylvania participated in the fight at North Anna and lost many men though Pollock said nothing about this in his letters home. He did, however, write much about the regiment's next major battle, Cold Harbor.

After launching a series of assaults against Lee south of the North Anna, Grant determined the Confederate lines there were too strong and on May 26 he began to deftly maneuver the army out of its position and cross them back north of the river. Once his men were fully across, Grant quickly turned east and then to the south and toward an obscure crossroads northeast of Richmond called Cold Harbor. Lee was initially deceived by Grant's movements, believing the Union army would attempt to sweep around his left rather than his right flank, but he would respond quickly and the familiar pattern would once more be repeated. Lee successfully got his men into position and his gray-and-butternut-coated soldiers established a strong line of fortifications and readied themselves for yet another onslaught. As the weary soldiers of the 48th Pennsylvania made their way toward Cold Harbor, they would first encounter Confederate soldiers near the Totopotomoy Creek and a place called Armstrong's Farm. There, on May 30 and 31, a series of sharp little fights broke out as the regiment pushed back Confederate skirmishers. Casualties were few but did include three of the regiment's best officers—Major Joseph Gilmour and Lieutenants William Hume and Samuel Laubenstein—all struck down either killed or mortally wounded by Confederate sharpshooters' bullets. Casualties were much higher over the next three days and particularly on June 3, when the regiment lost another 68 men.[30]

At Cold Harbor, the soldiers of Burnside's Ninth Corps held the far right of the Union line and the 48th Pennsylvania held the far right of the Ninth Corps's line, on the extreme right flank of the entire army. On June 3, the regiment assaulted the Confederate lines to their front and suffered heavily for it. They advanced to within a few yards of the Confederate position before orders were received to suspend further assaults and to dig in.[31] And there, in their hastily dug entrenchments at Cold Harbor, Lt. Pollock and what was left of the ever-thinning ranks of the 48th Pennsylvania would remain for the next week and a half. During this time, even though bullets continued to fly thickly overhead, Pollock wrote several letters home. He wrote about a close call he had on the fields of Cold Harbor and of his inability to make sense of either where they were or of Grant's intentions. And he also continued to write about those who had fallen, including Gilmour and so many other friends and fellow veterans who had served with the 48th since its formation some three years earlier. It was beginning to appear as if everyone was destined to fall, that their days were, as the saying goes, numbered. No doubt many of the soldiers spent the hours wondering, *who's next?* Death was ever-present and it was, indeed, drawing close to Lieutenant Pollock.

———•◦•———

May 31st 1864

My Dear Ma,
      I have not rec'd a letter from home since we left Chancellorsville but have written a letter to you every opportunity I have had. We were Skirmishing today and Maj. Gilmour[32] was

---

30. Gould, 187; Bosbyshell, 151-152.
31. Bosbyshell, 154-156; Gould, 188-194.
32. The loss of Major Gilmour struck a heavy blow to the entire regiment. Joseph Gould described Gilmour as "an excellent officer, quiet, unassuming, and as brave as man could be." He was, in short, " a perfect soldier." Oliver Bosbyshell echoed Gould's sentiments when he wrote that Gilmour was "beloved by all who knew his manly worth, one of the first men to offer his services to the government, and one who had from that hour given his entire time in the defense of the nation." Born on June 30, 1834, in Nova Scotia, Joseph Gilmour was the son of Scottish parents who subsequently settled in Pottsville, Pennsylvania. With the outbreak of civil war in April 1861, Gilmour served alongside Pollock in the Washington Artillerists. Gilmour was selected by Colonel James Nagle to raise a company of infantry, which became Co. H, 48th PA. On September 19, 1861, Gilmour was mustered into service as its captain. He was 27 years of

wounded in the leg & it had to be taken off. Lt. Hume of Co. B was wounded in the arm but will not lost it. Lt. Laubenstein Co. H. was killed.[33] Two other men were hit. I hope you rec'd all the letters I have written.

With much love to all.

I remain Your Affectionate Son

C.C.P.

On the Skirmish Line about 10 miles from Richmond June 4 1864

My Dear Ma

I was very much pleased to receive your letters, the one of the 20th a few days ago and the one of the 27th yesterday. We had another severe engagement yesterday and lost pretty heavily. Alex. Govan and James Allison were killed. Both were hit in the head and killed almost instantly.[34] Sergt. C.F. Kuentzler was wounded severely in the arm. John Hutton was struck on the back of the fingers and cut a little. He will

---

age and stood 5'11" in height. His complexion was listed as dark; his eye color blue, and his hair gray. By occupation, Gilmour was a hatter. Gilmour served with the regiment from the start, rising to the rank of major in July 1863. On May 31, 1864, and while nearly within sight of the spires and steeples of Richmond, Gilmour was shot in the left knee. It was a painful wound; the kneecap shattered. In a field hospital behind the lines, Gilmour's left leg was amputated. From there, he was borne via wagon to White House, Va., then via steamer to the Seminary Hospital in Georgetown, D.C., where he breathed his last on June 9, 1864. Three days later, Gilmour's remains were buried in Pottsville's Presbyterian Cemetery and the occasion, said Bosbyshell, "was marked by a great outpouring of the people, who loved and honored the dead hero." Francis Wallace, in his tribute to soldiers from Schuylkill County, recorded that Gilmour lay his "bright life on the altar of his country—a martyr to the cause nearest and dearest to his generous heart." (Wallace, 523-524; Bosbyshell, 152-153; Gould, 187).

33. Samuel Laubenstein had served in the regiment since the summer of 1861 when he had enlisted at the age of 22. He stood 5'8¼" in height and was, by occupation, a clerk. He listed his residence as Pottsville, though his remains were sent back to what was, presumably, his family's home in Schuylkill Haven where they were laid to rest in the Union Cemetery. William Hume was 20 years old when he enlisted in 1861. Like Laubenstein, Hume was also a clerk, though he resided in St. Clair. He was shot in the arm during the advance on May 31. The wound may not have appeared dangerous but, as Oliver Bosbyshell recorded, "the trying work of the campaign had so reduced his system that he failed to recover from the shock of the wound" and he would succumb to this wound within a matter of days. Hume's remains were buried in the Odd Fellows Cemetery in Pottsville. "These were good officers," reflected Bosbyshell, who "had proven themselves worthy on many fields of battle." (Bosbyshell, 153; Wallace, 527-528).

34. Cpl. Alexander Govan had served alongside Pollock in Company G since the formation of the company. He was eighteen when he enlisted and listed his profession as engineer. Pvt. James Allison was 27 years old when he entered Co. G, 48th PA, in February 1864. Previously he had served in the 7th PA Cavalry. Tragically, James would be the *fourth* son of Agnes Allison of Port Carbon, Pennsylvania, to die in the war. John and Alexander Allison of the 96th PA lost their lives at Salem Church in May 1863 while George Allison of the 56th PA had been mortally wounded at Spotsylvania. Few others paid as high a sacrifice during the war as Agnes Allison.

be back to the Company today. Wm. Martin was struck in the ankle and bruised pretty badly. The loss in the Regt. is 10 killed and 42 wounded I do not know anything new and have no idea what is going on.[35] The Rebs we were fighting yesterday left last night and we are now out as skirmishers but there are no Rebels in front of us. John Hodgson is well and quite anxious to hear from home. He has not had a letter for some time. Flanagan and Humble are all right. I had a ball cut a piece out of the top of my hat yesterday and knocked it about ten feet from me. It is the nearest I have ever had a ball come to me. Hoping you are all well I remain

Your Affectionate Son
With much love to all
C.C.P.

On the battlefield near the
Chicahominie Va.
June 5 1864

My Dear Ma
I wrote a letter to you yesterday but as I have an opportunity of writing a few lines again today I will embrace it. We moved yesterday from the position we occupied on the extreme right of the line to about the center and relieved a part of the 2nd Corps. Our Brigade is lieing in Reserve to-day in the second line of Rifle Pits and are as comfortable as can be expected under the circumstances. It commenced raining last night and it has been unpleasant ever since. I do not know whether I told you of Maj Gilmour having had his leg taken off. He was hit by a ball on the skirmish line. I was talking to him a few minutes before he was hit. The left wing of the Regt. was skirmishing that day and we lost Lt. Laubenstein killed and Lt. Hume wounded. I wish Pa would speak to Sandy Govan about his son. He was hit on the head by a musket ball and never spoke a word afterwards though he lived for some time. Bob Reid and Dan Donne buried him and took charge of his things. They are throwing some shells in the woods here which does not make it as comfortable as it might be. My dinner is just

---

35. Total casualties for the 48th PA at Cold Harbor on June 3 equaled 16 killed or mortally wounded, and 58 wounded. Kuentzler, Martin, and Hutton all survived their injuries.

ready and I will wait a few minutes before finishing. It consists of coffee, fired potatoes & crackers. I have finished dinner but had to put it off for a little while on account of shells dropping rather fast and get behind a log.

Hoping you are all well; I remain your affectionate Son
C.C.P.

With much love to all.
I am glad you have made up your mind to write oftener.

C.C.P.

I send you Lizzie Lawrence's photograph. Keep it at home until I send for it.

———————

June 7 1864
In the Rifle Pits on the Right
Flank of the Army of the Potomac
about 10 miles from Richmond

*M*y Dear Ma
I do not know on which side of Richmond we are but it is either North- or East of it. We are lieing in Rifle Pits in the woods on the edge of a swamp. The Rebs attacked us last evening about 4 PM and we kept it up until about dark. This morning they had all left our front and our skirmishers are out at the old place about a mile and a half in our front. Three of our Band were wounded yesterday by a shell and two others one belonging to Co. A & the other of Co E. That was all the casualties in the Regt. yesterday. We are not very comfortable since at present having to be always on the alert. However we are in good spirits and hoping we will soon be able to take Richmond. Everything has been very quiet for the last few days and they say the siege of Richmond has commenced. But we have no opportunity of learning anything I will always write to you every opportunity I get & hope you will do the same as it is a great comfort to me to get letters from home. I do not write any letters scarcely to anyone except home. I have rec'd two letters from Lizzie Lawrence and she asked me to send Pa's directions to her so if anything happened to me she would know of it. She writes some very patriotic letters to me and

says she knows I will not have an opportunity to write her very often. Hoping you are all well.

I remain Your Affectionate Son
C.C.P.

————◦•◦•◦————

June 12 1864
Near Coal [Cold] Harbor about
10 miles from Richmond

My Dear Ma

I rec'd your letter of the 21st yesterday and was much pleased to hear from home again. I think I received all the letters you write and hope you get all mine. I write to you almost every few days. Though at present there is very little to write about. I do not get away from the Regt.- and can find out nothing about what is going on. Frank Farquhar was here yesterday he is Chief Engineer of the 18th A.C. and is a Capt. now. He looks very well. I am sorry to hear Margie is getting along so poorly. I have not written to her for some time, but our opportunities for writing are such that she ought not expect it. I have nothing more to write about. We have been lieing in reserve in rear of the line of Rifle pits-and have nothing to do. Our baggage has been taken to White House Landing and stored on board of boats. The teams I guess are to be loaded with supplies for the Corps. We have enough to eat such as it is Hard Bread, Coffee & Fresh Beef. We managed to get a ham the other day which was quite a luxury. Hoping you are all well.

I remain Your Affectionate Son
C.C.P.

❋ ❋ ❋

THIS WOULD BE LIEUTENANT Curtis Pollock's final letter home; the last he would write to his "Dear Ma." Just five days later and on yet another sanguinary field, Pollock received his death wound. Removed from the front and taken by steamer to Georgetown, Pollock would draw his final pained breaths in a hospital there on June 23. He fell in the rush of victory, during what regimental historian Oliver Bosbyshell would later deem the 48th Pennsylvania's most brilliant battlefield success, while

Corporal Alexander Govan, Company G, 48th Pennsylvania, was killed in action at the Battle of Cold Harbor, June 3, 1863. (From Gould, The Story of the Forty-Eighth*)*

leading the men of Company G in an early morning assault against the Confederate lines outside Petersburg, Virginia.

Following the slaughter that was Cold Harbor, Grant's thinking had shifted. Having spent the past five weeks attempting to out maneuver Lee and draw the Confederate army into the open where it could be destroyed somewhere north or east of Richmond, Grant now set his sights on Petersburg, a city of some 18,000 residents located twenty miles to the south of the Confederate capital and an important transportation and supply base. With its warehouses, its road networks and its five rail

Much respected and highly popular, Major Joseph Gilmour died on June 9, 1864, from the effects of a wound he received as the 48th Pennsylvania approached Cold Harbor. (From the John D. Hoptak Collection)

lines radiating out from the city, Petersburg was keeping Lee's army supplied and fed. Should it fall, reasoned Grant, both Richmond and the Army of Northern Virginia would fall along with it. As he had done several times throughout the course of the campaign, Grant deceived Lee, successfully extracting the Army of the Potomac from in front of Lee's positions at Cold Harbor and ordering it south yet again. After having crossed the James River, Grant's blue-clad forces arrived opposite the Confederate defenses ringing the city on the afternoon of June 15. The defenders were heavily outnumbered but their ten-mile long line of entrenchments and fortifications—constructed in 1862 and known as the Dimmock Line—helped to offset some of the advantage held by the Union in terms of manpower. In addition, the Union efforts that day were ill-led and ill-coordinated, resulting in what many historians believe to have been a missed opportunity to carry Petersburg before Lee could respond. A portion of the Dimmock Line did collapse but Union forces were unable to exploit their gains and the Confederates simply dug new lines of trenches closer to the city. And as the hours passed, Lee's soldiers continued to arrive in greater strength, augmenting the city's few defenders and strengthening the defenses. The attacks resumed on June 16 and would continue for the next three days until Grant, finally realizing the futility of head-on assaults against well-fortified positions, shifted his thinking once more and called off further frontal assaults.

The initial attacks on Petersburg, launched by the various corps of the Army of the Potomac as well as soldiers from the Army of the James, were, overall, poorly executed and poorly led but there were some bright spots and some localized successes, especially on the Ninth Corps's front during the early morning hours of June 17. The previous day, Curtis Pollock and the soldiers of the 48th had marched away from their positions at Cold Harbor and crossed the James River, arriving in front of Petersburg later that afternoon and in time to witness soldiers of the army's Second Corps launch an unsuccessful attack against the entrenched Confederate line. Sometime around dusk, the regiment was led further to the left, marching south along a creek bed until they arrived at a position directly opposite Battery No. 15, a well-fortified angle in the Confederate lines. The opposing lines were very close and sometime around 10:00 p.m. on the night of June 16, Colonel Henry Pleasants ordered the men of Companies B & G to advance across to the Confederate side of the creek to reconnoiter. Creeping forward in the darkness—regimental historian Joseph Gould later wrote that that night was "dark as pitch"—the two companies came under fire and scampered back. Yet the question remained as to whether they were fired upon by friend or by foe and it fell to two men of Company B, Sergeant Andrew Wren and Private Jacob Wigner, to go forward once more to find out. Slowly they crept forward in the darkness. When nearing the line of earthworks,

A depiction of Union soldiers assaulting the Confederate defenses surrounding Peters-burg in June 1864. (Courtesy of the Library of Congress)

however, they were both grabbed and, by the collars of their uniform coats, pulled inside the Confederate lines, and thus became prisoners of war.[36]

While these two men ventured forth in the darkness, the rest of the regiment settled in for the night, catching what-ever sleep they could, knowing that the next day, they would most likely be called upon again to go into action. That next day—June 17—arrived all too soon. At 3:00 a.m. and in the total darkness, Colonel Pleasants quietly made his way from company to company, informing each of their commanders that they would soon be launching an attack. The men were to charge with bayonets fixed and all caps removed from the guns to prevent against the men from firing. The soldiers were soon stirred awake and, per Robert Reid of Pollock's Company G, the soldiers quietly attached their bayonets, removed the caps, and even secured their tin cups so there would be no rattling. "[T]hen we moved out of the works and crossed the creek. . .After getting the whole regiment over, we silently formed line; then, in utter darkness, moved to the right about one hundred yards, when, in a whisper, the command forward was given."[37]

36. Bosbyshell, 156-157; Gould, 195-197.
37. Gould, 201.

In his regimental history, Oliver Bosbyshell painted a vivid portrait of the morning's preparations and noted that Pleasants "informed the men of the danger before them, and directed that if any felt disinclined to make the assault, they had permission to remain where they were. There is no record or evidence of any kind that a single man of the regiment took advantage of this offer—not one stayed behind! Tin cups and coffee pots were so secured as to make no rattling sound, and directions were passed along in whispered accents. Bayonets were silently fixed . . . and the regiment moved quietly out of the old rebel works, left in front, with the stealth of Indians, over the creek where line of battle was formed, in utter darkness. Moving to the right, for about a hundred yards with panther-like tread, a whispered command 'forward!' was given, and the savage rush began."[38]

Brave Lieutenant Curtis Pollock was embarking on his final charge. Behind and alongside of him the soldiers of the 48th swept across the open though uneven ground between the opposing lines; it was still very much dark and eerily quiet; the only noise that of hundreds of feet tramping down upon the dew-covered grass and dirt. Away off to the right, however, some Union troops opened fire, which drew an immediate response from the Confederate line. The darkness was illuminated with the flash of the Confederate rifles. But still the soldiers of the 48th rushed on. "Directly into this fiery ribbon, belching its leaden hail through the ranks of the charging line, swept the Forty-Eighth," wrote Bosbyshell, while Reid boasted that "We went at them squarely, right into their firing line. Not one of our regiment returned a shot until we reached their works, when there was a short, sharp contest, and the line was ours. I still remember how my heart beat when starting on the charge, but it was forgotten in the glorious rush of the fight."[39]

It was an almost complete surprise and within a matter of minutes, the 48th Pennsylvania crashed into the Confederate lines and captured Battery No. 15. Hundreds of Confederates were captured. During the sharp engagement, the Irish-born Sergeant Patrick Monaghan of Company F noticed a few Confederate soldiers attempting to flee. He ran amongst them and demanded their surrender. Their hands went up and it was soon noticed that one of these Confederate soldiers was attempting

---

38. Bosbyshell, 157-158.
39. Bosbyshell, 158; Gould, 201-202.

to retreat with the flag of the 7th New York Heavy Artillery. The flag had been captured the day before and now Monaghan of the 48th re-captured it and later it would be returned to the New York regiment. For this action, Monaghan received the Medal of Honor. Robert Reid of Company G would also receive a Medal of Honor for his actions during this pre-dawn attack on June 17, 1864. Sweeping forward and rushing up and over the Confederate lines, Reid wrestled away the flag of the 44th Tennessee from its regimental color bearer, capturing those colors.[40]

"How the heart beat, and the pulse throbbed during that onslaught!" wrote Bosbyshell. "If fear or dread marked the supreme moment of the attack, it was banished completely in the glorious rush of the fight! What a harvest of prisoners—they were captured by the score, disarmed, and sent to the rear." As the skies continued to lighten that Friday morning, another Confederate redan about 100 yards further south became visible. Confederate cannons posted there soon erupted into the flank of the 48th. Quickly Pleasants organized the men for another attack and "like a savage torrent" the 48th charged forward again. "[T]he regiment fairly tore over those hundred yards and swept through the fort irresistibly. The enemy ran in great disorder by squads and singly to their left and rear." Two Confederate Napoleons fell into the hands of the 48th and the two guns were safely hauled, by hand, to the rear.[41]

Two cannons, two flags and two Medals of Honor, hundreds of prisoners and a good section of the Confederate line; it was a glorious victory for the 48th and for the Ninth Army Corps. All along Burnside's front, the morning attack had achieved much success. George Meade, commanding the Army of the Potomac, would recognize the success of the Ninth Corps in a note to Burnside, sent on that June 17: «It affords me great satisfaction to congratulate you and your gallant corps on the assault this morning, knowing the wearied condition of your men from the night march over twenty-two miles, and the continual movement this last night; their persistence and success is highly creditable.»[42]

For the actions of the 48th, Oliver Bosbyshell would later write that the attack on June 17, 1864, at Petersburg, "was

---

40. Gould, 202-206.
41. Bosbyshell, 158-161.
42. Gould, 205.

Quartermaster Sergeant Henry Krebs wrote to William Pollock to offer his condolences and to offer to help the Pollock family secure their son's possessions. Krebs also recalled the events surrounding Pollock's wounding. (From the John D. Hoptak Collection)

probably, in all its results, the most brilliant engagement for the Forty-Eighth of any in which it participated. Praise is due to every officer, from Colonel Pleasants down, and to every man who was in this grand assault, for the splendid record the work here accomplished . . ."[43]

A savage torrent—a glorious rush—yes; but it was also a costly one. As they had been throughout the course of the entire campaign—from the Wilderness to Cold Harbor—the ranks of the 48th were once more heavily thinned that Friday morning. Fifty soldiers were among the killed and wounded on June 17; fifteen more would join them the following day. Among those

43. Bosbyshell, 159.

who fell on June 17 was Lieutenant Curtis Clay Pollock. At some point during the day's actions, whether in the pre-dawn rush or once inside the Confederate lines, Pollock sustained a grievous wound to his right shoulder. He did his best to keep up good spirits and when asked by one of his sergeants how he felt, he responded by asking "Wasn't that a splendid charge?" Helped to the rear, Pollock was conveyed by ambulance to City Point and, from there, by steamer to the Seminary Hospital in Georgetown. Though painful, few believed the wound was dangerous, and most were optimistic about his recovery, especially after the bullet was removed from his shoulder. Yet less than a week later, on Thursday, June 23, 1864, the young lieutenant passed away, one month and a few days shy of his twenty-second birthday. It was believed that lockjaw, or tetanus, caused his death.

The final two letters contained in the Pollock collection are addressed to Curtis's father, William, and were written respectively by Thomas Bohannan and Henry Krebs, friends and comrades of the slain lieutenant who, for the past three years, had served alongside of him in the ranks of the 48th Pennsylvania. In addition to describing Pollock's fatal wounding and their efforts at getting his personal belongings returned to his family, Bohannan and Krebs also expressed their sympathies and condolences at the loss of so brave and so young an officer who, like so many others, gave his life fighting in defense of the Union.

Near City Point
July 6, 1864

*M*r. Pollock
    Sir

This morning I turned over your son's valise to the Agent of the Sanitary Committee. He promised me he would deliver it to the Express Office at Washington, D.C. It is in safe hands and I hope you will receive it in good order. I would have forwarded it before the present time but the difficulty was that there has not been any Express Office established here as yet.

I was very much surprised in hearing of Lieut's death. The morning he arrived at City Point from the battlefield he sent the ambulance driver to inform me of his accident. My quarters are ½ mile from City Point. I went immediately to see my

William Auman helped to remove the mortally wounded Pollock from the field at Petersburg. A First Defender, Auman would later come to command Company G, 48th Pennsylvania, and would ultimately rise to the rank of brigadier general in the U.S. Army, leading a famed attack alongside Teddy Roosevelt up San Juan Hill during the Spanish-American War. Auman lays at rest at Arlington National Cemetery. (Courtesy of Mr. Ronn Palm and the Museum of Civil War Images)

particular friend as I must say he was a favorite young man in the Regt and a brave soldier.

On my arrival at City Point the Ambulance Corps was preparing to have him carried on board the boat to be sent to Washington. I took him by the hand and asked him if his wound was dangerous. He seemed to think not and appeared to be very much pleased that his wound was not more serious. As soon as he was placed in a bunk on board the steam boat, I sat down and spoke to him a few minutes. He then requested me to get him his valise but at that time I was not able to get the valise as I had placed all the baggage belonging to officers of the Regiment on board a barge at White House to be sent

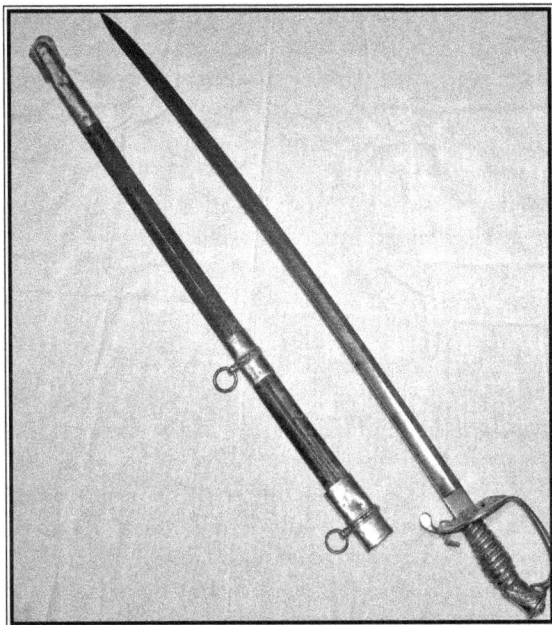

Lieutenant Curtis Pollock's Sword and Scabbard. (From the John D. Hoptak Collection)

around to City Point by water. The barge had not arrived at the time.

I bid the poor fellow good bye but not thinking at the time nor him either that it was our last farewell with each other. I hope he has gone to a happy home. I must come to a close by sending my kindest regards.

Yours Respectfully
Thomas Bohannan
1st Lt.
48 Penn v vol

W. Petersburg, Virginia
August 1, 1864

*M*r. Pollock—
Dear Sir:

Lieut. Bohannan having a press of business has request-ed me to answer for him your letter asking for information concerning Curtis' valise and other effects. Enclosed you will find the address (obtained from the Agent of the Sanitary Commission at City Point) to which the valise was sent, which I trust will enable you to get it, if it has not yet reached you.

Serg't [Richard M.] Jones, (now Lieut) of Company "G" thinks that his pistol must be in the valise.

Serg't [William] Aumen (now Lieut) Company "G" was near Curtis when he was wounded and assisted him from the field. He states that he was quite cheerful and in good spirits, though he suffered considerable pain. One of the his first expressions was "Wasn't that a splendid charge ?"

After he had walked some distance he said he felt faint and sank to the ground ere Lieut. Aumen could catch him. He soon revived and walked assisted by Lieut. Aumen to the Field Hospital.

A few hours after, he was taken in an ambulance to City Point. Lieut. Bohannan met him on the road. He spoke cheerfully and requested him to send his baggage home. He seemed to think his wound was slight, and that he was very fortunate in escaping so well, without the loss of a limb as there were many around him. Two hours' ride brought him to City Point, where there was boat in readiness to receive the wounded and as soon as she was loaded she started for Washington.

The baggage of our Corps was sent by water from White House and only arrived the day he left or it could have been sent with him. There is an overcoat with the Company baggage which was just discovered a day or two since. Lieut. Bohannan will see Major Bosbyshell about it, and if it is Curtis' will send it by express.

The writer of this will see Lieut. Aumen and see if he has any additional particulars, he will, no doubt, be pleased to give them.

All the members of the Company and of the Regiment unite in the highest praise of his bravery and courage in battle as well as his example as a friend and companion. His death and the of Lieut. [Henry] Jackson has caused a deep feeling of gloom and sadness to pervade Company "G" which will not easily be dispelled. They will live long in the memories of those who knew them to love and respect them.

Trusting that the condolence of a friend and former member of Company "G" is not here out of place, I beg to subscribe myself.

Very Respectively Yours,
Harry Krebs

⊷⊜ EPILOGUE ⊜⊷

---◆---

I T IS NOT KNOWN exactly how or even when William and Emily Pollock first learned of their son's death, though news of his passing did appear in the June 25 edition of the *Miners' Journal*, printed just two days after he died. "We are pained to learn that Lieut. Curtis C. Pollock, of Co. G, 48th Regt., died in Washington on Thursday last from the effects of a wound received in battle," the paper reported, "He was a brave, capable officer, and his loss will be severely felt."[1] It was felt, certainly, by the Pollock family—by his mother and father and his six younger siblings—as well as by their friends in his hometown of Pottsville. It was also felt within the ranks of the 48th Pennsylvania and by those who had once served alongside the young officer. William Clemens, for example, a lieutenant in the U.S. Signal Corps who had grown up with Curtis and who had marched off to war with him in April 1861 with the Washington Artillery, read of Pollock's death on June 28. In a letter to his parents, one can detect the pain and the grief Clemens felt upon discovering the sad news:

> "I saw today in a [*Miners'*] *Journal* of last Saturday a notice of the death of Curt Pollock. I could scarcely contain myself when I read it; I was so shocked and grieved. Pollock was a noble fellow, a brave, fearless and efficient officer, always in the foremost rank of battle, leading on his gallant men. In the death of Lieut. Pollock the country loses one of its best and bravest officers, and I one of the best friends I had in the army. He would do anything in his power for me and I am sorry that he has been called so soon to his God; he was too good to live. It is dreadful to contemplate the great loss of life during this war; oh, that it may soon come to an end."[2]

---

1. *Miners' Journal*, Saturday, June 25, 1864.
2. William W. Clemens to family, June 28, 1864, The Civil War Letters of Lt. William Clemens, U.S. Signal Corps, Courtesy of the Signal Corps Association (1860-1865) www.civilwarsignals.org

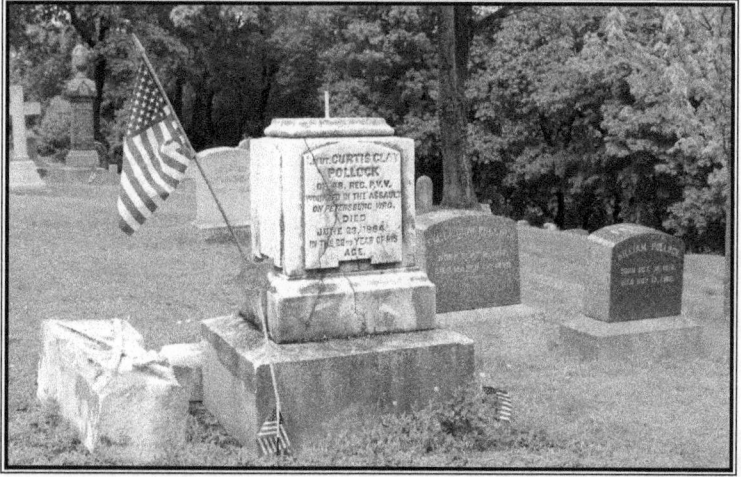

The Final Resting Place of Lieutenant Curtis Pollock in the Charles Baber Cemetery, Pottsville, Pennsylvania. The graves of Curtis's "Dear Ma" Emily Pollock, and his father William, can also be seen here. Sadly, Curtis's stone has been vandalized over the years. (Hoptak Photograph)

More tributes would follow. In late 1865, a short biography of Pollock, written by Francis Wallace and the editors of the *Miners' Journal*, appeared in the book, *Memorial to the Patriotism of Schuylkill County in the American Slaveholders' Rebellion*. "His conduct as an officer was without reproach," wrote the authors. "Although firm in the discharge of his duty, he never allowed an opportunity to pass for doing a kind office for any of his men, and many have testified to his kindness of heart, and sympathy in their long and weary marches. His coolness and courage on the battle-field were remarkable in one so young. Never absent from his post in danger, he inspired others by his presence of mind and undaunted courage." Thirty years later, in his regimental history, Oliver Bosbyshell declared that Pollock was "literally fearless of danger."[3]

America's fratricidal war would, of course, continue long after Pollock's death though the fighting at Petersburg would wind to a slow and bloody grind. Following the slaughter of June 17-18 and deciding against any more frontal assaults against the entrenched Confederate positions south and east of the city, General U.S. Grant chose, instead, to settle in while contemplating his next move. The days of open field attacks and linear

---

3. Wallace, 530-531; Bosbyshell, 159.

formations were seemingly over and, as the soldiers on both sides dug in and experienced the cruel, unforgiving realities of life in the trenches, a new kind of warfare developed—stagnant, callous, and very deadly. Yet soon after the armies took up position in their trenches outside Petersburg, a spectacular effort was made to break the deadlock, an effort made by none other than the soldiers of Pollock's very own regiment, the 48th Pennsylvania Infantry.

On June 25—indeed the very same Saturday that news of Pollock's death first appeared in Pottsville in the pages of the *Miners' Journal*—the men he had once served alongside put pick and shovel to earth and began digging a tunnel that would ultimately terminate directly under a portion of the Confederate lines southeast of Petersburg known as Elliott's Salient. The attacks of June 17-18 at Petersburg, during which Lt. Pollock and so many others had fallen, had carried the soldiers of the Union's Fifth and Ninth Corps to points very near the Confederate lines. Just one hundred or so yards in front of the position taken up by the 48th loomed Elliott's Salient, a Confederate fortification held by a Virginia artillery battery and a brigade of South Carolina infantry. According to one account, while walking along his lines, Lt. Col. Pleasants overheard one of his men grumble, "We could blow that damn fort out of existence if we could only run a mine under it." Pleasants, a civil mining engineer, soon after developed a plan, compiled a list of all the skilled miners in the regiment, and took his proposal to his superior officers. After receiving the approval of General Ambrose Burnside, Pleasants and the men of the 48th began to dig. Just one month later—working under severe hardship, with improvised mining tools, and with virtually no support or help from the army—the tunnel was completed. It stretched 511 feet in length and, at the end, two lateral galleries were dug to house the wooden magazines which were soon filled with 8,000 pounds of powder. Then, early on a Saturday morning—July 30, 1864—the mine was fired. In an instant, a hole was literally blasted in the Confederate lines: 125 feet in length, 60 feet in width, and, in places, 30 feet in depth.

A door was blown wide open. Henry Pleasants and the men of the 48th had presented the Union army and its commanders a tremendous opportunity to break the stalemate at Petersburg and crush the Confederate army, caught unawares by the tremendous magnitude of the blast. But it was not to be. As it turned out, the follow up attacks were so badly botched and bungled that the entire endeavor culminated in one of the worst Union defeats of the entire war at the aptly-named Battle of the Crater. Pleasants and his weary, mud-covered soldiers of the 48th Pennsylvania could do nothing but watch, seething in anger or shaking their heads in utter disbelief that their remarkable achievement could be so badly miscarried. Still, though, despite the fiasco that ensued at the Crater, the extraordinary efforts of the 48th in successfully tunneling under the Confederate lines would forever etch their names in the history books.

Of course, by the time the mine exploded, and over 300 quiet miles away, the earthly remains of Lt. Curtis Pollock had long since been laid to rest. They had arrived in Pottsville on Tuesday, June 28—exactly one month shy of what would have been Pollock's twenty-second birthday—and taken to the Pollock home. That evening the house was open for those wishing to pay their final respects. The next day, on June 29, 1864, a funeral was held and the remains of Curtis Pollock were laid to rest, interred within the tranquil confines of what was then known as the Mount Laurel Cemetery but which today is known as the Charles Baber Cemetery.

And there today the remains of Curtis Pollock continue their silent repose, laying in eternal rest next to those of his father, William, who passed away at age 86 in 1902, and those of his mother—his "Dear Ma" Emily—who drew her last breaths on March 15, 1895, in her seventy-seventh year.

Bosbyshell, Oliver C. *The 48th in the War: Being A Narrative of the Campaigns of the 48th Regiment, Infantry, Pennsylvania Veteran Volunteers, During the War of the Rebellion.* Philadelphia: Avil Printing Company, 1895.

Goolrick, William K. and the Editors of Time-Life Books. *Rebels Resurgent: Fredericksburg to Chancellorsville.* Alexandria, Virginia: Time-Life Books, 1985.

Gould, Joseph. *The Story of the Forty-Eighth: A Record of the Campaigns of the Forty-Eighth Regiment Pennsylvania Veteran Volunteer Infantry During the Four Eventful Years of its Service in the War for the Preservation of the Union.* Philadelphia: Alfred M. Slocum, Printers, 1908.

Hennessy, John J. *Return to Bull Run: The Campaign and Battle of Second Manassas.* New York: Simon & Schuster, 1993.

Hess, Earl. *The Knoxville Campaign: Burnside and Longstreet in East Tennessee.* Knoxville: The University of Tennessee Press, 2012.

Hoptak, John D. *First in Defense of the Union: The Civil War History of the First Defenders.* Bloomington, Indiana: AuthorHouse, 2004.

O'Reilly, Francis A. *The Fredericksburg Campaign: Winter War on the Rappahannock.* Baton Rouge: Louisiana State University Press, 2003.

Rafuse, Ethan S. *McClellan's War: The Failure of Modernization in the Struggle for the Union.* Bloomington: Indiana University Press, 2005.

Sauers, Richard A. *A Succession of Honorable Victories: The Burnside Expedition in North Carolina.* Dayton, Ohio: Morningside House, 1996.

———. "Laurels for Burnside: The Invasion of North Carolina: January-July 1862." *Blue & Gray Magazine*, Vol. V, Issue 5, May 1988.

Stoker, Donald. *The Grand Design: Strategy and the U.S. Civil War*. New York: Oxford University Press, 2010.

Thompson, Heber S. *The First Defenders*. N.p.: 1910.

Wallace, Francis B. *Memorial to the Patriotism of Schuylkill County in the American Slaveholders' Rebellion*. Pottsville, Pennsylvania: Benjamin Bannan, 1865.

Woodbury, Augustus. *Major General Ambrose E. Burnside and the Ninth Army Corps: A Narrative of the Campaigns in North Carolina, Maryland, Virginia, Ohio, Kentucky, Mississippi and Tennessee, during the War for the Preservation of the Republic*. Providence, Rhode Island: S.S. Rider & Brother, 1867.

Wren, James. *From New Bern to Fredericksburg: Captain James Wren's Diary: February 20, 1862-December 17, 1862*. Edited by John Michael Priest. Shippensburg, Pennsylvania: White Mane Publishing Company, 1990.

———◆•◆•◆———

JOHN D. HOPTAK is the author of several books, including *The Battle of South Mountain*, *Confrontation at Gettysburg*, *First in Defense of the Union*, and *Antietam: September 17, 1862.* He is also a frequent contributor to such periodicals as *Civil War Times*, *America's Civil War*, and *Pennsylvania History.* Having previously served as an Interpretive Park Ranger at Antietam National Battlefield, Hoptak is currently employed as a Ranger at Gettysburg National Military Park. A lifelong student of the American Civil War in general, Hoptak's special interest lies in the wartime history of his native Schuylkill County, Pennsylvania, and particularly the 48th Pennsylvania Volunteer Infantry. Hoptak maintains a website dedicated to the regiment, which can be found at www.48thpennsylvania.blogspot.com

www.ingramcontent.com/pod-product-compliance
Lightning Source LLC
Chambersburg PA
CBHW021353090426
42742CB00009B/836